Learning to Read Across Languages

This book systematically examines how learning to read occurs in diverse languages, and in so doing, explores how literacy is learned in a second language by learners who have achieved at least basic reading skills in their first language. As a consequence of rapid globalization, such learners are a large and growing segment of the school population worldwide, and an increasing number of schools are challenged by learners from a wide variety of languages, and with distinct prior literacy experiences. To succeed academically these learners must develop second-language literacy skills, yet little is known about the ways in which they learn to read in their first languages, and even less about how the specific nature and level of their first-language literacy affects second-language reading development.

This volume provides detailed descriptions of five typologically diverse languages and their writing systems, and offers comparisons of learning-to-read experiences in these languages. Specifically, it addresses the requisite competencies in learning to read in each of the languages, how language and writing system properties affect the way children learn to read, and the extent and ways in which literacy learning experience in one language can play a role in subsequent reading development in another. Both common and distinct aspects of literacy learning experiences across languages are identified, thus establishing a basis for determining which skills are available for transfer in second-language reading development.

Learning to Read Across Languages is intended for researchers and advanced students in the areas of second-language learning, psycholinguistics, literacy, bilingualism, and cross-linguistic issues in language processing.

Learning to Read Across Languages

Cross-Linguistic Relationships in First- and Second-Language Literacy Development

Edited by
Keiko Koda
Annette M. Zehler

Routledge
Taylor & Francis Group

NEW YORK AND LONDON

First published 2008
by Routledge
270 Madison Ave, New York, NY 10016

Simultaneously published in the UK
by Routledge
2 Park Square, Milton Park, Abingdon, Oxon OX14 4RN

*Routledge is an imprint of the Taylor & Francis Group,
an informa business*

© 2008 by the Taylor & Francis Group

Typeset in Sabon by
RefineCatch Limited, Bungay, Suffolk
Printed and bound in the United States of America on acid-free paper by
Walsworth Publishing Company, Marceline, MO

Library of Congress Cataloging in Publication Data
A catalog record has been requested for this book

ISBN 10: 0–8058–5611–0 (hbk)
ISBN 10: 0–8058–5612–9 (pbk)
ISBN 10: 0–203–93566–7 (ebk)

ISBN 13: 978–0–8058–5611–8 (hbk)
ISBN 13: 978–0–8058–5612–5 (pbk)
ISBN 13: 978–0–203–93566–8 (ebk)

Contents

List of figures

Preface

As a consequence of rapid globalization, students with a mother tongue different from the societal language are a large and growing segment of the school population. These students must develop second language literacy skills in order to succeed academically, and often do so on the basis of at least some initial level of literacy experience in their first language. Despite the great importance of literacy development among language minority students, little is known about the ways in which these students learn to read in their first languages, and even less is known about how their prior literacy experience affects second language reading development. The primary goal of *Learning to Read across Languages* thus is to systematically examine successive biliteracy development, that is, literacy learning in a second language that occurs after learners have achieved at least basic reading skills in their first language. Accordingly, the volume provides detailed descriptions of five typologically diverse languages together with their writing systems, as well as comparisons of learning-to-read experiences in these languages.

The volume is an expansion of a federally-funded project, Research on the Transfer of Literacy Skills from Languages with Non-Roman Script to English: Feasibility and Pilot Study (ED–01–CO–0042/0002), awarded to Development Associates, Inc. The earlier project was prompted by the U.S. Department of Education's recognition of the need to expand scientific knowledge on how second language reading proficiency in English evolves. The research focused on learners whose first language writing systems differ substantially from that of English. The investigation centered on identifying the literacy skills children develop through their first language reading experience and the implications of these skills for learning to read in English as a second language. Specifically, the project examined reading skill development and transfer in five non-Roman script languages (specified by the U.S. Department of Education): Arabic, Chinese, Khmer, Korean, and Lao. Four of the five are included in this volume with updated and expanded literature reviews. A chapter describing Hebrew language and literacy has been added, primarily because Hebrew literacy has been most extensively studied among languages employing non-Roman scripts.

The volume provides descriptions of reading acquisition in these typologically diverse languages by addressing (a) the requisite competencies in learning to read in each of the five languages; (b) how language and writing system properties affect the way children learn to read; and (c) the extent and ways in which literacy learning experience in one language impacts on reading development in another. These chapters thus illustrate how language, writing system, and learning to read are interconnected. Through these analyses, moreover, the volume clarifies both common and distinct aspects of literacy learning experience across languages, and in so doing, establishes a basis for determining which skills are available for transfer in second language reading development.

Acknowledgments

This volume is an outgrowth of the project, *Research on the Transfer of Literacy Skills from Languages with Non-Roman Script to English: Feasibility and Pilot Study*, funded by the U.S. Department of Education, Office of English Language Acquisition. In the project, Development Associates, Inc., in collaboration with Carnegie Mellon University, conducted analyses of five languages (Arabic, Chinese, Khmer, Korean and Lao), reviewed the research on the transfer for these languages, developed recommendations and a specific design for a research study, examined resources available and other feasibility issues, and conducted a pilot test for the proposed tasks and implementation plan. We wish to acknowledge the important role of our sponsor, the Office of English Language Acquisition (OELA) of the U.S. Department of Education in providing guidance and assistance.

We also would like to extend our gratitude to Dr. Richard Tucker, Head, Department of Modern Languages, Carnegie Mellon University, for his support and Carnegie Mellon project team members, Hisae Fujiwara, Megumi Hamada, Etsuko Takahashi, Yukiko Wada, and Ran Zhao, for their valuable assistance in the literature reviews and linguistic analyses. We are grateful to Development Associates, Inc., for its support, and to Judy Lewis, Chhany Sak-Humphry, and Wayne Wright for input on the literature review for the Khmer language, and Hyekyung Sung for input on the literature review for the Korean language. Our appreciation is also extended to Yanhui Zhang, Chan Lu, and Pooja Reddy at Carnegie Mellon University for their assistance in manuscript and index preparations. Continuous support and guidance from Naomi Silverman, Commissioning Editor at Lawrence Erlbaum Associates, greatly facilitated the overcoming of many impediments.

Finally, but importantly, our respective families deserve our deepest gratitude for their patience, support, and encouragement.

1 Introduction

Conceptualizing reading universals, cross-linguistic variations, and second language literacy development

Keiko Koda and Annette M. Zehler

Reading is an essential component of academic learning, as well as a foundation for becoming an informed member of the broader community. Failure to achieve adequate reading proficiency denies students access to the essential tool for further learning. Students suffer academically when they are unable to make the transition from oral language skills to achieving basic decoding competence and comprehending various types of texts. They increasingly fall behind in their schooling, and are at greater risk of dropping out. Sadly, this has been the case with too many children in today's schools, and understandably there has been concern when students struggle in learning to read.

These concerns take on increasing complexity among the growing number of language-minority students who receive formal instruction in a language other than their mother tongue. In 2002, there were approximately four million English language learners in grades K-12, constituting roughly 8.4 percent of the estimated total student population. While two-thirds of these students are in the lower elementary grades, the remaining third are in middle and high schools (Kindler, 2002). As we seek ways to promote skilled readers, it is extremely important to address the needs of these students.

Given this end, the volume's primary objective is to explore principled approaches examining the impacts of prior literacy experience on reading development in a second language. It provides theoretical perspectives through which such impacts are conceptualized, and then presents sequential analyses as the methodological foundation for identifying variations in literacy experience in typologically diverse languages. Collectively, the analyses make it possible to examine the specific ways in which literacy skills developed in one language alter reading development in another.

The problem

A recent large-scale synthesis on literacy research involving language-minority students (August & Shanahan, 2006) concludes that literacy in the first language is a potential facilitator in literacy development in a second language. However, many researchers have acknowledged that much remains to be explored as to the relationship between first- and second-language learning to read (August & Hakuta, 1998; Snow *et al.*, 1998). Although it has long been recognized that those already literate in one language progress faster and achieve higher levels in second-language reading development (e.g. Bernhardt, 2003), little is known about the specific ways literacy experience in one language facilitates reading development in another. Obviously, there is a pressing need for clarifying the precise nature of the cross-linguistic relationship in literacy development in bilingual students.

The issues at hand, however, are extremely complex, because second-language literacy encompasses a broad range of learners, including those of different ages, and with diverse first-language backgrounds. Probing the fundamental question of how literacy in one language affects reading development in another requires an extensive consideration of the many disparate circumstances in which literacy is learned in both first and second languages. The investigations must, therefore, include learners with different first languages as well as those at different stages of reading acquisition in those languages.

These complexities are further compounded by the distance between the languages involved, since distance predicts how similar (or different) literacy learning experiences in the two languages will be. The distance thus determines, in considerable part, to what degree second-language learning-to-read will be facilitated by prior literacy experience through cross-language transfer. Less facilitation can be expected to occur when the two languages are distinct than when the two are related. In the absence of coherent frameworks, the distance effects, although considerably discussed on a speculative basis, remain to be adequately explained.

The learning context is another factor adding complexity to the cross-linguistic relationship in literacy development. Since literacy learning does not occur in a vacuum, the context in which literacy has been learned in the first language must be taken into account. To illustrate, Arabic-speaking children learn to speak a local dialect at home, and then learn Modern Standard Arabic for both oral and written communication in school. For these children, an additional language—for example, English as a foreign language—represents a second written language, and a third oral language. Another example can be drawn from Chinese heritage-language learners in the U.S. These children learn to speak Chinese at home, receive primary literacy instruction in English in school, and pursue additional literacy in Chinese in a weekend school. For them, their second oral language (English) represents a first written language, and their first oral language (Chinese) is a second written language. Finally, there are students who enter schools in a host country without prior schooling experience and with only very rudimentary, if any, reading skills in their first language.

Obviously, circumstances of "prior literacy" learning differ considerably among second-language learners and the reading skills acquired through "prior literacy" vary accordingly. Hence, these circumstances, and variations therein, must be adequately described and understood because they explain, at least in part, the different developmental paths needed in learning to read in a second language among diverse groups of learners.

Given the complexity of the issues to be addressed, it is perhaps not surprising that there is only a limited body of research to draw upon. As will be further noted in several of the chapters in the volume, much of the research on second-language reading has focused on alphabetic first- and second-languages, and on early elementary grade students. Research involving middle- and high-school students to date remains heavily restricted (Zehler *et al.*, 2003). Also, many of the studies on record have examined aggregated groups of students from several different first languages, and thus do not isolate the impacts of prior literacy experience stemming from a particular first language or a particular learning context.

As the first step in initiating systematic investigations of the cross-linguistic relationship in second-language literacy development, we have laid out a set of fundamental questions to guide subsequent conceptualizations:

- Do reading skills developed in diverse first languages differ from one another?
- If so, in what ways do they differ?
- Which specific skills transfer across languages?
- Under what conditions does transfer occur?
- What factors affect cross-language reading skills transfer?
- To what extent, and in what ways, do transferred first-language competencies affect learning to read in a second language?
- Do the transferred competencies compensate in any way for underdeveloped linguistic knowledge in second-language reading development?
- If, in fact, transferred first-language competencies play a role in learning to read in a second language, what are the implications of the first-language influences for instructional practice?

In this volume, we attempt to explore a principled approach to addressing these questions, first, by identifying the universal and language-specific constraints on learning to read in typologically diverse languages, and second, by clarifying how literacy competencies developed in one language are incorporated in learning to read in another. Based on these conceptualizations, we outline procedures for analyzing the properties of five languages and their writing systems to identify the competencies shaped through literacy experience in these languages, and to examine how these competencies can be applied to reading acquisition in another language.

The scope of the analyses

Reading, as a complex cognitive process, involves a number of operations, each of which requires diverse sub-skills for its execution. At the same time, reading development, as a socially constructed pursuit, is shaped and constrained by everyday experiences of members in a particular socio-cultural community. Inevitably, theories of reading acquisition must incorporate the broad range of competencies to be acquired, as well as the varied social contexts in which literacy is learned. Given such diversity in both the competencies involved and the contextual factors affecting their acquisition, no single theory can be all encompassing. It is imperative, therefore, that the scope of investigation be clarified at the outset.

First, in this volume, reading is viewed as a psycholinguistic construct, and as such, the requisites for its acquisition are conceptualized as the cognitive and linguistic resources needed for print information extraction (decoding) and for text meaning construction (comprehension). The psycholinguistic orientation simply reflects the expertise of the contributing authors and in no way intends to discredit other perspectives and approaches.

Second, metalinguistic awareness—the ability to identify, analyze, and manipulate language forms—is the primary focus in the analyses in this volume. Here again, this privilege by no means implies that metalinguistic awareness is the only construct contributing to learning to read or pertaining to cross-language transfer. The restricted scope is necessary simply because the exploration is still in its infancy, seeking empirical procedures for tracking uses of particular skills across languages.

Serious attention is also given to decoding development. Since decoding is the process of extracting linguistic information from print, it benefits directly from metalinguistic awareness. Accordingly, the extent to which first-language metalinguistic awareness relates to variations—both qualitative and quantitative—in second-language, decoding can be taken as an index of an impact stemming from prior literacy experience, thereby serving as a basis for estimating such an impact on second-language learning to read. Insofar as decoding is a critical first step in literacy acquisition, it is hoped that the current exploration will be extended to other reading sub-skills—comprehension skills, in particular—in future investigations.

The conceptual frameworks

Reading is a multi-dimensional pursuit, involving a large number of sub-component processes. The complexity increases exponentially in second-language reading since virtually all of its operations involve two, or more, languages. To understand how children learn to read in a second language, it is necessary to consider what "involving two languages" means, how such "dual-language involvement" affects learning to read in a second language, and how the aggregated impacts can be empirically examined. Theory of language transfer, therefore, is central to the current exploration, because it clarifies how first-language literacy skills come into play in second-language learning to read, thereby explaining the developmental variations attributable to prior literacy experience.

Theory of reading universals is also critical because it specifies the learning-to-read requisites imposed on all learners in all languages. Therefore, by comparing how the requisite tasks are accomplished in diverse languages, we can identify the language-specific constraints and describe similarities and differences in learning-to-read experiences systematically across languages. Importantly, accurate descriptions of such variations, in turn, will permit further explorations of how second-language reading development is constrained by disparate demands imposed by the properties specific to the two languages involved.

Metalinguistic awareness is equally integral to the current exploration. Inasmuch as reading is embedded between spoken language and the writing system (Perfetti, 2003), its acquisition requires the linking of the two systems (Perfetti & Liu, 2005; Nagy & Anderson, 1999). Accordingly, in learning to read, children must first understand which language elements are encoded in the writing system, and then recognize how these elements are encoded. Metalinguistic awareness plays a pivotal role in guiding both these processes that are critical in learning to read.

Although metalinguistic ability expedites the initial task in reading acquisition, substantial print decoding and encoding experience are necessary for its refinement. In this regard, metalinguistic awareness and literacy are developmentally reciprocal, and therefore, the resulting metalinguistic competencies are assumed to reflect the specific ways spoken language elements are graphically represented in the writing system. Developmental reciprocity thus has a significant methodological implication for second-language reading research. Because of the reciprocity, the specific metalinguistic competencies likely to transfer can be identified through careful analysis of the writing system, thus making it possible to measure and trace the identified competencies empirically.

There are additional reasons why metalinguistic awareness should be the primary focus in the current exploration. Tracing reading-skill transfer among young second-language learners is a tricky enterprise. Validation of "transfer" entails an empirical demonstration of similar processing behaviors across the languages involved. However, this is difficult to achieve with young learners whose first-language literacy is still evolving. Since specific facets of metalinguistic awareness are associated with distinct aspects of literacy learning and print information processing, prior literacy experience can be described in terms of specific metalinguistic capabilities. This, in turn, provides a solid basis for predicting which specific capabilities are "transfer-ready" at a given point in time among a particular age group of second-language learners. Further, because of its abstract nature, meta-linguistic awareness, if properly measured, should be less vulnerable than language-processing skills to linguistic variables such as frequency and vis-ual/conceptual familiarity. Conceivably, then, it can yield a more stable picture of the cross-linguistic relationship in first- and second-language literacy development.

The analyses

A sequence of analyses was carried out in order to identify the principal "learning-to-read" competencies in five typologically diverse languages. The analysis procedures involved the following steps: (a) identifying the spoken language elements that are encoded in the writing system; (b) describing how these elements correspond to graphic symbols; (c) based on the descrip-tions, isolating the metalinguistic insights required for deducing how the identified spoken elements are related to graphic symbols in the writing system; and (d) comparing the requisite metalinguistic insights in the focal language with those in English. This final step in the analyses is vital because English, as the denominator in the comparisons, provides a basis for identi-fying similarities and differences in the learning-to-read requirements in the languages analyzed. These languages include Arabic, Chinese, Hebrew, Khmer (Cambodian), and Korean. Outlined below are the questions that guided the analyses:

1   How many symbols are there in the writing system?
2   What information is conveyed by each graphic symbol in the writing system?
3   How are individual symbols combined to form a word?
4   How is a word's phonological information represented by graphic symbols?
5   Which morphological information is graphically shown in the writing system?
6   How is it represented by graphic symbols?
7   What should children know to be able to deduce how the spoken language elements correspond with graphic symbols in the writing system?
8   What differences and similarities distinguish the metalinguistic com-petencies in this language and those in English?
9   In what ways does first language "learning-to-read" experience affect the manner and rate of reading skill acquisition in English as a second language?

Organization of this volume

To reiterate, the volume aims at establishing theoretical and methodological foundations for examining the impacts of first-language literacy on learning to read in a second language. The theoretical underpinnings for conceptualizing influences of prior literacy experience are presented in Part I. In the opening chapter, Perfetti and Dunlap describe what is entailed in learning how one's writing system encodes one's spoken language. By demonstrating the universal dependence of reading on spoken language, and the accommodation of this universality to the properties of a particular writing system, the authors clarify the universal principles and cross-language variations in the learning-to-read requirements. In the next chapter, on the premise that learning to read is essentially metalinguistic, Kuo and Anderson explain the specific contributions of metalinguistic awareness to reading acquisition in all languages and writing systems. They then describe how its facets can be identified, measured, and compared across languages. In the third and last chapter of the section, Koda synthesizes the key concepts of reading universals and metalinguistic awareness to propose a model clarifying the precise ways in which prior literacy experience facilitates, through cross-language transfer, reading development in a second language. More specifically, the model offers explanations of how, and under what conditions, previously-acquired competences transfer across languages, and how the transferred competencies are incorporated in second-language learning to read. Collectively, the three chapters in Part I establish the bases—both theoretical and empirical—for identifying the requisites for reading acquisition, for comparing similarities and differences in these requisites across languages, and for tracing the impacts of prior literacy experience on second-language reading development.

The chapters in Part II present descriptions of five typologically diverse languages and their respective writing systems (Arabic in Chapter 5, Chinese in Chapter 6, Hebrew in Chapter 7, Khmer in Chapter 8, and Korean in Chapter 9). Each chapter explains (1) what metalinguistic competencies are required for learning how elements of the language in question are graphically represented in the writing system; (2) how these competencies differ from those in English; and (3) how literacy experience in this language affects learning to read in English as a second language.

The chapters are structured in similar formats to offer parallel descriptions of the metalinguistic awareness and other competencies that enable a child to learn to map between spoken language elements and the writing system that encodes those elements. The parallel format should allow systematic comparisons of the learning-to-read requisites across the five languages. The chapters also provide reviews of empirical studies involving children learning to read the languages as their first language; studies describing patterns in learning to read in English as a second language by native speakers of these languages; and studies on learning to read in these languages as a second language.

The closing chapter offers a summary that highlights the differences and similarities in the requirements for learning-to-read in the five languages, and discusses their implications for cross-language transfer within the proposed model. The chapter also recapitulates the major findings of research on second-language learning to read by native speakers of the five languages in order to identify voids in the research and provide suggestions for future research directions.

References

Akamatsu, N. (1999) The effects of first language orthographic features on word recognition processing in English as a second language. *Reading and Writing: An Interdisciplinary Journal*, 11(4), 381–403.

August, D. & Hakuta, K. (eds.) (1998) *Educating language–minority children*. Washington, DC: National Academy Press.

August, D. & Shanahan, T. (eds.) (2006). Executive summary: Developing literacy in second-language learners: report of the National Literacy Panel on Language-Minority Children and Youth. Mahwah, NJ: Lawrence Erlbaum.

August, D., Calderon, M., & Carlo, M. (2001) Transfer of skills from Spanish to English: A study of young learners. Updated review of current literature relevant to the technical issues in the implementation of the study. Washington, DC: Center for Applied Linguistics.

Bernhardt, E. (2003) Challenges to reading research from a multilingual world. *Reading Research Quarterly*, 38(1), 112–17.

Durgunoglu, A. Y., Nagy, W. E., & Hancin, B. J. (1993) Cross-language transfer of phonemic awareness. *Journal of Educational Psychology*, 85, 453–65.

Fowler, A. E., & Liberman, I. Y. (1995) The role of phonology and orthography in morphological awareness. In L. B. Feldman (ed.), *Morphological aspects of language processing* (pp. 157–88). Hillsdale, NJ: Lawrence Erlbaum Associates.

Goswami, U. & Bryant, P. (1990) *Phonological skills and learning to read*. Hove, UK: Lawrence Erlbaum Associates.

Kindler, A. (2002) Survey of the States' Limited English Proficient students and available educational programs and services: 2000–2001 summary report. Report prepared for the U.S. Department of Education, Office of English Language Acquisition, Language Enhancement and Academic Achievement for Limited English Proficient Students (OELA). Washington, DC: National Clearinghouse for English Language Acquisition and Language Instruction Educational Programs.

Koda, K. (1998) The role of phonemic awareness in second language reading. *Second Language Research*, 14(2), 194–216.

Koda, K. (1999) Development of L2 intraword orthographic sensitivity and decoding skills. *Modern Language Journal*, 83(1), 51–64.

Koda, K. (2000) Cross-linguistic variations in L2 morphological awareness. *Applied Psycholinguistics*, 21(3), 297–320.

Nagy, W. E. & Anderson, R. C. (1999) Metalinguistic awareness and literacy acquisition in different languages (pp. 155–60). In D. Wagner, R. Venezky, & B. Street (eds.), *Literacy: an international handbook*. New York: Garland.

Perfetti, C. A. (2003) The universal grammar of reading. *Scientific Studies of Reading*, 7, 3–24.

Perfetti. C. A. & Liu, Y. (2005) Orthography to phonology and meaning: comparisons across and within writing systems. *Reading and Writing*, 18, 193–210.

Snow, C. E., Burns, M. S., & Griffin, P. (eds.) (1998) *Preventing reading difficulties in young children*. Washington, DC: National Academy Press.

Wang, M., Koda, K., Perfetti, C. A. (2003) Alphabetic and non-alphabetic L1 effects in English semantic processing: A comparison of Korean and Chinese English L2 learners. *Cognition*, 87, 129–149.

Zehler, A. M., Koda, K., and Sapru, S. (2003) Research on the transfer of literacy skills from languages with non-Roman script to English: Feasibility and pilot study. Final report to the U.S. Department of Education, Office of English Language Acquisition. Arlington, VA: Development Associates, Inc.

Part I
Theoretical underpinnings

2 Learning to read

General principles and writing system variations

Charles A. Perfetti and
Susan Dunlap

In learning to read, what is it that one learns? Reading educators have stressed the goal of learning to read in variations around meaning; e.g. learning to construct meaning, to get meaning from print, to comprehend. Although the goal of reading is indeed to obtain meaning from written language, this falls short of specifying what is actually learned. One general answer to the question of what is learned in learning to read was proposed by Perfetti & Zhang (1995): learning to read is learning how one's writing system encodes one's language. This claim reflects the view that reading is fundamentally about converting graphic input (letters, words, characters) to linguistic-conceptual objects (words, morphemes, and their associated concepts). Moreover, what really forces this view of learning to read is the fact that the world presents learners with different writing systems. In what sense is learning to read in English like learning to read in Korean, Arabic, or Chinese? Each language is written in one or more distinctive graphic forms. In each case, the graphic forms are different in appearance and in how they connect to the language. What they have in common is that the learner must figure out how the graphic forms work—how they map onto the learner's spoken language.

If the mapping involves a second language, one that the learner is still acquiring, the learning problem is the same in general (learning the new mapping), although it is severely complicated by the simultaneous acquisition of a second language and, in some cases, a second writing system or orthography. The advantage of first language (L1) literacy acquisition is that it can build on a well-established language system that a child has acquired, with little effort, prior to literacy instruction. If a second writing system is also involved, as when a Chinese learner acquires English, this presents an additional learning task, although one that in general should provide a relatively mild obstacle compared with learning the language itself. Learning to read in a new language (L2) would be facilitated to some extent if reading has universal properties that apply to all writing systems and all orthographies across all languages.

But are there universals in reading, or only a set of specific problems posed by each writing system and language? Comparative writing research shows both the universal dependence of reading on language and the accommodation of this universality to the properties of the writing system (Perfetti, 2003; Perfetti *et al.*, 2005). The most basic universal is the Language Constraint on Writing Systems: writing systems encode spoken language, not meaning. Put to rest by research on logographic systems (Chinese, Japanese kanji) is the idea that reading in such systems implements a simple visual form-to-meaning process that allows the reader to bypass spoken language. Instead, reading appears to depend on language in the most fundamental way: when a reader encounters printed words, he or she understands their meaning within the context of the language, not as signs that derive their meaning independently. This language constraint allows a second universal, The Universal Phonological Principle (UPP; Perfetti *et al.*, 1992). The UPP expresses the generalization that word reading activates phonology at the lowest level of language allowed by the writing system: phoneme, syllable, morpheme, or word (for research in support of this conclusion, see Tan & Perfetti, 1998; Perfetti *et al.*, 2005).

In summary, if there are universal principles, they must accommodate both the language constraint and variations within writing systems. Reading is a process that is embedded in both the language system and the writing system. Universals, therefore, must attend to the nature of both the graphic input and the nature of the linguistic-conceptual objects to which they connect. The Universal Phonological Principle does that. Finally, universals must take into account the properties of the developing human mind that allow the learning of such connections. Beyond universals are the specific variations in languages, orthographies, and writing systems that confront the learner.

In what follows we elaborate these general claims in a way that we hope is relevant for the broad practical issues of learning to read across languages. We begin by examining the basic properties of written language that matter for issues of reading.

Writing systems, scripts, and orthographies

The first thing a literate English speaker notices about written Arabic or Hindi is how different both look from written English. Similarly, Hebrew, Tamil, Khmer, Chinese, Japanese kana, and Korean all look different from English. Interestingly, to a reader familiar with the Roman alphabet, these last three look similar to each other, despite the fact that they represent three fundamentally different writing systems. Figure 2.1 shows some examples of the differences in the appearance of writing, illustrating the variability in both the appearance of writing (the script) and in the fundamental design of the writing system.

Scripts vary not only across writing systems, but also within a specific orthography. Thus English is printed in a Roman script, and children learning to read and write in English, after learning printed Roman letters, learn

Language	Writing system	Script example
English	Alphabetic	All human beings are born free and equal in dignity and rights. They are endowed with reason and conscience and should act towards one another in a spirit of brotherhood.
Dutch	Alphabetic	Alle mensen worden vrij en gelijk in waardigheid en rechten geboren. Zij zijn begiftigd met verstand en geweten, en behoren zich jegens elkander in een geest van broederschap te gedragen.
Spanish	Alphabetic	Todos los seres humanos nacen libres e iguales en dignidad y derechos y, dotados como están de razón y conciencia, deben comportarse fraternalmente los unos con los otros.
Korean	Alphabetic (Hangul)	모든 인간은 태어날 때부터 자유로우며 그 존엄과 권리에 있어 동등하다. 인간은 천부적 으로 이성과 양심을 부여받았으며 서로 형제애의 정신으로 행동하여야한다.
Arabic	Alphabetic (Consonantal)	يولد جميع الناس أحرارًا متساوين في الكرامة والحقوق. وقد وهبوا عقلاً وضميرًا وعليهم ان يعامل بعضهم بعضا بروح الإخاء.
Hebrew	Alphabetic (Consonantal)	כל בני האדם נולדו בני חורין ושווים בערכם ובזכויותיהם. כלם חוננו בתבונה ובמצפון, לפיכך חובה עליהם לנהג איש ברעהו ברוח של אחוה.
Lao	Alphabetic (Tonal)	ມະນຸດທຸກຄົນເກີດມາມີສິດເສລີພາບ ແລະ ສະເໝີໜ້າກັນໃນທາງກຽດສັກສີ ແລະ ທາງສິດ. ເຂົາເຈົ້າລ້ວນມີ ເຫດຜົນ ແລະ ມະໂນທັມ ແລະ ຄວນປະພຶດຕໍ່ກັນ ໃນທາງພີ່ນ້ອງ.
Khmer	Alphabetic (Syllabic)	មនុស្សទាំងអស់កើតមកមានសេរីភាព និងភាពស្មើៗគ្នាក្នុងសិទ្ធិនិងសេចក្ដីថ្លៃថ្នូរ។ មនុស្សគ្រប់រូបសុទ្ធតែមានវិចារណញ្ញាណនិងសតិសម្បជញ្ញៈ ហើយត្រូវប្រព្រឹត្ដចំពោះគ្នាទៅវិញទៅមកក្នុងស្មារតីជាបងប្អូន។
Kannada	Alphabetic (Syllabic)	ಎಲ್ಲಾ ಮಾನವರೂ ಸ್ವತಂತ್ರರಾಗಿಯೇ ಜನಿಸಿದ್ದಾರೆ. ಹಾಗೂ ಘನತೆ ಮತ್ತು ಹಕ್ಕುಗಳಲ್ಲಿ ಸಮಾನರಾಗಿದ್ದಾರೆ. ವಿವೇಕ ಮತ್ತು ಅಂತಃಕರಣ ಗಳನ್ನು ಪಡೆದವರಾದ್ದರಿಂದ ಅವರು ಪರಸ್ಪರ ಸಹೋದರ ಭಾವದಿಂದ ವರ್ತಿಸಬೇಕು.
Chinese	Morphosyllabic (Logographic)	人人生而自由，在尊嚴和權利上一律平等。他們賦有理性和良心，並應以兄弟關係的精神互相對待。

Figure 2.1 Examples of writing systems.

to write in a cursive script. A modern computer font set may contain dozens of different scripts for the same alphabet. As illustrated in Figure 2.2, these visual differences within languages can be striking, but are usually superficial. Underneath their variability in appearance, these script variations within English, Chinese, and Hebrew each represent a single orthography and a single writing system. In contrast, note the graphic forms in Figure 2.3.

At a glance, it might seem that these are script differences, too. Instead, they are deep differences, not in script, but in writing system. Represented are the world's three major writing systems: alphabetic, syllabic, and "logographic." (The logographic designation for Chinese is common, but arguably misleading; see DeFrancis, 1989.) The defining feature of a writing system is its mapping principle—graph to phoneme (alphabetic), graph to syllable (syllabic), and graph to word or morpheme (logographic). Korean Hangul shows that we can represent alphabetic writing without a linear array of letters, but rather with a syllable-size square.

English	Print	CAPITALIZED or lower case Serif Font or San Serif Font
	Cursive	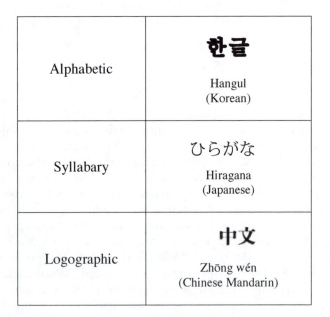
Chinese	Traditional	漢
	Simplified	汉
Hebrew	With vowels	בָּרְעָהוּ
	Without vowels	ברעהו

Figure 2.2 Examples of different scripts in English, Chinese, and Hebrew. Where the script differences within English and Chinese are purely visual, the Hebrew script differences mark linguistic information. However, both Hebrew scripts (with and without vowels) are alphabetic.

Alphabetic	한글 Hangul (Korean)
Syllabary	ひらがな Hiragana (Japanese)
Logographic	中文 Zhōng wén (Chinese Mandarin)

Figure 2.3 The three types of writing systems.

Japanese is especially interesting because it can be written in all three types of writing systems (although only one of its syllabic kana systems is shown in Figure 2.3). One can write Japanese in a syllabary way (hiragana and katakana) or in a "logographic" way (kanji). The kanji system is a borrowing of Chinese characters (a logography), so each kanji graph corresponds to a word, pronounced (to complicate matters) either as it would be in Chinese (the "on" reading) or in Japanese (the "kun" reading). In addition, as an aid to foreign learners, Japanese can be written in "romaji," an alphabetic writing system using Roman letters.

With these examples, we can sharpen the distinction between superficial appearance and writing system design. A script is a systematic expression of visual forms for writing. A writing system expresses the basic principle that maps graphic units onto language units. Thus, Chinese and English differ in writing system design. The Chinese writing system maps graphs (characters) onto words and morphemes, units of meaning, and is thus logographic. English, Italian, and Danish writing systems map graphs onto speech sounds (phonemes) and are thus alphabetic. The Japanese kana system maps graphs onto spoken syllables, and thus is a syllabary. Korean, despite its visual departure from Italian and English, is nonetheless alphabetic because the graphs map to phonemes.

One final distinction is needed: an orthography is the implementation of a writing system to a specific language. Thus, written English is not a distinct writing system but an orthography. It differs from Italian orthography, although both represent alphabetic writing systems. Within alphabetic writing systems, orthographies vary in the transparency of mappings between letters and phonemes. Italian and Finnish are very transparent (or shallow), English is relatively nontransparent (deep or opaque), and Danish falls in between. As Figure 2.4 illustrates, transparency can be considered as a dimension along which orthographies can be ordered. The possible consequences for such an ordering are significant for learning to read. A learner can confidently connect a letter to a sound in the shallower or more transparent orthographies. However, the basis for such confidence wanes as one moves to the deeper or more opaque orthographies.

Which of these aspects of written language—script, orthography, and writing system—make a difference for reading? Perhaps all of them do. At the script level, there appears to be little evidence that, within a given orthography (e.g. English), script variations deeply affect reading. Some of the effects of scripts on readers are a matter of visual familiarity, and such effects can be modified with experience, as illustrated in studies that alter the normal orientation of printed input (e.g. Kolers, 1976, 1985). In learning to read, a child usually encounters a restricted number of closely related scripts, and this relative uniformity may aid the learning of graphic forms. Although a lack of clear evidence makes this conclusion tentative, it is probably safe to assume that, compared with orthography and writing systems, the superficial visual forms are not a major source of difficulty in learning.

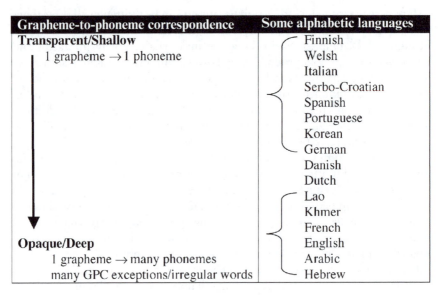

Grapheme-to-phoneme correspondence	Some alphabetic languages
Transparent/Shallow 1 grapheme → 1 phoneme	Finnish Welsh Italian Serbo-Croatian Spanish Portuguese Korean German Danish Dutch Lao Khmer French
Opaque/Deep 1 grapheme → many phonemes many GPC exceptions/irregular words	English Arabic Hebrew

Figure 2.4 Orthographic depth of various languages.

However, because reading begins with visual input, the visual forms of the graph do matter for the visual stages of reading, as has been shown by differences between Chinese and English in the degree of involvement of right hemisphere visual areas (Tan *et al.*, 2005a).

Orthography

In the case of orthography, it appears that there can be significant effects on learning to read. Because of the distinction we must make between writing system and orthography, the most meaningful comparisons for orthographic effects are those within a writing system. Such comparisons are available only for alphabetic systems. The orthographic depth hypothesis (Frost *et al.*, 1987; Katz & Feldman, 1983; Katz & Frost, 1992) asserts that the continuum of orthographic transparency illustrated in Figure 2.4 influences the strategies adopted by readers. The more shallow or transparent the orthography—that is, the more reliable the correspondence between graphemes and speech segments—the more the reader uses a print-to-sound decoding strategy. The deeper or less transparent the orthography, the more the reader uses a direct look-up of the word, without grapheme-speech decoding.

Research has been directed at orthographic comparisons that involve the less transparent English compared with more transparent orthographies, such as German and Welsh. The research suggests that German children and adults trust their orthography to implement a reliable grapheme-phoneme conversion, whereas English children and adults come to rely more on orthographic whole-word reading (Frith *et al.*, 1998; Landerl & Wimmer, 2000; Wimmer & Goswami, 1994). Thus, German children read pronounceable non-words nearly as well as real words, whereas English children do much more poorly on non-words. Although the interpretation of such results has some difficulties, the carefulness of the studies allows the interpretation that readers of the two orthographies differ in how they approach letter strings. German readers are more likely to treat a string of letters as decodable, English readers are more likely to first try to find the whole word that the string represents. Similar conclusions come from studies comparing children in Wales, who learn to read in English as well as in Welsh, a highly consistent alphabetic system (Ellis & Hooper, 2001).

Another way to understand the differences in orthographic depth is by observing the size of the units that readers use in mapping the graphemes to pronunciations. The unreliability of English grapheme-phoneme mappings may lead to more variability in the size of units that are successful in the orthography-to-phonology mappings. German, although it too has some inconsistencies (Ziegler *et al.*, 1997), provides a more uniform mapping pair at the lowest level allowed by writing systems (grapheme-phoneme). English has lower mapping consistency at the grapheme-phoneme level, but higher consistency at the rime level, the vowel plus consonant ending of a syllable (Kessler & Treiman, 2001, 2003; Treiman *et al.*, 1995). Instead of decoding letter-by-letter, readers of English may use a larger portion, or "grain size," of the printed word to map onto spoken language. This perspective, known as the grain-size hypothesis, can be applied across writing systems as well (see Wydell & Butterworth, 1999; Ziegler & Goswami, 2005). Transparent alphabetic systems apply a small-grain mapping; and syllabaries, which map graphs to syllables, apply a larger-grain mapping.

Writing system

Alphabetic reading can involve the use of letter-phoneme mappings, a level of mapping that can support both learning to read and adult skilled reading because the alphabetic system maps graphic units to phonemes. In contrast, the Chinese logographic and the Japanese kanji systems map graphic units to morphemes and words; they do not allow phoneme-level mappings to function in either learning to read or in skilled reading. Instead, they allow reading to proceed from graphic form to meaning and from graphic form to syllable. Notice that the graphic forms map not only to meaning, but also to pronunciation. The spoken syllable indeed is activated during silent skilled reading in Japanese kanji and in Chinese (Perfetti & Zhang, 1995).

Japanese writing allows the implication of syllable-level mappings on reading to be seen clearly. Japanese kanji (grapheme-word or grapheme-morae) and Japanese kana (grapheme-syllable) are very different in writing system design. However, both potentially provide relatively uniform mapping pairs from a graphic form to a spoken form. The learner can come to acquire these mappings, whether the corresponding spoken units have meaning or are only syllables that are parts of meaningful words. And because the mappings involve a relatively large-grain spoken unit, the syllable, they may be learned by a reader who has trouble learning alphabetic mappings. Indeed Wydell and colleagues (Wydell & Butterworth, 1999; Wydell & Kondo, 2003) reported the case of a bilingual child who, although dyslexic in English (an inconsistent small-grain size system), could easily read both kana and kanji (consistent larger-grain size systems).

These observations emphasize the differences in reading due to writing systems. Syllabaries and logographs provide larger spoken units for graphic mappings than alphabets. The greater accessibility of syllable units compared to phonetic units can affect reading acquisition and the process of skilled reading. However, universals emerge across different writing systems as well. One misconception about Chinese is that it is an exception to the principle that writing systems encode spoken language because it is pictographic, mapping referents and concepts directly. A more sophisticated form of this misconception is that Chinese, although not mainly pictographic, picks out the meaning level of the language to the exclusion of the phonology. This view treats Chinese as a morpheme-based system.

The first misconception is corrected by the observation that only about one or two percent of currently used Chinese characters have identifiable pictographic content (DeFrancis, 1989). Figure 2.5 illustrates the evolution of the form of the characters for "horse" and for "fish" in the clear direction away from literal depictions and toward abstraction. In Figure 2.5, it is difficult to discern the referent-object in the presently used traditional and simplified characters, no matter how pictographic the original appeared in its discovery in the Shang dynasty oracle bones (1000 BCE or earlier; DeFrancis, 1989; see also Luk & Bialystok, 2005).

With the abstract nature of the character established, the second issue is the claim that Chinese is morphemic. This description of Chinese is correct but incomplete and therefore slightly misleading. The characters do represent morphemes, but they also represent syllables. Thus, a character is morpho-syllabic, corresponding not to an abstract formless piece of meaning, but usually to a spoken Chinese syllable that is also a morpheme. Thus, to re-use the horse example, the character represents not horsiness but the Chinese single syllable word /ma/3 that means horse. (The number following the syllable indicates one of four pitch contours or "tones" that are part of all Chinese syllables.) This simple fact means that a Chinese character can be read to correspond to a meaning, to a spoken word, or to both. Because Chinese does not have graphic elements that correspond to phonemes, it is not alphabetic. But the writing unit does correspond to a meaning-bearing spoken language unit—the syllable. Thus it maps spoken language, as do all writing systems. Chinese is more complex than this simple example suggests, because most characters are compounds, the combination of two or more components (characters or radicals). One of the two components often gives

	fish	**horse**
Oracle Bone Script Shang and Yin Dynasties *c.* 1400–1200 B.C.E.	𩵋	馬
Large Seal Script Zhou Dynasty *c.* 1400–1200 B.C.E.	魚	馬
Small Seal Script Qin Dynasty 221–207 B.C.E.	魚	馬
Traditional Script Han Dynasty 207 A.D.–present	魚	馬
Simplified Script People's Republic of China 1949–present	鱼	马
Pinyin People's Republic of China 1958–present	y	mǎ

Figure 2.5 Evolution of Chinese characters from pictographs to abstract character.

Source Information adapted from omniglot.com

information about pronunciation (the phonetic radical) and one often gives information about meaning (the semantic radical). Figure 2.6 provides an example of this kind of phonetic-semantic compounding. The character /ri/4 (sun) combines with the character for green (/qing/1), which donates its pronunciation to the compound as a whole. Thus the compound is also pronounced /qing/2 and means sunshine or clear weather.

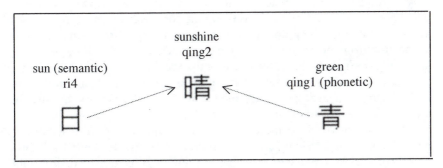

Figure 2.6 Chinese compound character with semantic and phonetic radicals.

However, this example does not do justice to the range of combinations that can occur in phonetic compounds, which make up the vast majority of characters. In most compounds, the phonetic component does not give a full mapping to the correct syllabic pronunciation. Sometimes the component and the character share a phoneme or two, other times nothing at all. On average, the potential phonetic part of the compound is more likely to have a pronunciation different from the character as a whole than it is to match it, even disregarding tone. (See Perfetti, 2003 for examples.)

With this brief and incomplete description of Chinese writing, we come to the simple point that Chinese maps spoken language as well as meanings. A character, whether simple or compound, associates with a spoken syllable (often a one-syllable word) that has a meaning. The speech mapping is non-compositional; that is, there is no part of the character that corresponds to a phoneme. But the mapping is highly deterministic; a given character is usually associated with a single syllable, allowing a consistent connection between writing and speech. Thus, the universal principle that writing systems map phonology unites the two highly contrasting writing systems: logographic (Chinese, Japanese kanji) and alphabetic. It encompasses as well the straight syllabary system of Japanese kana. All writing systems map graphic units to spoken language units.

Writing systems influence the implementation of the universal phonological principle

If all writing systems honor the Universal Phonological Principle, then we should expect to find evidence that reading in any writing system involves the use of phonology. Indeed, the evidence suggests that for skilled readers of Chinese, phonology is part of normal silent reading, including word identification (Perfetti & Liu, 2005; Perfetti *et al.*, 2005). It would be a mistake to conclude from this, however, that reading is identical across writing systems or that learning to read is unaffected by the writing system. The similarity of reading across writing systems lies at the highest and most general level. The differences lie in the details and, of course, details matter.

With respect to skilled reading, the Chinese use of phonology appears to be different from the alphabetic use of phonology. Reading a character uses a connection from the graphic form (the character) to its meaning, and a connection from the graphic form to its pronunciation, more or less in parallel. (See Perfetti *et al.*, 2005, for one way to model this structure.) Reading a character can activate its pronunciation first or its meaning first, but there is no necessary sequencing in which the pronunciation comes first to mediate the meaning. More fundamental is that the activation of phonology must await the orthographic identification of a character. It is "addressed phonology," based on retrieving an association of the character with a syllable-morpheme in the language. In Chinese, phonology is activated threshold style, triggered by the reader's representation of the character reaching its identification threshold (Perfetti *et al.*, 2005). In an alphabetic system, the phonological activation does not wait until an orthographic identification of the word is complete, but rather is immediately begun with identification of a letter or two, and "cascades" as more letters are identified from left to right (Coltheart *et al.*, 2001). These differences occur within the few hundred milliseconds it takes to identify a letter string as a word and to produce either its pronunciation or meaning (Perfetti, Liu, & Tan, 2005). Thus, the product of the identification is not necessarily different across writing systems. Only the rapid intermediate processes that bring this about are different.

In the case of learning to read, writing system differences also matter and may be simpler to observe. Although there is much variability in the teaching of English reading, the successful procedures somehow must help the learner acquire the alphabetic principle. The letters correspond not to meaning but to sound. The path to this learning may vary, but the successful result is more or less the same, and learners who fail to acquire the specific mappings will not succeed at reading. In learning to read Chinese, what is acquired is not the alphabetic principle, nor even a corresponding syllabary principle (which would apply to Japanese kana), but associations between specific character forms and their corresponding syllable morphemes. These associations are learned through a level of practice at writing as well as reading that is substantially more than what occurs in alphabetic learning (Perfetti & Zhang, 1995; Tan *et al.*, 2005b). Children in mainland China begin by learning alphabetic pinyin, which then supports the introduction of characters. In Hong Kong, the learning follows the traditional direct approach, with no alphabetic foundation. In either case, the product of learning is the ability to identify each character as a meaning-bearing syllable that occurs in the spoken language.

This is not to say the phonology is not relevant in learning Chinese. Ho and Bryant (1997) and others point to a predictive role of phonological awareness in learning to read Chinese, just as there is in English. However, morphological awareness, as one would expect, is also important (McBride-Chang *et al.*, 2003). A recent study (Tan *et al.*, 2005b) adds to the picture the importance of writing in learning to read Chinese characters. Tan *et al.* found that character-copying skill showed a much stronger association with children's character reading than did phonological awareness. Character-writing skills may be especially relevant for the specific character learning that is required for Chinese reading. To learn written Chinese is to acquire a lexicon of individual characters that follow an explicit compositional structure, but one that does not represent phonemes.

The larger picture is that reading, because of the Language Constraint, always takes the reader from a graphic form to language and to meaning. Conceptual understanding is not direct, but rather is mediated through language. This means that writing engages a reader's knowledge of phonology and morphology at the word level, and knowledge of syntax at the sentence level. Knowledge of a wide range of culturally embedded language and non-linguistic conventions is also very important for competent reading at all levels, and these become increasingly important beyond the level of the sentence. Our focus here is on the reading of words because this is where the writing system and the orthography make their major contribution. We turn now to a closer examination of how writing systems and language affect learning to read.

Learning to read in different languages and different writing systems

Across all languages and writing systems, the task of the learner is to learn how to obtain meaning from printed words and larger units of text. And for this, learners have to figure out how their writing system encodes their language. The first challenge for a learner of an alphabetic system is to appreciate that the smallest units of writing are arbitrary mappings of minimal, semantically meaningless units of speech—phonemes, not syllables or whole words. Each writing system presents its own distinctive mapping challenge. There has been sufficient comparative research to support some conclusions on how these challenges matter for learning. Indeed, the recognition that the world's variety of writing systems, orthographies, and scripts are relevant for understanding literacy acquisition is evidenced by the recent publication of a Handbook of Orthography and Literacy (Joshi & Aaron, 2005).

Comparisons within alphabetic writing systems

Much of the research on learning to read has been conducted with native speakers of English who were learning to decode words in their alphabetically written language. However, compared to most other modern languages, decoding English is rather difficult, owing to its inconsistent grapheme-phoneme correspondences. As illustrated in Figure 2.4, English is one of the least transparent of alphabetic writing systems, exceeded perhaps by Hebrew and Arabic when they are written without vowel markings. Resolving inconsistent connections between letters and phonemes and between letter strings and words places a demand on English word reading that is greater than for more transparent orthographies, such as Italian (e.g. Paulesu *et al.*, 2000, 2001) or Welsh (e.g. Ellis & Hooper, 2001; Spencer, 2001). For example, the dominant mapping for the letter "o" in the rime unit "-one" is its pronunciation in "bone," "tone," and "lone." When the reader encounters "gone," there is a conflict between this dominant letter-phoneme mapping and the pronunciation of "gone." As the dual-route models (Coltheart *et al.*, 2001) explicitly recognize, and connectionist models must capture in other ways, there are two pathways to get to a word's pronunciation, and sometimes, as in "gone," they are in conflict. In fact, even in skilled reading there is a small price to pay in reading time for such conflicts, at least when the word is encountered infrequently. The reader has to, in effect, weigh knowledge of the letter-level mapping against knowledge of the word-level mapping. For learners, these conflicting pathways necessitate the use of error-prone reading strategies (Frith *et al.*, 1998). Although one can, because of these problems, characterize English as a "dyslexic" orthography (Spencer, 2000; see also Wydell & Butterworth, 1999), it is important to recognize that dyslexia appears to be general and not restricted to opaque orthographies nor even to alphabetic writing (e.g. Stevenson, 1984; Ziegler & Goswami, 2005). Nevertheless, there are specific challenges to word reading posed by an alphabetic writing system whose orthographic implementation deviates from its mapping principle as often as English does. To illustrate this, it is useful to contrast the English case with other alphabetic orthographies.

Compare English and Welsh, for example, both of which use a Roman-based alphabet. English uses 26 letters (graphemes) to represent 44 sounds (phonemes). Most letters have multiple possible pronunciations depending on the word context. The letter "g" has at least three different sounds (e.g. in "garage" or "giraffe" or "thing") or can be silent (e.g. "gnome"). Vowel sounds are especially unreliably mapped in English (e.g. "give" and "five"). The complex mappings and exceptions to decoding generalizations that characterize English are largely absent in Welsh. Indeed, Welsh letter-sound mappings are so consistent that Welsh dictionaries do not include pronunciation entries after each word in the way that English dictionaries do. Welsh uses 21 letters from the same Roman-based alphabet (some of them in two-letter digraphs such as "ch" or "ff") to represent roughly 40 sounds. But unlike English, Welsh has nearly one-to-one mapping for single consonants with some digraph combinations, and vowel sounds are spelled by single vowels, marked vowels, or diphthongs. With the exception of some initial letters altered by a Celtic system of mutations, Welsh is a transparent orthography. For instance, the letter "g" predictably sounds like /g/. It is this grapheme-to-phoneme predictability in Welsh relative to English that leads to different decoding strategies in the two cases.

Ellis and Hooper (2001) showed that six and seven-year-old children learning to read Welsh were able to implement their alphabetic mapping more easily than children learning to read English. The children were well matched in other relevant variables. Welsh children learn both English and Welsh in school, with geographical region (associated with language dominance) determining which language they learn to read first. The Welsh-reading children tended to use a decoding strategy based on letter-sound correspondences, which reliably predict the correct word pronunciation in their language. This strategy was apparent in their overall stronger reading ability and in the kinds of errors they made when they did misread words. They also correctly read aloud a greater number of low-frequency words, even some words for which they could not report the correct meaning. On the other hand, English-reading children had difficulty reading many words, even those for which they knew the meanings. And when they made errors, these errors were less likely to share many phonemes with the target word, as if higher weight were given to a whole-word route based on partial visual analysis of the letters. In effect, the evidence is that children learning English learned to use the alphabetic procedure unreliably and did not generalize it to decode new words.

One might wonder whether these cross-linguistic differences are simply due to instructional differences. Shallow orthographies lend themselves more readily to phonics instruction and phonics instruction appears to be used for all shallow orthographies. Instruction in English has tended to de-emphasize phonics. However, Ellis and Hooper (2001) controlled for this and a number of other factors by using participants in the same geographic region of Northern Wales who received equivalent phonics instruction in their respective classrooms. Language was the primary factor that differed. That differences were nevertheless found between Welsh and English readers lends support to the hypothesis that the orthographic transparency influences the reading strategies that learners acquire. Decoding letters to phonemes is more adaptive in a shallow orthography than in a deep orthography, and children learning to read appear to tune their reading to the functional properties of their orthography.

This demonstration that the consistency of orthography-to-phonology mappings can lead to different reading strategies fits well within the broad theoretical outlines of how word identification works. We noted above the assumption of dual-route theories that there are two ways to read printed words (Coltheart *et al.*, 2001). One is via an assembled (sublexical) pathway along which letters are mapped to phonemes, which are assembled into larger units. This route depends on reliable mappings, and works well for Welsh and German and for other shallow orthographies. The other pathway is an addressed or lexical route, in which the word corresponding to a full-word letter pattern is retrieved. This path is needed for irregular or exception words, words whose assembled letter-phoneme mappings fail to match the target pronunciation. Since English has many irregular words, children successfully learning to read English will learn to use the lexical pathway for many words. In fact, it is possible that they will come to use this pathway for all words, a strategy that will fail for words that readers have not experienced before or whose frequency has been too low to establish an addressable representation. For such children, whole-word or sight recognition comes to completely outweigh the letter-sound mappings. Although dual-route models provide a natural account of these phenomena, single route models, with the use of multi-layer networks, can also do so (Plaut, 1999; Plaut *et al.*, 1996; Seidenberg & McClelland, 1989). Additionally, models with learning mechanisms have the potential to account for how different orthographies might lead to different reading strategies (Harm & Seidenberg, 1999).

The two different strategies (henceforth "sublexical" and "lexical") lead to different types of errors, as shown in the English-Welsh studies. The lexical strategy leads readers, when they make errors, to respond with real words based on shared letters or partial visual overlap with the target word, for example, responding "near" for the word "never." The sublexical strategy leads to errors with high phonemic overlap with the target word, even when that means producing non-words (Ellis & Hooper, 2001). This difference in error patterns has also been found in comparisons of English with German, a transparent orthography. Wimmer and colleagues (e.g. Frith *et al.*, 1998; Landerl, Wimmer, & Frith, 1997; Wimmer & Goswami, 1994) have shown that German children decode words relying on the sublexical strategy, that is, grapheme-phoneme conversion, whereas English children decode words relying on a lexical strategy. The German children gave more non-word responses, indicating they were sounding out new words at the expense of lexicality, and remaining faithful to learned letter-sound correspondences. The English children were more likely to respond incorrectly with a real word that looked similar to the target item. Overall, English children made more errors than German children when reading both non-words and low frequency words, again lending support for the orthographic depth hypothesis.

Further evidence for orthographic factors comes from a comparison of English with Italian, which is orthographically very transparent. Paulesu and colleagues (Paulesu *et al.*, 2000, 2001) showed both behavioral and brain differences for native speakers of Italian versus English. Generally, both Italian and English participants read real words faster than non-words, indicating that lexicality, that is, whether a letter string is a word, plays a role even in a shallow orthography. However, Italian participants were faster than their English participants at reading both real words and non-words. Using positron emission tomography (PET), Paulesu found many common brain regions for Italian reading and English reading: left inferior frontal and pre-motor cortex, left temporal gyrus, left fusiform gyrus, and right superior temporal gyrus. Most of these left hemisphere regions were activated more in reading non-words than in reading words. In addition to these regions that were activated by both languages, there were regions whose activation was specific to each of the two languages. English reading activated the left posterior inferior temporal and inferior frontal gyrus. Italian reading activated the left superior temporal gyrus and inferior parietal cortex (planum temporale). The interpretation linking this pattern to the orthographic differences is that the superior temporal region is more active in Italian, because this region supports the sublexical letter-phoneme procedures that are encouraged by Italian's transparent orthography. The greater role of the left frontal and posterior inferior temporal regions for English may implicate English's greater reliance on a lexical procedure. Although there is some uncertainty in how to characterize the functionality of the brain's reading network in detail, the network is likely to be tuned by the reader's experience with word reading. If the orthography shapes a strategy that is adaptive to its use of sublexical versus lexical pathways, then the reading network will come to reflect this adaptation (Fiez, 2000).

The manifestations of dyslexia also seem to be affected by orthography. Readers of a shallow orthography may have reading problems, but these problems are less likely to involve sublexical phonology and more likely to involve slow reading rates and poor spelling (Landerl *et al.*, 1997). Dyslexic readers of English show these deficits in addition to impaired phonological decoding and phonological awareness (Ziegler & Goswami, 2005). Furthermore, the neuroimaging study of Paulesu (2001) that compared French, Italian, and English found differences in brain activity for normal and dyslexic readers. For the dyslexic groups, compared with a non-reading baseline task, reading produced less activity in left hemisphere areas (middle, inferior, and superior temporal cortex) that were involved in normal reading of deep orthographies. Dyslexics also showed more activity in the left planum temporale, thought to be involved in processing shallow orthographies. One interpretation of this pattern is that the dyslexics were processing deep orthographies (English and French) as if they were shallow, that is, applying letter-phoneme decoding to irregular words. The dyslexic group did not have greater activation in any brain region relative to the control group. However, the controls did show greater activation in several regions relative to the dyslexic group: superior temporal gyrus, middle temporal gyrus, inferior temporal gyrus, and middle occipital gyrus. There were no orthography-specific effects among the three dyslexic groups. This again lends support to the notion that different strategies (alphabetic vs. whole word) possibly recruit different brain regions.

Korean provides an important comparison in that it is alphabetic but quite different in appearance from the horizontal arrangement of letters seen in most alphabetic writing. Instead of a horizontal arrangement, Korean letters are configured in square blocks that correspond to syllables. Most blocks represent a CVC syllable, with the initial consonant and vowel depicted on the top and the final consonant on the bottom (see Figures 2.1 and 2.3). The Korean reader can decode words at the subsyllabic level rather than the whole word level because the orthography represents an alphabetic writing system. Yoon, Bolger, Kwon, and Perfetti (2002) found that Korean children as young as five years old were sensitive to subsyllabic units within written Korean and that their preferred subsyllabic structure was body + coda (for "pin," /pI/ + /n/), rather than the onset + rime (/p/ + /In/) as it is in English. Such a difference in subsyllabic structure could arise because of the script—the visual differences between Korean and English in how the alphabet is displayed—or because of linguistic differences. Based on the fact that the preference differences were observed in speech as well as reading, Yoon *et al.* (2002) suggested it is a linguistic difference. Given our emphasis here on writing and orthography, this conclusion provides an equally important consideration. The language, not just the writing system, is critical in learning to read. Specific facets of language influence the development of the writing system and the orthography, and they influence the language units the reader uses in reading.

Finally, notice that the languages we have examined here—Welsh, German, Italian, and Korean—are just a few examples of orthographically shallow alphabetically written languages. Many other languages including those discussed in other chapters of this book are shown in Figure 2.4. For example, both Spanish and Dutch are high on the transparency scale. French, vowel-less Arabic, Lao, and Khmer, are less transparent, closer to English. All of these languages use alphabetic writing systems. We turn in the next section to non-alphabetic languages.

Comparisons across writing systems

Compared with alphabetic systems, both the Chinese and Japanese writing systems represent larger units of speech—syllables rather than phonemes. Chinese characters represent an onset-rime unit that by itself can usually be a one-syllable word, or can be combined to form multiple-character words. A beginning reader must learn and memorize the corresponding spoken syllable/morpheme for each new character. Approximately 2,000 distinct orthographic forms (characters) must be learned for a Chinese speaker to be considered basically literate (Kennedy, 1966). Given the design principle of Chinese, characters cannot be decoded at the level of graph to phoneme, as is possible in alphabetic writing. Furthermore, although characters correspond to syllables, Chinese is not a syllabary, which would require a systematic mapping from a meaningless (and productive) graphic unit to a spoken syllable, as occurs in Japanese kana. The characters map to meaningful morpheme-level syllables at a low level of systematicity. This structure appears to promote a whole character approach to reading.

In its kanji system, Japanese borrows the form of Chinese characters and, as we previously noted, applies either a Japanese ("kun") or a Chinese ("on") pronunciation to them. In contrast, Japanese kana is a writing system that uses a distinct graph for each possible syllable in the language. Once a reader has learned a few dozen correspondences, reading is a matter of combining syllables into multisyllabic words. Katakana and hiragana are the two types of kana syllabaries used in Japanese. The grain size of Japanese kana is smaller (one syllable of a multi-syllable word) than that of kanji (whole word). Reading at these two different levels of writing systems may involve different mixes of basic reading processes and may draw on somewhat different cognitive resources.

Shafiullah and Monsell (1999) conducted a study of reading processes using naming and semantic categorization tasks while continually switching between two types of scripts (kana and kanji). They found a very small (13 ms) but significant cost of switching between kana and kanji, but no cost of switching within the two equally transparent forms of kana (katakana and hiragana). This suggests that reading either type of syllabary involves shared kana orthographic processes; their differences are at the script level, not the system level. Kana processes and kanji processes, however, are different at the system level; the processes are sufficiently distinct to require different cognitive procedures; and a switch from one to the other bears some cost. Consistent with this conclusion is the finding that kana (syllabic) stimuli produce faster pronunciations than do kanji (whole word), whereas kanji stimuli produce faster semantic judgments, perhaps due to a more lexical approach to reading whole words (Shibahara *et al.*, 2003). This implies that different reading processes develop in specific adaptation to the basic mapping structures of these two writing systems.

Differences in the reading processes required by different writing systems may also be reflected in the neural organization of reading in the brain. Several brain-imaging studies suggest that Chinese reading and alphabetic reading recruit distinctive as well as overlapping brain regions. This general conclusion emerges from two reviews and meta-analyses of several such studies reported by Bolger *et al.* (2005) and by Tan *et al.* (2005a). Moreover, even within the Chinese writing system, there is evidence that different brain regions support different units of linguistic processing. Siok, Jin, Fletcher, and Tan (2003) investigated syllabic versus phonemic processing in an fMRI study in which native speakers of Mandarin made homophone judgments and initial consonant judgments on pairs of Chinese characters. Results showed that syllabic processing, as seen in the homophone judgment task, recruited areas of the left middle frontal cortex, whereas phonemic processing, as seen in the onset judgment task, recruited the left inferior prefrontal gyri. This result suggests that separate brain regions have functions that support distinctive processes at the phoneme level compared with the syllable level, even in a single writing system where stimuli are held constant across tasks.

Adult learning of a new writing system

When adults learn to read in a new writing system they face challenges beyond those faced by the native language reader. Lacking a native knowledge of the spoken language, they must learn the spoken language while simultaneously learning to read the written language. Furthermore, writing system differences across languages may provide unique challenges for the learner. For example, how does a native Chinese speaker learn to read English? Conversely, how does a native English speaker learn to read Chinese?

Addressing these learning questions can begin with another question: the relationship between reading in L1 and L2 across the two writing systems. Liu and Perfetti (2003) studied native Chinese speakers who were fairly fluent in English by recording event-related brain potentials (ERPs) during Chinese and English word reading. Specifically, participants performed a delayed-naming task with high- and low-frequency words in Chinese and

English. The ERP recording showed clear differences between L1 Chinese and L2 English, beginning with ERPs that reflected early (100–200ms) graphic processing. In effect, Chinese characters showed slightly faster orthographic recognition than English words, and Chinese high-frequency words showed faster orthographic recognition than low-frequency words. Occipital area activation (reflecting visual-orthographic processing) was longer for L2 (English) words than L1 (Chinese) words, and longer for low-frequency words compared to high-frequency words in L1. Thus, graphical analysis requires more processing time for L2 than for L1 and for less familiar items compared with more familiar words. This graphic analysis is prior to phonological and semantic analysis.

Furthermore, source localization of the Liu and Perfetti (2003) ERP data showed some common brain regions for the two languages, as well as some brain regions distinctively involved in one or the other language. In line with general understanding of the brain's reading network, both Chinese and English showed early encoding of graphic forms in posterior visual areas, with later phonological and semantic processing involving anterior areas of the reading network. Language-distinct brain regions emerged also within the first 100–200 ms of word reading. Chinese high- and low-frequency words specifically recruited bilateral occipital regions, whereas English high-frequency words recruited only the left occipital cortex. Within 300– 400 ms, Chinese activated right prefrontal regions, and English activated medial frontal regions. Thus even for speakers who have gained some fluency in both Chinese and English, we see differences between the two languages in the time course of word reading and in the brain regions that support word reading.

With such differences established, the question becomes whether learners of Chinese come to show language-specific patterns of the same type as shown by Chinese-English bilinguals. Liu *et al.* (2005) studied native speakers of English who learned a limited set of Chinese characters. Participants learned the pronunciation, the meaning, or both the pronunciation and meaning of 60 Chinese characters in the course of a three-day training period. Following learning, participants viewed the Chinese characters they had learned along with novel Chinese characters and English words in an fMRI procedure. Comparisons across conditions showed more activation for learned Chinese characters relative to English words at several areas, including a bilateral pattern in medial, middle frontal, insula, occipital, fusiform, and superior parietal regions. Conversely, English words produced more activation than learned Chinese words at bilateral superior and inferior frontal regions as well as middle and superior temporal gyri. The pattern for these learners while they were viewing Chinese overlapped in key regions found for native speakers of Chinese. These include both bilateral visual cortex (compared with left hemisphere for English) and the middle frontal gyrus, an area that seems specific to Chinese character reading (Tan *et al.*, 2005a). This suggests that, although there may be a universal brain network for reading, the network makes accommodations to the specific features of the writing system (the system accommodation hypothesis, Perfetti & Liu, 2005). Especially remarkable is how rapid at least some of this accommodation is, perhaps as soon as real learning is underway.

Finally, a related study investigated native speakers of English who were learning Chinese in a university setting (Nelson *et al.*, 2005). FMRI data collected after one year of classroom study showed that English speakers recruited new brain regions that have been shown to be used by Chinese readers, especially bilateral visual and visual-temporal cortex, as previously found (Liu *et al.*, 2005). Nelson and colleagues (2005) included an informative comparison with Chinese-English bilinguals. These readers showed high overlap in the visual brain regions for Chinese and for English. Specifically, the bilinguals showed, for both English and Chinese, the Chinese pattern of bilateral activation as opposed to the alphabetic pattern of left hemisphere dominance. This pattern may suggest that, whereas English speakers learning Chinese show brain network accommodation to the new system, a system that cannot be decoded phonemically like their L1, Chinese speakers who have learned English may use the same whole-word reading strategy for L1 Chinese and for their new L2 English. The too-simple idea here is that Chinese readers may read English as they do Chinese. It remains to be seen whether this is a characteristic of high levels of skill in the new system or one that really depends on the writing system. On the latter formulation, one might say something like Chinese-style reading can handle all systems, whereas alphabetic-style reading is specialized for alphabets. Again, this is a too-simple account that will be modified as we learn more about how the brain responds to learning to read.

These three studies of Chinese and English reading suggest that two very different languages with fundamentally different writing systems share reading processes, beginning with graphic encoding and including the retrieval of both phonological and semantic constituents of words. The brain's reading network shares much of its functionality across languages and writing systems, consistent with the existence of language-general processes in reading. The orthographic-phonological and semantic processes that operate in word-reading are similar across languages, but the time course of these processes depends on frequency or familiarity of words either within a language or across languages. In one's native language, a reader initiates more quickly and completes the processing of graphic forms and moves to pronunciation and meaning. Nevertheless, language-specific characteristics, including the writing system's mapping principles, the visual aspects of the script, and the orthographic consistency, determine variations in the details of these processes. These details are visible as variations in the contributions of specific components of the brain's reading network.

Transfer across systems

Finally, we turn to an issue raised by our discussion of learning across writing systems. Is the acquisition of reading in a second language dependent on the match between the first and second writing system? First, we observe that the match between L1 and L2 is a factor in the acquisition of a second language. The competition model (Bates & MacWhinney, 1987; MacWhinney, 1997) explicitly predicts that learners of L2 will have problems where their L1 grammar provides a point of difference in some grammatical feature. The parallel question is whether orthographies and writing systems present comparable points of match and mismatch.

An obvious candidate is the mapping system. For a Chinese native speaker, there is a mapping mismatch in learning an alphabetic system. Chinese children (in the mainland) learn the pinyin alphabet first, and thus they are familiar with alphabets when they encounter English or some other alphabetic system. However, pinyin is virtually never encountered in Chinese writing for adults, and it is not clear that later learning to read in English, especially as an adult, benefits much from knowledge of pinyin. The fact that pinyin is transparent, may further limit its easy transfer to the nontransparent orthography of English, particularly since pinyin is orthographically transparent.

Let us consider the Chinese L1 learner of English L2 compared with the Korean L1 learner of English L2. If mapping principles can be transferred, then the Korean learner has an advantage over a Chinese learner in learning an alphabetic system. Korean makes a solid comparison with Chinese for two reasons: Korean is linguistically distant from English, and its square, syllabic-size units do not resemble the alphabet used in English.

Wang, Koda, and Perfetti (2003) compared Korean L1 and Chinese L1 adults in their English reading. Their skill level in English was comparable, allowing the question to focus on the reading strategies used for English. If mapping transfers, despite the differences in visual appearance, then Korean readers may use the same sublexical (letter-phoneme) strategy that works in reading Korean in reading English as well. By contrast, Chinese readers may attempt to transfer their lexical (holistic) strategy to English, as implied by the brain imaging results (Nelson *et al.*, 2005) for Chinese bilinguals reading English. Wang *et al.* tested (2003) their Korean-English and Chinese-English bilinguals for their relative reliance on phonological and orthographic processing in English word identification. The hypothesis was that Korean would support sublexical strategies that result in phonological processing, whereas Chinese would support visual-lexical strategies that would show effects in orthographic processing. This hypothesis was tested in a semantic category judgment task that required participants to decide whether an English word belonged to a semantic category. Korean ESL learners showed a homophone effect: more false positive errors to homophones of category exemplars (e.g. Is bare an animal?) than to spelling controls. Chinese ESL learners showed a reduced homophone effect that depended on spelling similarity: only when homophones were visually similar to exemplars (creek, creak) did they make errors (cf. knows, nose). Chinese bilinguals also performed more poorly in a phonological awareness task, compared with Korean readers. Wang *et al.* suggested that writing system mapping principles are subject to transfer to new languages, and that the relative match of the mappings for Korean and Chinese produced the observed effects.

Wang *et al.* (2003) also pointed out that such results might also reflect language differences rather than writing system effects. This is a serious problem for studies of comparative reading generally, and for transfer effects in L2 in particular. Although it is nearly impossible to control fully for language factors (as opposed to orthography and writing system factors), the language factors are very important. They also have not been studied much in comparative reading research, which has focused mainly on written language factors. As the Korean-English comparisons of Yoon *et al.* (2002) suggest, it is very likely that language factors will emerge as important. These factors, after all, shape the writing system. English orthography is inconsistent partly because it has a very large vocabulary that derives from different languages with different phonologies. Further, written English has undergone only modest spelling changes compared with the larger changes in pronunciations that the spellings map. Chinese writing, or so it has been argued, is a poor candidate for an alphabet because of its many homophones and its tone system. Observations such as these make it apparent that the language itself inevitably affects reading: first through how it has influenced writing, and second through how it affects the output—the linguistic representations—of reading.

Summary and conclusions

In learning to read, part of the learning process is to figure out how the writing system encodes the reader's language. Because all writing systems work through language rather than through non-language concepts (the Language Constraint on Writing), there is a universal problem to be solved by all learners. The great variety of writing at the script level presents a problem for learning that may be relatively easily overcome. However, the fundamental principles of the writing system and the details of the orthography present deeper challenges for the learner, while the universal role of phonology in reading provides a common grounding.

For a child learning to read, the print-to-language mapping is the fundamental learning task. This task is challenging for different reasons in different systems. In Chinese, the problem is hundreds of characters to memorize with limited productivity possible. In English, the problem is the compromise made with the alphabetic principle, leaving many irregular letter-to-sound mappings. We focused more on the English problem than the Chinese problem here. We reviewed a sample of the research that makes clear that in the family of alphabetic systems, the reliability of letter-phoneme mappings makes a difference for reading and learning to read in alphabetic systems. More generally, the size of the phonological unit mapped by the basic graphic unit, which varies across writing systems, may define the learning problem for the child. As a learner figures out the workings of the writing system and its orthography, there is an accommodation to these writing factors. This accommodation may be seen in the strategies for identifying words, as English readers develop a more lexical strategy while readers of transparent orthographies develop sublexical strategies.

At the writing system level, the accommodation is even more profound. The universal phonology is implemented in different ways across writing systems in skilled adult reading. One example is phonological activation, which may be implemented by a threshold procedure (Chinese) or a cascaded procedure (alphabetic). Learning to read in a second system presents a complex problem for the learner that involves language differences, that is, an incomplete learning of the second language prior to learning to read it. However, the writing system differences appear to be important beyond the language factors. Recent imaging research suggests that the brain network for reading accommodates to properties of the writing system, although this may be truer for learning Chinese than for learning an alphabetic system.

In the context of learning to read English, an especially important set of questions concerns the effect of the L1 (first language) and WS1 (first writing system) on learning to read in L2. At least one study illustrates the possibility that mapping principles learned as part of L1 reading are transferred to a second writing system, suggesting that Chinese readers learn to read English using a lexical strategy, whereas Korean readers transfer their sublexical strategy. There is much to learn about this possibility and about the role of language factors themselves in learning to read in a second language.

Acknowledgment

The authors acknowledge the support of the National Science Foundation for the work of this chapter. Some of the research reviewed was supported by National Science Foundation Award # BCS–0113243 to the first author. Additional support for the preparation of the chapter came from the Pittsburgh Science of Learning Center (NSF Award # 0354420).

References

Bates, E. & MacWhinney, B. (1987) Competition, variation, and language learning (pp. 157–93). In B. MacWhinney (ed.), *Mechanisms of language acquisition.* Hillsdale, NJ: Lawrence Erlbaum Associates, Inc.
Bolger, D. J., Perfetti, C. A., & Schneider, W. (2005) Cross-cultural effect on the

brain revisited: universal structures plus writing system variation. *Human Brain Mapping*, 25, 92–104.

Coltheart, M., Rastle, K., Perry, C., Langdon, R., & Ziegler, J. (2001) DRC: A dual route cascaded model of visual word recognition and reading aloud. *Psychological Review*, 108(1), 204–56.

DeFrancis, J. (1989) *Visible speech: the diverse oneness of writing systems.* Honolulu, HI: University of Hawaii Press.

Ellis, N. & Hooper, A. M. (2001) Why learning to read is easier in Welsh than in English: Orthographic transparency effects evinced with frequency-matched tests. *Applied Psycholinguistics*, 22, 571–99.

Fiez, J. A. (2000) Sound and meaning: how native language affects reading strategies. *Nature Neuroscience*, 3(1), 3–5.

Frith, U., Wimmer, H., & Landerl, K. (1998) Differences in phonological recoding in German and English-speaking children. *Scientific Studies of Reading*, 2, 31–54.

Frost, R., Katz, L., & Bentin, S. (1987) Strategies for visual word recognition and orthographic depth: A multilingual comparison. *Journal of Experimental Psychology: Human Perception and Performance*, 13(1), 104–15.

Harm, M. W. & Seidenberg, M. S. (1999) Phonology, reading acquisition, and dyslexia: insights from connectionist models. *Psychological Review*, 106(3), 491–528.

Ho, C. S. & Bryant, P. (1997) Phonological skills are important in learning to read Chinese. *Developmental Psychology*, 33, 946–51.

Joshi, R. J. & R. G. Aaron (eds.) (2005) *Handbook of orthography and literacy.* Mahwah, NJ: Lawrence Erlbaum Associates.

Katz, L. & Feldman, L. B. (1983) Relation between pronunciation and recognition of printed words in deep and shallow orthographies. *Journal of Experimental Psychology: Learning, Memory, and Cognition*, 9, 157–66.

Katz, L. & Frost, R. (1992) The reading process is different for different orthographies: the orthographic depth hypothesis (pp.67–84). In R. Frost & L. Katz (eds.), *Orthography, phonology, morphology, and meaning. Advances in psychology*, Vol. 94. Oxford, England: North-Holland.

Kennedy, G. A. (1966) *Minimum vocabularies of written Chinese.* New Haven, CT: Far Eastern Publications, Yale University.

Kessler, B. & Treiman, R. (2001) Relationship between sounds and letters in English monosyllables. *Journal of Memory and Language*, 44, 592–617.

Kessler, B. & Treiman, R. (2003) Is English spelling chaotic? Misconceptions concerning its irregularity. *Reading Psychology*, 24(3–4), 267–89.

Kolers, P. A. (1976) Reading a year later. *Journal of Experimental Psychology: Human Learning and Memory*, 2, 554–65.

Kolers, P. A. (1985) Skill in reading and memory. *Canadian Journal of Psychology*, 39, 232–9.

Landerl, K. & Wimmer, H. (2000) Deficits in phoneme segmentation are not the core problem of dyslexia: evidence from German and English children. *Applied Psycholinguistics*, 21, 243–62.

Landerl, K., Wimmer, H., & Frith, U. (1997) The impact of orthographic consistency on dyslexia: A German-English comparison. *Cognition*, 63, 315–34.

Liu, Y. & Perfetti, C. A. (2003) The time course of brain activity in reading English and Chinese: an ERP study of Chinese bilinguals. *Human Brain Mapping*, 18, 167–75.

Liu, Y., Dunlap, S., Fiez, J., & Perfetti, C. A. (2005) Learning to read characters: an fMRI study of controlled learning of orthographic, phonological, and semantic constituents. Paper presented at the 12th annual meeting of the Society for the Scientific Study of Reading, Toronto, Ontario.

Luk, G. & Bialystok, E. (2005) How iconic are Chinese characters? *Bilingualism: Language and Cognition*, 8(1), 79–83.

MacWhinney, B. (1997) Second language acquisition and the competition model (pp. 113–142). In A. M. B. de Groot & J. Kroll (eds.). *Tutorials in bilingualism: psycholinguistic perspectives*. Mahwah, NJ: Lawrence Erlbaum Associates.

McBride-Chang, C., Shu, H., Zhou, A., Wat, C. P., & Wagner, R. K. (2003) Morphological awareness uniquely predicts young children's Chinese character recognition. *Journal of Educational Psychology*, 95, 743–51.

Nelson, J., Liu, Y., Fiez, J., & Perfetti, C. A. (2005) Learning to read Chinese as a second language recruits Chinese-specific visual word form areas. Paper presented at the 12th annual meeting of the Society for the Scientific Study of Reading, Toronto, Ontario.

Paulesu E., Démonet, J.-F., Fazio, F., McCrory, E., Chanoine, V., Brunswick, N., Cappa, S. F., Cossu, G., Habib, M., Frith, C. D., & Frith, U. (2001) Dyslexia: cultural diversity and biological unity. *Science*, 291, 2165–7.

Paulesu, E., McCrory, E., Fazio, F., Menoncello, L., Brunswick, N., Cappa, S. F., Cotelli, M., Cossu, G., Corte, F., Lorusso, M., Pesenti, S., Gallagher, A., Perani, D., Price, C., Frith, C. D., & Frith, U. (2000) A cultural effect on brain function. *Nature Neuroscience*, 3(1), 91–6.

Perfetti, C. A. (2003) The universal grammar of reading. *Scientific Studies of Reading*, 7, 3–24.

Perfetti, C. A. & Zhang, S. (1995) Very early phonological activation in Chinese reading. *Journal of Experimental Psychology: Learning, Memory, and Cognition*, 21, 1, 24–33.

Perfetti, C. A. & Tan, L. (1998) The time course of graphic, phonological, and semantic activation in Chinese character identification. *Journal of Experimental Psychology: Learning, Memory, and Cognition*, 24(1), 101–18.

Perfetti, C. A. & Liu, Y. (2005) Orthography to phonology and meaning: comparisons across and within writing systems. *Reading and Writing*, 193–210.

Perfetti, C. A., Liu, Y., & Tan, L. H. (2005) The lexical constituency model: some implications of research on Chinese for general theories of reading. *Psychological Review*, 112, 43–59.

Perfetti, C. A., Zhang, S., & Berent, I. (1992) Reading in English and Chinese: evidence for a "universal" phonological principle (pp. 227–48). In R. Frost & L. Katz (eds.). *Orthography, phonology, morphology, and meaning. Advances in psychology*, Vol. 94. North-Holland: Oxford, UK.

Plaut, D. C. (1999) A connectionist approach to word reading and acquired dyslexia: extension to sequential processing. *Cognitive Science*, 23, 543–68.

Plaut, D. C., McClelland, J. L., Seidenberg, M. S., & Patterson, K. (1996) Understanding normal and impaired word reading: computational principles in quasi-regular domains. *Psychological Review*, 103, 56–115.

Seidenberg, M. S. & McClelland, J. L. (1989) A distributed, developmental model of word recognition and naming. *Psychological Review*, 96, 523–68.

Shafiullah, M. & Monsell, S. (1999) The cost of switching between kanji and kana while reading Japanese. *Language and Cognitive Processes*, 14, 567–607.

Shibahara, N., Zorzi, M., Hill, M. P., Wydell, T., & Butterworth, B. (2003) Semantic effects in word naming: evidence from English and Japanese kanji. *The Quarterly Journal of Experimental Psychology*, 56A(2), 263–86.

Siok, W. T., Jin, Z., Fletcher, P., & Tan, L. H. (2003) Distinct brain regions associated with syllable and phoneme. *Human Brain Mapping*, 18, 201–7.

Siok, W. T., Perfetti, C. A., Jin, Z., & Tan, L. H. (2004) Biological abnormality of impaired reading is constrained by culture. *Nature*, 431, 71–6.

Spencer, K. (2000) Is English a dyslexic language? *Dylexia*, 6, 152–62.

Spencer, K. (2001) Differential effects of orthographic transparency on dyslexia: Word reading difficulty for common English words. *Dyslexia*, 7, 217–8.

Stevenson, H. W. (1984) Orthography and reading disabilities. *Journal of Learning Disabilities*, 17, 296–301.

Tan, L. H. & Perfetti, C. A. (1998) Phonological codes as early sources of constraint in Chinese word identification: a review of current discoveries and theoretical accounts. *Reading and Writing: An Interdisciplinary Journal*, 10, 165–200.

Tan, L. H., Laird, A. R., Li, K., & Fox, P. T. (2005a) Neuroanatomical correlates of phonological processing of Chinese characters and alphabetic words: a meta-analysis. *Human Brain Mapping*, 25, 83–91.

Tan, L. H., Spinks, J. A., Eden, G. F., Perfetti, C. A, & Siok, W. T. (2005b) Reading depends on writing, in Chinese. Proceedings of the National Academy of Sciences of the USA, 102, 8781–5.

Treiman, R., Mullennix, J., Bijeljac-Babic, R., & Richmond-Welty, E. D. (1995) The special role of rimes in the description, use, and acquisition of English orthography. *Journal of Experimental Psychology: General*, 124, 107–36.

Wang, M., Koda, K., & Perfetti, C. A. (2003) Alphabetic and non-alphabetic L1 effects in English word identification: A comparison of Korean and Chinese English L2 learners. Cognition, 87, 129–49.

Wimmer, H. & Goswami, U. (1994) The influence of orthographic consistency on reading development: word recognition in English and German children. *Cognition*, 51, 91–103.

Wydell, T. N. & Butterworth, B. (1999) A case study of an English-Japanese bilingual with monolingual dyslexia. *Cognition*, 70, 273–305.

Wydell, T. N. & Kondo, T. (2003) Phonological deficit and the reliance on orthographic approximation for reading: a follow-up study on an English-Japanese bilingual with monolingual dyslexia. *Journal of Research in Reading*, 26, 33–48.

Yoon, H. K., Bolger, D. J., Kwon, O. S., & Perfetti, C. A. (2002) Subsyllabic units in reading: a difference between Korean and English. In L. Verhoeven, C. Elbro, & P. Reitsma (eds.), *Precursors of functional literacy*. Amsterdam/Philadelphia: John Benjamins Publishing Company.

Ziegler, J. C. & Goswami, U. (2005) Reading acquisition, developmental dyslexia, and skilled reading across languages: a psycholinguistic grain size theory. *Psychological Bulletin*, 131, 3–29

Ziegler, J. C. Stone, G. O., & Jacobs, A. M. (1997) What is the pronunciation for -ough and the spelling for /u/? A database for computing feedforward and feedback consistency in English. *Behavior Research Methods, Instruments, & Computers*, 29, 600–18.

3 Conceptual and methodological issues in comparing metalinguistic awareness across languages

Li-jen Kuo and Richard C. Anderson

It has generally been agreed in the literature that metalinguistic awareness plays a critical role in reading development (e.g. Gombert, 1992; Mattingly, 1984; Nagy & Anderson, 1998). Yet despite the agreement, the term "metalinguistic awareness" has not received a consistent interpretation and thus tends to refer to different constructs in different studies. Resolving these inconsistencies is important because the conceptualization of "metalinguistic awareness" provides the theoretical framework that guides research designs, data analyses, and interpretations of findings. Understanding differences in the conceptualization of "metalinguistic awareness" is particularly important when it comes to cross-language research, because only with a consistent framework can comparisons across languages be meaningful. Otherwise, there is no way to be certain whether the differences found in cross-language studies result from different courses of metalinguistic awareness development across languages or from different conceptualizations of metalinguistic awareness.

We will begin this chapter with a discussion of the multiple interpretations metalinguistic awareness has received in reading research. The discussion does not intend to yield a *correct* definition of metalinguistic awareness. Instead, it aims to offer researchers a more critical lens to examine cross-linguistic reading studies by highlighting the different cognitive components and linguistic domains that have been considered in the conceptualization of metalinguistic awareness. The next section outlines major subtypes of metalinguistic awareness relevant to reading development and raises issues that need to be considered in assessing the metalinguistic awareness of second language learners and comparing their performance with the performance of monolingual children. The third section discusses conceptual and methodological issues in studying cross-language transfer. We conclude this chapter with a summary and a proposal for directions for future research.

Defining metalinguistic awareness

Metalinguistic awareness can be broadly defined as the ability to "reflect on and manipulate the structural features of languages" (Nagy & Anderson,

1998, p. 155). Whereas in ordinary language use, attention is given to the message conveyed through language, metalinguistic awareness entails directing attention to language itself, to the means that convey the message. Several cognitive components have been proposed to distinguish the mental activities involved in metalinguistic awareness from ordinary language use.

First, some researchers have argued that metalinguistic activities require explicit mental representations of language properties, whereas in ordinary language use, structural properties of language are left implicit (e.g. Bialystok, 2001; Gombert, 1992). Bialystok (2001) described metalinguistic knowledge as the knowledge "that is made explicit during language acquisition (p. 127)." However, having explicit mental representations of language properties does not necessarily entail the ability to verbalize these language properties. For example, a child who understands that doable, but not readable or computerable, are permissible affixed words in English may not be able to articulate the distributional properties of the suffix "-able" (i.e. "-able" can only be attached to verbs and not to adjectives or nouns). Still, he or she may have the mental representation of this rule, which becomes explicit in a context where metalinguistic activity is required.

Second, metalinguistic research varies in whether the emphasis is on the declarative or procedural aspects of cognitive processes (for a thorough review, see Gombert, 1992). For research that emphasizes the declarative aspect of cognitive processes, metalinguistic awareness is conceptualized more in terms of the ability to treat language as an object of analysis (e.g. Pratt & Grieve, 1984; Van Kleeck, 1982). Metalinguistic awareness thus involves declarative knowledge with which one can reflect upon and manipulate the structural and functional aspects of language. Other research on metalinguistic awareness puts more emphasis on the procedural aspect of cognitive processes. In this view, metalinguistic activity is characterized as "a part of treatment of language" during production or comprehension (Gombert, 1992, p.3). What differentiates this aspect of metalinguistic awareness from ordinary language use is the intentional control and monitoring of language processes (Cazden, 1976; Hakes, 1980). The procedural aspect of metalinguistic awareness enables people to shift their attention from the content transmitted in the language to the properties of language during production or comprehension. Some researchers have argued that both declarative and procedural aspects of cognitive processes need to be considered in discussing metalinguistic development (Bialystok, 2001; Bialystok & Ryan, 1985; Tunmer et al., 1984). For example, Bialystok (2001; see also Bialystok and Ryan, 1985) proposed that metalinguistic activities consist of two dimensions of cognitive process—representational analysis and attentional control. In her view, metalinguistic awareness involves both the analytical ability to reflect upon and manipulate formal properties of language and the attentional control of the mental mechanism that operates language processing. It should be noted that the declarative-procedural distinctions are not binary categories. The two aspects of cognitive process may coexist in many metalinguistic processes, but with different degrees of involvement.

Consciousness probably raises the most controversy of all concepts attendant to the definition of metalinguistic awareness. Bialystok (2001) argued that the concept of consciousness does not contribute to defining metalinguistic awareness because both metalinguistic activities and linguistics activities must be operated consciously. Gombert (1992), on the other hand, envisioned a central role for consciousness as an explanatory concept in metalinguistic development. According to his developmental model, a stage prior to the acquisition of metalinguistic awareness is the acquisition of epilinguistic control. In the epilinguistic control stage, children gradually organize implicit knowledge of language accumulated through multiple co-occurrences of a particular linguistic form with its pragmatic context. Children may have some control over their language use, but such control is primarily functional rather than reflective. For example, children at this stage may repair their own ungrammatical utterances in speech. However, the epilinguistic detection of ungrammatical utterances is triggered by a breakdown in communication rather than a conscious realization that the produced form is inconsistent with the implicit knowledge of language they have developed. The repair is done more at a surface level to remove dissonance of the utterance with its pragmatic context than at an abstract level with a generalized understanding of language properties. According to Gombert, it is not until the metalinguistic awareness stage that children begin to have conscious management of their language use, which is beyond functional control and reaches the level of intentional reflection.

Gombert (1992) proposed a final stage of metalinguistic development, the automation of metaprocesses. As in the epilinguistic stage, control of language processes is normally unconscious during automated metaprocesses. What distinguishes automated metaprocesses from epilinguistic processes is the possibility of conscious access to metalinguistic knowledge. If a problem disrupts automatic functioning, automated metaprocesses—but not epilinguistic processes—can gain conscious access to metalinguistic knowledge. In Gombert's model, consciousness is a critical cognitive component that differentiates different stages of metalinguistic development.

Gombert's stage theory was proposed primarily to capture metalinguistic development in first language learning. It is doubtful that all of the theory is applicable to second language learning. For example, Gombert (1992) argued that "the absolute prerequisite for this consciousness (in the metalinguistic awareness stage) is epilinguistic control. Only that which has already been mastered at a functional level can be so at a conscious level" (p. 190). However, this may not always be true for second language learners. Second language learners may be explicitly taught some metalinguistic knowledge from the outset before they have achieved any epilinguistic control of the second language. Thus, although they do not have perfect functional control of the language, they may nonetheless have conscious access to metalinguistic knowledge. For example, second language learners of English may not always be accurate in aspect inflection of verbs during conversation, but they can still consciously direct attention to that property of language in a metalinguistic task. In other words, for second language learners, lack of functional control does not always preclude conscious access to metalinguistic knowledge.

Research on metalinguistic awareness varies not only in its emphasis on different cognitive components, but also in the type of metalinguistic skills and the scope of metalinguistic knowledge it encompasses. In terms of the type of metalinguistic knowledge, some branches of research put more emphasis on the ability to identify and manipulate linguistic units, whereas others focus more on the sensitivity to the distributional patterns of these linguistic units. For example, existing research on phonological awareness has primarily investigated children's ability to identify and manipulate sound units of different sizes, whereas in research on morphological awareness, both the ability to identify morphemes and sensitivity to distributional constraints in use of morphemes have received attention. In terms of the scope of metalinguistic knowledge, some researchers have maintained that it must be broader, or at a more abstract level, than knowledge about a particular language (e.g. Bialystok, 2001; Boutet et al., 1983, as cited in Gombert, 1992). Bialystok (2001) argued that "metalinguistic knowledge minimally needs to include the abstract structure of language that organizes sets of linguistic rules without being directly instantiated in any of them" (p. 123). However, few existing studies of metalinguistic awareness tap the abstract cross-language level of knowledge, because usually only language-specific items are used in the assessments (an exception is Chen et al., 2004). Nonetheless, the view that metalinguistic knowledge can be universal, rather than language-specific, provides a promising framework for future investigations of metalinguistic awareness.

Assessing metalinguistic awareness across languages

Phonological awareness

Phonological awareness refers to the ability to reflect upon and manipulate phonological units in a language and may entail sensitivity to the phonological structure of the language. Three nested levels of phonological awareness have been identified as important in children's literacy development: syllable awareness, onset-rime awareness, and phoneme awareness (Treiman & Zukowski, 1991). Syllable awareness is the ability to recognize the syllabic units in spoken language. Onset-rime awareness refers to the insight that syllables may be segmented into an onset and a rime. The onset of a syllable is the initial consonant or consonant cluster before the vowel. The remaining part of the syllable, which consists of the vowel and perhaps a final consonant or consonant cluster, is the rime of the syllable. Phoneme awareness refers to the insight that syllables can be further segmented into finer units, phonemes, which are the smallest distinctive units of speech identified by speakers of a language. There appears to be a general developmental progression from the awareness at the syllable level, awareness at the onset-rime level, and, finally, awareness at the phonemic level (Goswami, 1999).

Phonological awareness is the most extensively studied aspect of metalinguistic awareness. This emphasis is likely a reflection of the fact that most of the research has been conducted with children learning to read an alphabetic script (Nagy & Anderson, 1998). Research has consistently shown that the ability to reflect upon and manipulate sublexical phonological units is critical in the early development of children learning to read an alphabetic script (e.g. Bradley & Bryant, 1983; Caravolas & Bruck, 1993; Cossu *et al.*, 1988; Holligan & Johnston, 1988; Porpodas, 1993; Schneider & Naslund, 1999; Wimmer *et al.*, 1994). Phoneme awareness has proved to be a stronger predictor of reading achievement than other measures of reading readiness or IQ (Juel *et al.*, 1986; Stanovich *et al.*, 1984; Tunmer & Nesdale, 1985; Vellutino & Scanlon, 1987). This body of research suggests that having an explicit representation of phonological units facilitates the learning of phonology-orthography relations in an alphabetic script, and thus accelerates early literacy development. There has been debate about whether phonological awareness is a precursor to reading or a consequence of learning to read. This debate may be resolved within an interactive view: onset-rime awareness usually emerges prior to receiving any formal literacy instruction, while more subtle phonological concepts, such as phoneme awareness, tend to develop as a consequence of learning to decode.

Awareness of phonological units has also been the most vigorously studied aspect of metalinguistic awareness in second language reading research. Several patterns have emerged from existing research that has compared the phonological awareness of monolingual children and bilingual children. First, at least prior to literacy instruction or at the early stage of literacy development (within one year), bilingual children generally demonstrate heightened phonological awareness in their second language as compared to monolingual children who speak that language as their native language (e.g. Bialystok *et al.*, 2003; Bruck & Genessee, 1995; Campbell & Sais, 1995; Chen *et al.*, 2004; Liow & Poon, 1998; Mumtaz & Humphreys, 2001). This advantage is especially pronounced when the bilingual children's native language: (a) has simpler and more regular phonological structures (e.g. Italian, which has only five vowels and no dipthongs, in Campbell & Sais, 1995); (b) has more salient segmental units (e.g. French, which has more salient syllables than English, in Bruck & Genessee, 1995; and Cantonese, which has a greater number of syllables and tones than Mandarin Chinese, in Chen *et al.*, 2004); or (c) is orthographically transparent (e.g. Bahasa Indonesian, in Liow & Poon, 1998; Urdu, in Mumtaz & Humphreys, 2001). However, bilingual children do not seem to have an advantage in phonological awareness when their first and second language have very different phonological structures (Bialystok *et al.*, 2003).

Second, consistent with research on first language reading research, the development of phoneme awareness in a second language is contingent upon literacy instruction and the orthographic transparency of the language. Bilingual children who can read and write in a more transparent native language and are learning to read in a second language are more likely to have a higher level of phoneme awareness in the second language than monolingual children who speak that second language as their native language (e.g. Liow & Poon, 1998). However, bilingual children who are not literate in their native language may not enjoy such an advantage (e.g. Bruck & Genesee, 1995). There has been little exploration of whether bilinguals who have a native language with less complicated phonological structure or more opaque writing system would also show an advantage in phonological awareness over their monolingual peers (an exception is Bialystok *et al.*, 2003).

A caveat needs to be expressed regarding the assessment of phonological awareness in a second language. Ordinarily, the mastery of receptive skills precedes the mastery of production skills (Brown, 1994). Furthermore, acquisition of a high level of phonological production skill may not be attainable beyond certain critical age period (Gass & Selinker, 1994). For example, Tahta *et al.*, (1981) found that American children's ability to imitate intonational patterns in French and Armenian declined drastically after the age of eight. However, not being able to produce certain phonological features does not preclude the ability to recognize them in speech (Brown, 1994). It seems probable to us that second language learners, who speak a second language with a strong foreign accent, are often able to understand native speakers of the second language perfectly well. If this is true, when selecting a task to assess the phonological awareness in a second language, one needs to take into account the possible gap between production skills and receptive skills. A child who cannot pronounce bat and bate accurately may still make the distinction in his or her mental representations of /æ/ and /eɪ/, and thus other things being equal, this child might not necessarily experience greater difficulty in decoding than children capable of accurate pronunciation.

Thus, for second language learners, receptive tasks (e.g. judgment tasks), rather than production tasks (e.g. phoneme deletion, blending), may tap into the level of phonological awareness that is more directly related to decoding. This could be true even though the more demanding production tasks explain additional variance in reading, because the additional variance may come from sources not directly related to the mapping between graphemes and representations of phonological units. For example, second language learners with more accurate pronunciation may have had more opportunity to interact with the native speakers because their language is more comprehensive. Having more exposure to input with better quality may thus in turn promote the overall proficiency in the second language. If this is what was happening, then phonological awareness tests would serve as an indicator of a social process, not mark a proximate cause.

In first language reading research with alphabetic scripts, phonological awareness is considered important because it involves prerequisite skills needed for decoding, or mapping between graphemes and phonological units. Furthermore, because most alphabetic scripts encode segmental features but not suprasegmental features, only awareness of syllables, onset-rimes, and phonemes has received much attention in reading research (Goswami, 1999).

However, the contribution of phonological awareness to reading development probably goes beyond the mapping between graphemes and phonemes and thus the scope of phonological awareness should be broader and involve more than reflecting on and manipulating phonological units. Additional levels of phonological awareness that should be considered are awareness of suprasegmental features and awareness of the phonological structure of a language.

Speech sounds can be characterized not only in terms of segmental units, but also in terms of suprasegmental features, notably tone and stress. In many languages, the tone, or pitch contour, of a syllable makes a difference in meaning. For example, Mandarin Chinese syllables are pronounced with one of four tones that have a crucial role in determining the possible meanings of a syllable. The syllable /ma/ may mean "mother" in a high pitch, "hemp" in a high-rising pitch, "horse" in a low-falling-then-rising pitch, and "scold" in a high-falling pitch. In other languages, such as languages of sub-Saharan Africa, tone not only distinguishes different words but also marks grammatical features.

Another suprasegmental feature is stress. Stress is a property of syllables. When a syllable is stressed, it is longer and louder than other syllables in the same word or phrase. In some languages, the placement of stress on a word follows a predictable pattern. For example, in Czech, stress is almost always placed on the first syllable of a word, and in French, almost always on the final syllable of a phrase (Jannedy *et al.*, 1991). In other languages, although the placement of stress is less predictable, it can make a difference in meaning. For example, in English, the word "record" functions as a noun when the stress falls on the first syllable, but as a verb when the stress falls on the second syllable.

In addition to lack of attention to suprasegmental features, a further overlooked area in research on reading is the ability to reflect upon phonological structures in a language. Research from developmental psycholinguistics has shown that one of the preliminary stages in language development is to parse continuous speech into strings of lexically viable segments (Johnson *et al.*, 2003). Identification of possible word boundaries in continuous speech requires an understanding of not just individual phonological units in the language, but also how these units are combined with each other or synchronized with suprasegmental features.

Two of the most widely studied word boundaries cues are phonotactic regularities (e.g. Mattys & Jusczyk, 2001) and stress patterns (e.g. Cutler & Butterfield, 1992; Jusczyk *et al.*, 1993; McQueen *et al.*, 1994; Morgan & Saffran, 1995). Phonotactic regularities refer to the distributional pattern of possible sound combinations in a word. For example, /ŋ/ is a common offset in English words (e.g. king, thing) but cannot be an onset in English; /h/ is a common onset in English, but cannot end a word; and /pf/ is a good onset in German, but not in English. Stress pattern may also provide cues to word boundaries. As mentioned earlier, stress in Czech is almost always placed on the first syllable of a word. Thus, being able to identify stressed syllables and having the insight that they mark the beginning of a word would facilitate word segmentation in spoken Czech. In English, although the stress patterns are not as predictable as in Czech, the majority of the content words are trochaic (with strong-weak stress pattern), and it has been suggested in first language acquisition research that this dominant stress pattern can be utilized by English-speaking infants to identify word boundaries (e.g. Morgan & Saffran, 1995).

Awareness of the phonological structure of a language may be particularly important for second language learners because it offers an analytical framework to segment speech in the new language. Understanding what are the possible sound combinations in a new language may also help learners assimilate and retain phonological strings in the language. All these advantages would expedite incidental learning of new vocabulary and thus influence the overall literacy development in the second language.

Semantic awareness

Semantic awareness refers to the knowledge about how meanings are organized in language and the sensitivity to different semantic domains. For example, in English the meaning of a verb rarely includes an action plus its object (Nagy & Scott, 1990). According to Nagy and Gentner (1990), understanding the pattern of word meanings may facilitate the process of constructing and evaluating hypotheses about the possible meanings of unfamiliar words, thus affecting rate of vocabulary learning.

Assessment of semantic awareness has not received much attention in reading research. One of the pioneering studies was conducted by Nagy and Scott (1990) with students in seventh and tenth grade and college undergraduates. The students were asked to rate the plausibility of the novel meanings of nonsense words. The findings suggested that skilled adult readers are sensitive to the semantic regularities in the English lexicon.

To our knowledge, semantic awareness has not been systematically studied in second language reading research. However, it could be an important aspect of metalinguistic awareness for second language learners, because the way meanings are organized in the lexicon may vary from language to language. Thus, second language learners might have to develop a new semantic system in order to efficiently acquire the vocabulary in the new language, which would in turn affect their reading development in the new language.

Morphological awareness

Morphological awareness refers to the ability to reflect upon and manipulate morphemes and to control word formation processes. Morphemes are the smallest phonological units that carry semantic information. The most common word formation processes are inflection, derivation, and compounding. Inflectional morphemes typically mark syntactic or semantic relations between different words in a sentence without altering the meaning or the part of speech of the stem. For example, verbs may be marked by inflectional morphemes for tense, aspect, mood, and voice. Nouns may be inflectionally marked for agreement with other words in the sentence in terms of gender, case, and number. It should be noted that inflection does not always operate through suffixation. Some languages use infixes. For example, the verb stem for "write" in Tagalog is /sulat/. Its infinitive form "to write" is formed by inserting the infix -um- within the stem, and thus, /sumulat/. Other languages use reduplication. For example in Indonesian, the plural form for "house", /rumah/, is /rumahrumah/.

Derivation involves the addition of a morpheme to change the part of speech or the meaning of a base morpheme. Compared with inflectional morphemes, derivational morphemes are usually less productive and more restrictive in terms of what types of base morphemes they can be combined with. For example, in English, -able can only be attached to verbs but not to nouns to form adjectives. Finally, compounding refers to the formation of new words by combining two or more words. The words that are the parts of a compound can be free morphemes (e.g. aircraft), derived words (e.g. air conditioner), inflected words (e.g. energy-saving), compounds (e.g. car insurance salesman), or bound roots (e.g. telescope, telephone, television, telegram).

Morphological awareness has not received much attention in first language reading research until recently (e.g. Assink & Sandra, 2003; Carlisle, 2003; Ku & Anderson, 2003). Yet there are reasons to believe that there should be a strong relationship between morphological awareness and learning to read in either a first or a second language. First, morphemes not only have semantic but also phonological and syntactic properties (Mahony *et al.*, 2000). Morphological awareness is thus integrally related to other aspects of language knowledge and may provide a "more general index of metalinguistic capability" than phonological or syntactic awareness considered alone (Carlisle, 1995, p. 192).

Another reason to relate morphological awareness and learning to read is concerned with the way the mental lexicon of skilled readers is organized. Psycholinguistic studies involving adult participants have consistently shown that morphological information is utilized when processing complex words (Nagy *et al.*, 1989; Napps, 1989; for a review, see Clahsen *et al.*, in press; and Harley, 2001). For example, root frequency has been found to have an effect on the processing of morphologically complex words in alphabetical languages (e.g. Burani & Caramazza, 1987; Niswander *et al.*, 2000). In research involving speakers of logographic languages such as Chinese, similar results in support of such morpheme-based mental lexicon models have been obtained (e.g. Zhou & Marslen-Wilson, 1994; Zhou & Marslen-Wilson, 1995). The fact that the mental lexicon of adult skilled readers is morphologically organized suggests that morphological knowledge may serve as an important framework to store words efficiently (Sandra, 1994). Thus, children with more developed morphological knowledge may have an advantage of acquiring and retaining morphologically complex vocabulary. Expedited learning of morphologically complex vocabulary is crucial because such vocabulary may make up of 60 percent of the new words acquired by school-aged children (Anglin, 1993; Nagy & Anderson, 1984). Given that vocabulary is a strong indicator of reading performance (Anderson & Freebody, 1981), morphological awareness should play a significant role in reading development.

One of the major reading difficulties faced by second language learners is limited vocabulary knowledge (Droop & Verhoeven, 2003; Garcia, 1991, 2000; Verhoeven, 2000); thus it is reasonable to assume that morphological awareness should play an even greater role in second language reading development. There has been some indirect evidence in support of this assumption. For example, studies that have looked at the use of cognates by Spanish-English bilingual children have shown that high-performing and low-performing bilinguals differ in their ability to strategically search for cognates in Spanish when encountering unknown words in an English text (Jimenez *et al.*, 1996), and that awareness of a cognate relationship between Spanish and English increases markedly with age (e.g. Hancin-Bhatt & Nagy, 1994). These studies in fact investigated grapho-morphological awareness because they used only written assessments. This is in contrast to most morphological awareness studies, which use primarily oral tasks to minimize the interference from lack of decoding ability (for a review, see Carlisle, 2003). However, the studies on use of cognates demonstrated that recognizing morphological units can facilitate the learning of vocabulary in a typologically related language.

An intriguing research question that remains to be explored in the field is whether children who are exposed to two languages would be able than monolingual children to see the morphological structures in a language, which the monolingual children might take for granted. In other words, would exposure to two languages render abstract word formation rules more accessible and explicit? This is an area that deserves further investigation in future research.

Syntactic awareness

Syntactic awareness refers to an understanding of how words in a language are strung together to form sentences. This process involves two major subcomponents. The first subcomponent is concerned with word order. Languages differ in terms of how words are distributed within phrases and how phrases are distributed relative to each other within sentences. For example, English has prepositions, and a preposition is always located at the beginning of a prepositional phrase (e.g. "in the kitchen"). Japanese, however, has postpositions; these correspond to the prepositions in English, except that the postpositions are normally located at the end of a phrase (e.g. "the kitchen in"). English is usually referred to as an SVO (Subject-Verb–Object) language because, in a declarative sentence, the subject usually precedes the verb and an object, if present, usually follows the verb. Other word order variations, such as SOV, are also quite common in world languages.

The second subcomponent involved in syntactic awareness is the selection of a word form consistent with its grammatical role in a sentence; this has sometimes been more precisely termed in the literature as morphosyntactic awareness (e.g. Gaux & Gombert, 1999). In many languages, the form can be the inflection of a word according to grammatical rules such as agreement in tense, aspect, number, gender or case; or it can be the derivative of a word according to its syntactic status in a sentence. In some other languages, the form entails inserting an additional marker word, such as the object-marker /ba/3 in Chinese.

Bilingual speakers need to differentiate the word orders in the two languages and may need to adopt a word order frame that is not consistent with the one they acquired from their native language. Thus, bilingual children may be confused at some point in their language development. At the same time, because they have two syntactic systems to compare, they are also more likely to attend to abstract levels of syntactic structure which monolingual children may simply take for granted.

A number of studies have provided empirical evidence that bilingual children may develop somewhat heightened syntactic awareness as compared to their monolingual counterparts (Bialystok, 1988; Bialystok & Majumder, 1998; Cromdal, 1999; Galambos & Goldin-Meadow, 1990; Galambos & Hakuta, 1988; Ricciardelli, 1992). Using a word-order correction task, Ricciardelli (1992) found that the Italian-English bilingual children who had attained a high level of proficiency in both languages outperformed their monolingual English-speaking peers, even though the bilingual children had slightly smaller English vocabularies. Consistent with this finding, Bialystok (1988) reported that French-English balanced bilinguals, whose English proficiency was lower than the proficiency of their monolingual counterparts, performed better on a syntax correction task. However, the advantage was not found in partial bilinguals who had similar proficiency in English but lower proficiency in French than the fully bilingual children. These findings not only suggest that bilingual children may have more advanced syntactic awareness, but also highlight the importance of first language proficiency in the development of second language syntactic awareness.

The effect of bilingualism on syntactic awareness also manifests itself in bilingual children's ability to reflect upon their native language. Galambos and Hakuta (1988) investigated the performance of Spanish-English bilinguals with varying degrees of language proficiency on a Spanish grammaticality judgment task. An interaction was found between native language proficiency (proficiency in Spanish) and the degree of bilingualism (proficiency in English). For bilingual children with equally high proficiency in Spanish and English, performance on the more difficult items positively correlated with their proficiency in English. For bilinguals with low levels of proficiency in their native language, the effect of bilingualism was similar across items of varying levels of difficulty.

To explore in more detail how the developmental pattern of syntactic awareness in bilingual children is different from that in monolingual children, Galambos and Goldin-Meadow (1990) distinguished between three levels of syntactic awareness in their grammatical judgment task: to detect syntactic errors, to correct the errors they detected, and to explain their corrections. In a cross-sectional study, they compared Spanish-speaking monolinguals, English-speaking monolinguals, and Spanish-English bilinguals aged 4:5 to 8:00 on a grammatical judgment task. The results show that monolingual children and bilingual children followed the same course of development, moving from being able to detect syntactic errors, to correct them, and then to explain the correction. The bilingual children in prekindergarten were able to give more grammar-oriented corrections and fewer content-oriented corrections than their monolingual counterparts, but this difference disappeared at kindergarten and grade one. The overall findings suggested that bilingual experience may accelerate the transition from a content-based to a form-based approach to language, but the advantage might not be maintained when children are older.

Based on her analysis-control framework, Bialystok (1988) also proposed an elaborated experiment designed to investigate how children differentiate form from content. Two dimensions of language, meaning and form, are manipulated to yield four types of sentences in the grammatical judgment test: (1) grammatically correct and semantically correct; (2) grammatically incorrect but semantically meaningful (called incorrect); (3) grammatically correct but semantically not meaningful (called anomalous); and (4) grammatically incorrect and semantically meaningless. The two key conditions are the incorrect items and the anomalous items. According to Bialystok (1988), to detect the errors on the incorrect items, a child has to refer to some principle of language structure, which is a process that requires the analysis of linguistic knowledge. To make the correct judgment on the anomalous items, a child needs to focus the attention on the form, and intentionally suppress the meaning of the sentence, which requires a high level of control of attention.

Using the foregoing design, Bialystok (1988) conducted a study with a group of first-grade Italian-English bilingual children. She found that the children performed similarly on the anomalous items, but children who had better proficiency in Italian scored higher on the incorrect items. This finding was replicated by Cromdal (1999) using the same design with a group of Swedish monolingual children and two groups of English-Swedish bilingual children with similar proficiency in English but different levels of proficiency in Swedish. Despite having a significantly smaller Swedish vocabulary, the partial bilingual group performed overall approximately the same as their monolingual Swedish peers in all conditions. The highly balanced bilinguals and the Swedish monolinguals did not differ in vocabulary size in Swedish, but the highly balanced bilinguals outperformed the monolinguals on the incorrect items. Yet in a later study with this paradigm, Bialystok and Majumder (1998) found that, although French-English bilingual children had an advantage in solving attention control items, they performed at the same level as their monolingual English-speaking peers on the analysis items. Taken together, these studies suggest that bilingualism has a positive effect on the ability to attend to the form of language. However, whether bilingualism enhances metalinguistic awareness depends upon level of proficiency in both languages.

In contrast to the foregoing studies, a set of studies by Siegel and her collaborators has repeatedly reported that—except for children with a Slavic native language background—bilingual children do not have any advantage in syntactic awareness over monolingual children (Abu-Rabia & Siegel, 2002; Chiappe & Siegel, 1999; Chiappe *et al.*, 2002; Da Fontoura & Siegel, 1995; D'Anguiulli *et al.*, 2001; Leseaux & Siegel, 2003; Lesaux *et al.*, 2003; Lesaux *et al.*, 2003; Lipka & Siegel, 2003a; 2003b; Siegel & Lipka, 2003). In these studies, bilingual children were found to lag behind their monolingual peers in the development of syntactic awareness, even when they were matched with their monolingual counterparts in word and pseudoword reading (Abu-Rabia & Siegel, 2002; Chiappe & Siegel, 1999; Da Fontoura & Siegel, 1995; Lesaux & Siegel, 2003) or in reading comprehension (Siegel & Lipka, 2003). In a study with Italian-English bilingual children, although the bilingual children outperformed their monolingual peers on word reading and pseudoword reading, they performed no better than the monolingual children on the syntactic awareness task (D'Angiulli *et al.*, 2001).

The disparity in the studies by Siegel and her collaborators and the studies by Galambos, Bialystok and others may arise from several sources which highlight some key factors underlying the relationship between bilingualism and the development of syntactic awareness. First, the way syntactic awareness was assessed in the two sets of studies is quite different. Most of the studies that reported no bilingual advantage assessed syntactic awareness with an oral cloze task. In this task, children are asked to supply a missing word in an orally presented sentence. Although the items in the cloze task were constructed to tap into several aspects of syntactic knowledge—such as agreement in tense, aspect, and number—for native speakers, the task could require only epilinguistic control rather than explicit syntactic awareness. For example, a native speaker of English may find it easy to fill in the right article in a cloze task without being able to explain why. A second-language learner, though not always able to answer the cloze task questions correctly, may have a more explicit understanding of how definite and indefinite articles function in English sentences. The linguistic representations of bilingual children may be more explicit, but the representations may comprise grammatical knowledge that is not always correct. Another possible problem with the cloze task is that it allows children to attend to meaning as well as to form, and thus may not sufficiently stress children's ability to manipulate or reflect upon language form.

Second, bilingual children's proficiency in their native language was not taken into account in many of the studies using the oral cloze task. Other research suggests that the effects of bilingualism may depend on degree of bilingualism (Diaz, 1985; Hakuta & Diaz, 1985). Thus, it remains unclear from these studies whether bilingualism simply does not facilitate the development of syntactic awareness or whether many of the bilinguals enrolled in these studies had not yet reached the threshold of proficiency in their second language for a metalinguistic advantage to emerge.

A general caveat needs to be raised concerning the role played by second language instruction in the emergence of syntactic awareness. Grammar has long been an important topic in second language curricula, and grammaticality judgment/correction tasks are commonly used by second language teachers to assess student progress. Therefore, when comparing bilingual children with monolingual children on grammaticality judgment/correction tasks, researchers need to take into account whether the bilingual children appear to have heightened syntactic awareness because of their greater familiarity with the tasks. None of the studies described above explicitly addressed this issue. Nevertheless, because the bilingual children in these studies were mostly young (between six to eight years of age), and were mostly in immersion programs, one can probably assume that these children did not have much explicit instruction in grammar or exercise with grammaticality judgment/correct tasks. However, when studying older bilingual children, or children in transitional second language programs where a grammar-oriented curriculum is likely to be used, researchers need to interpret data from grammaticality judgment/correction tasks cautiously and avoid attributing to bilingualism an advantage that is the byproduct of a particular kind of second language instruction.

Another general caveat about research on syntactic awareness is that the measures used tend to stress peripheral aspects of syntax such as knowledge of past tense forms, apt choice of prepositions, and agreement in number and aspect, but ignore or under-stress central aspects of syntax, such as the organization and distribution of syntactic units. Therefore, it is not surprising that existing research suggests that syntactic awareness has only a limited role in the literacy development of bilingual children (e.g. Geva & Siegel, 2000; Mutter & Diethelm, 2001).

Cross-language research on syntactic awareness is still in an early stage of development. Several areas need to be further explored. So far, nearly all the studies that report a positive effect of bilingualism on syntactic awareness have been conducted with bilinguals who were speaking Romance or Germanic languages that have parallel syntactic structures. Little is known about whether such an advantage would also appear among bilinguals who speak two languages that are typologically more distant. It remains unclear in current research whether the advantage that bilinguals sometimes have comes primarily from accelerated development of the overlapping syntactic structures in the first and second languages, or from increased attention to syntax arising from the saliency of non-overlapping structures. These could be distinguished by assessing bilinguals who speak typologically more distant languages and by examining their responses to the individual items in the grammaticality judgment tasks in both languages in more detail.

Finally, syntactic awareness should be examined over a wider range of ages. The effect of syntactic awareness may be less pronounced in young children's reading, because the biggest challenge for beginning readers, at least those reading an alphabetic script, is the mapping between graphemes and phonemes. It is likely that once children pass through the stage of learning basic grapheme-phoneme mapping skills, the effect of syntactic awareness would emerge in reading comprehension, as is suggested in some studies of first language reading (Nation & Snowling, 2000).

Grapho-phonological awareness

Grapho-phonological awareness refers to insight into how orthography encodes phonological information. This is usually assessed in a word-reading or word-decoding test. Pseudowords are usually used in the test to avoid confounding sight word familiarity. Performance on these word-reading tests is often assumed to be a satisfactory indicator of reading achievement in first language reading research, because word reading is highly correlated with reading comprehension (e.g. Siegel, 1993; Tunmer *et al.*, 1988). Word reading has also been a common assessment in cross-language reading research (e.g. Comeau *et al.*, 1999; Durgunoglu *et al.*, 1993). However, there is reason to doubt that there is inevitably a strong relationship between word reading and reading comprehension among second language readers.

Unlike first language readers, who are usually able to access the meaning of a word once the word is phonologically decoded, second language readers tend to have a smaller oral vocabulary in their second language (e.g. Droop & Verhoeven, 2003; Garcia, 1991, 2000) and, therefore, successful word decoding in a second language does not guarantee access to meaning. As indicated in some recent data, the relationship between word reading and reading comprehension may be weaker for bilingual children or second language learners. For example, in a study of fourth grade Spanish-English bilingual children who primarily used Spanish at home and English at school, Durgunoglu *et al.* (2002) did not find significant correlations between English word recognition and English reading comprehension or between Spanish word recognition and Spanish reading comprehension. Droop and Verhoeven (2003) reported relatively weaker correlations between word reading and reading comprehension for bilingual readers in a study that compared the literacy development of monolingual Dutch children with minority children from a Turkish or Moroccan background. Despite having superior performance in word reading, the minority children lagged behind their monolingual peers in Dutch reading comprehension. For the minority children, performance on Dutch oral receptive and productive vocabulary was a stronger predictor of Dutch reading comprehension than Dutch word reading. Taken together, these studies suggest that findings from a word reading task or grapho-phonological awareness task need to be interpreted with special caution in cross-language reading research.

Grapho-morphological awareness

Grapho-morphological awareness refers to the ability to reflect upon how semantic information is encoded in the orthography and how orthography provides cues to meaning. It is parallel to, but more specialized than, morphological awareness, which entails insight into relationships between meaning and phonological form. Importantly, there are cases in which written language provides information about meaning not available in spoken language. For example, the Chinese writing system has a unique graphic component called the semantic radical. Radicals usually provide reliable although partial information about the meanings of characters, but do not convey any phonological information. For example, most of Chinese characters that have female-related meanings—such as 媽 (mother), 姨 (aunt), 姐 (older sister), 妹 (younger sister)—contain the female radical 女 on the left. Another example of a grapho-morphological feature is the marking of nouns with capital letters in German orthography.

Grapho-morphological awareness is important for discriminating homophones, words that share the same pronunciation, but have different meanings and often have different orthographic forms. Examples in English include to, too, and two, and bear and bare. This type of grapho-morphological awareness is particularly important in languages with an abundance of homophones, such as Chinese.

Grapho-morphological awareness may play an important role in segment-ing orthographic strings into morphemes (Nunes *et al.*, 2003). This could work interactively with segmentation into syllables and other aspects of grapho-phonological analysis (Taft, 1991). Grapho-morphological aware-ness may have a role in processing varied orthographic representations of the same morphemes—which might be termed allomorphographs—as in the endings of the following English words: dog→dogs versus bunny→bunnies or react→reaction versus convert→conversion.

Research has shown that grapho-morphological awareness can play an important role in literacy development when grapho-morphological fea-tures in a language are plentiful and informative. For example, seman-tic radical awareness and homophone awareness have been found to be important in Chinese children's development of literacy skills (e.g. Ho, *et al.*, in press; Ho *et al.*, 1999; Li *et al.*, 2002; Nagy *et al.*, 2002; Shu & Anderson, 1997).

Grapho-morphological awareness is not a widely studied aspect of meta-linguistic awareness in second language reading research. Its potential importance is illustrated by a study by Hancin-Bhatt and Nagy (1994) with Spanish-English bilingual children. They showed that the recognition of cognates depended on the orthographic overlap of the cognate pairs. The ability to recognize cognate stems, which usually share orthographic forms in Spanish and English, increased steadily with age, but the ability to recog-nize systematic relationships between Spanish and English suffixes remained fairly limited.

Our conjecture is that grapho-morphological awareness is more import-ant for second language readers than first language readers. This ought to be especially true in the common situation in which people have more facility in reading their second language than in speaking it. We are not aware of direct evidence for this conjecture, but indirect evidence comes from studies show-ing that grapho-morphological information is especially important for deaf readers (Gustad, 2000).

Cross-language transfer of metalinguistic awareness

There has been a resurgence of interest in cross-language transfer in second language reading research during the past two decades. The idea of transfer in second language acquisition can be traced back to the Contrastive Analysis approach (Lado, 1957; for a review, see Selinker & Gass, 1994), which attempted to explain second language development based on the analysis of the similarities and differences between the native language and the second language. While the early development of cross-language transfer research was heavily influenced by comparative linguistics and behaviorism, recent research has evolved to view second language learners as playing a more active role in utilizing knowledge and experience gained from one language in the learning of another language. This shifted view was explicitly theorized in Cummins' interdependence hypothesis (1978, 1979, 1981, 1994):

> To the extent that instruction in a certain language is effective in promoting proficiency in that language, transfer of this proficiency to another language will occur, provided there is adequate exposure to that other language (either in the school or environment) and adequate motivation to learn that language. (1981, p. 29)

Cummins (1980, 1991) made a distinction between basic interpersonal communicative language skills and cognitive/academic language proficiency. The former refers to contextualized language use, such as everyday conversation, whereas the latter refers to the proficiency in somewhat decontextualized language use, which usually does not have immediate interpersonal communicative purpose, such as reading and writing. Cummins argued that while basic interpersonal communicative language skills may develop separately in different languages, cognitive/academic language proficiency should be common across languages. Furthermore, it is this common proficiency in decontextualized language use that serves as the basis for cross-language transfer of literacy skills.

Much of the evidence Cummins drew upon to support his interdependence hypothesis came from studies that show strong correlations between students' scores on academic assessments in two languages (for a review, see Cummins, 1991, 1994). In the past decade, researchers have tried to identify the aspects of language proficiency or cognitive ability that are common and thus may be transferable across languages. In this research, phonological awareness (e.g. Cisero & Royer, 1995; Comeau *et al.*, 1999; Durgunoglu *et al.*, 1993; Gottardo *et al.*, 2001; Lindsey *et al.*, 2003; Luk, 2003; Verhoeven, 1994), morphosyntactic awareness (e.g. Gottardo *et al.*, 2001; van Gelderen *et al.*, 2004; Verhoeven, 1994), word reading (Comeau *et al.*, 1999; Durgunoglu *et al.*, 2003; Gottardo *et al.*, 2001; Lindsey *et al.*, 2003; Luk, 2003; Verhoeven, 1994); reading comprehension (e.g. van Gelderen *et al.*, 2004; Verhoeven, 1994) and reading strategies (e.g. van Gelderen *et al.*, 2004) have been systematically studied.

Like the early investigations of interdependence, the studies conducted have been correlational in nature. Two types of cross-language relationship have been examined: (1) cross-language transfer of a particular aspect of metalinguistic awareness; and (2) cross-language contribution of a particular aspect of metalinguistic awareness to reading achievement. With regard to the first type of relationship, cross-language transfer has been evaluated in correlations between metalinguistic measures in two languages (e.g. Gottardo *et al.*, 2001; Luk, 2003) or in regression analyses where the metalinguistic awareness in the source language at Time 1 was used to predict metalinguistic awareness at Time 2 (e.g. Lindsey *et al.*, 2003) or the gain of metalinguistic awareness in the target language from Time 1 to Time 2 (e.g. Cisero & Royer, 1995). With regard to the second type of cross-language relationship, transfer has been mostly examined in hierarchical regressions analyses and structural regression modeling. Durgunoglu *et al.* (1993) looked at whether phonological awareness and word reading in the source language made independent contributions to word reading in the target language. Gottardo *et al.* (2001) and Luk (2003) examined the unique contribution of phonological awareness in the source language to word reading in the target language after controlling for the phonological awareness in the target language. Comeau *et al.* (1999) studied transfer by showing that there was no difference in the amount of target language word decoding variance explained by a separate measure of phonological awareness in the source language or by a combined measure of phonological awareness in the source and the target language. Using structural equation modeling, Verhoeven (1994) explored a number of possible models of cross-language transfer in the development of two languages.

Several methodological issues need to be considered with respect to existing research on cross-language transfer. First, more attention should be paid to whether observed cross-language relationships are mediated by other factors, such as working memory or nonverbal intelligence. In a study with Cantonese-English bilingual children, Luk (2003) found that with working memory and nonverbal intelligence as covariates, the cross-language correlations in word reading decreased significantly, whereas the cross-language correlations in phonological awareness remained significant, a finding which implied different underlying linguistic-cognitive mechanisms. Luk interpreted the findings to mean that performance on phonological awareness tasks operates through processes that are universal and language-independent, while word reading involves script-dependent processing. Luk's analysis illustrates the importance of considering potential latent cognitive factors in cross-language transfer research.

Second, more precision is needed in identifying the mechanism of cross-language transfer. Does transfer occur only when two languages have specific overlapping features (e.g. when a particular phoneme or grapheme–phoneme relationship occurs in both languages)? Or, can transfer occur when languages have non-overlapping parallel features (e.g. adverbial marking in English, -ly and in French, -ment)? Cross-language transfer is more compelling when it occurs with non-overlapping parallel features. For example, in a study of Spanish-English bilingual children, Durgunoglu *et al.* (1993) separated the English word-decoding items that had different phonological representations in Spanish from those that relied on the same grapheme-phoneme conversion rules in English and Spanish. Performance on these non-overlapping and overlapping sets of items were compared for two groups of Spanish-English bilingual children who were similar in Spanish word reading ability but differed in Spanish phonological awareness. The finding was that the difference between the two groups of bilinguals was more pronounced on the non-overlapping items than on the overlapping items, suggesting that the bilingual children with superior phonological awareness did not simply treat English words as Spanish words, but, in fact, applied abstract metalinguistic insights across languages.

Third, as pointed out by some authors (e.g. Verhoeven, 1994), what correlational studies can show is the association of language skills and metalinguistic insights across languages. A correlation, even one consistently found, falls short of providing direct evidence for cross-language transfer, because transfer inherently entails a causal relationship. A causal interpretation of correlational evidence becomes credible only when alternative interpretations can be ruled out and, in cross-language research, the number of plausible alternatives is inevitably large.

Summary and conclusions

The rapid progress of research on metalinguistic awareness and second language reading is exciting to observe. At the same time, it is disturbing to note the many gaps in knowledge, inconsistencies, conceptual lacunae, and failures of apparently similar lines of research to yield converging results. Perhaps these problems are inevitable considering that this is a young field addressing difficult issues that push social and behavioral science concepts and methods to the limit.

Levels or varieties of metalinguistic awareness are not clearly differentiated in existing research. The empirical warrant for the banner concept of awareness, and synonymous or related concepts such as explicit representation, intentional reflection, and conscious control, is weak. It seems fair to say that most research findings could be interpreted without appeal to awareness or, at least, that very few findings demand this interpretation. Children are seldom asked for explanations for fear this would be beyond their expressive ability. While the ability to verbalize may not be an appropriate test of awareness in all circumstances, the fact is that an intelligible explanation for a choice or an action, as exemplified in Galambos and Goldin-Meadow's (1990) study of syntactic awareness, constitutes straightforward evidence that the child has an explicit representation or conscious control.

Fundamental questions about metalinguistic awareness still have not been decisively answered. Under some conditions, bilingualism appears to heighten aspects of metalinguistic awareness. However, the importance of heightened awareness to the actual linguistic performance is not firmly established. To quote a piece of folk wisdom, "Bilinguals may be able to talk the talk, but does this enable them to walk the walk?" A study that goes further toward answering this question than many is the one by Durgunoglu *et al.*, (1993) which found that, among two groups of Spanish-English bilingual children equated in word-reading knowledge, the group with higher levels of phonological awareness was better able to pronounce English words that have grapheme-phoneme correspondences not found in Spanish.

Coverage of facets of metalinguistic awareness is spotty in existing research. The most intensively investigated facet is phonological awareness. This reflects the fact that frameworks for reaching research were established in studies with English-speaking children. Whether these frameworks are the most appropriate for studies of children who speak other languages should be re-examined.

Even phonological awareness has not been comprehensively studied, however. As we concluded earlier, research has been preoccupied with whether children can reflect on and manipulate phonological units of different sizes. Meanwhile, the important topics of suprasegmental features, phonotactics, and the phonological structure of languages have been virtually ignored. Research on metalinguistic insights related to reading comprehension—semantic awareness, syntactic awareness, morphological and grapho-morphological awareness—is still underdeveloped. Most attention has been directed to metalinguistic awareness and performance in a second language. Attention should also be given to whether knowing an additional language leads children to think more metalinguistically about their native language.

Particularly at "higher levels" of metalinguistic awareness, research needs to do a better job of taking account of previous familiarity with words and phrases, world knowledge, and linguistic and situational context as factors influencing performance. As we argued earlier, when studying the relationship between aspects of metalinguistic awareness and second language reading, reading comprehension should be assessed instead of, or in addition to, measures of word reading, because for second language readers, successful decoding does not guarantee comprehension.

The social and educational reasons for studying immigrant children are understandable, but this does not always lead to the best science because of the virtual impossibility of matching immigrant bilingual children with native monolingual children on all critical factors. Supplementary studies in countries in which most children learn to read in a second language could provide a vital check on findings of studies with immigrant children. An example is the study by Chen *et al.* (2004) comparing the phonological awareness of Cantonese-speaking children from the south of China learning to speak and read Mandarin in school with that of Mandarin-speaking children from the north of China.

There is excessive reliance on correlational methods in research on metalinguistic awareness and second language learning. Analysis of covariance, hierarchical regression analysis, and structural equation modeling provide useful tools for weighing the relative importance of factors, but it is an illusion that a causal model can be established by statistical legerdemain. Wherever possible, experimental research should be conducted. Consider the following Gedanken experiment ("thought experiment") on cross-language transfer: Spanish-speaking kindgartners in El Paso or East Los Angeles are screened for Spanish phonemic awareness. A random half of the children with performance below a threshold receive phonemic aware-ness training. All of the children are retested for phonemic awareness in Spanish and also in English. Later, if the investigator has the patience and the grant has not run out, reading development in Spanish and English is tracked.

We end with the thought that, when investigating the question of whether exposure to two languages promotes metalinguistic awareness, simply com-paring bilinguals with monolinguals is not sufficient. Research needs to investigate whether a bilingual advantage or disadvantage is conditioned on the level of native language and second language proficiency, and the struc-tural complexity of the native language and the second language. Some but not all existing research tries to address the question of whether the effect of bilingualism on metalinguistic awareness depends upon the specific relation-ship between the two languages involved. That is, taking into account whether the additional language the bilingual children know has simpler or more transparent linguistic structures (e.g. less complicated consonant clus-ters; more salient syllable structures; fewer tones; less complicated marking of case, gender, aspect, and tense) or a more or less opaque writing system than the native language.

References

Abu-Rabia, S. & Siegel, L. S. (2002) Reading, syntactic, orthographic, and working memory skills of bilingual Arabic–English speaking Canadian children. *Journal of Psycholinguistic Research*, 31, 661–78.

Altmann, G. T. M., Garnham, A., & Dennis, Y. (1992) Avoiding the garden path: eye movements in contexts. *Journal of Memory and Language*, 31, 685–712.

Anderson, R. C. & Freebody, P. (1981) Vocabulary knowledge. In J. Guthrie (ed.), *Comprehension and teaching: research reviews* (pp. 77–117). Newark, DE: International Reading Association.

Anglin, J. M. (1993) Vocabulary development: a morphological analysis. *Mono-graphs of the Society for Research in Child Development* 58, Serial #238.

Assink, E. & Sandra, D. (2003) *Reading complex words: cross-language studies.* Dordrecht, the Netherlands: Kluwer.

Bialystok, E. (1988) Levels of bilingualism and levels of linguistic awareness. *Devel-opmental Psychology*, 88, 560–7.

Bialystok, E. (2001) *Bilingualism in development: language, literacy and cognition.* Cambridge, UK: Cambridge University Press.

Bialystok, E. & Ryan, E. B. (1985) Toward a definition of metalinguistic skill. *Merrill-Palmer Quarterly*, 31, 229–51.

Bialystok, E. & Majumder, S. (1998) The relationship between bilingualism and the development of cognitive processes in problem-solving. *Applied Psycho-linguistics*, 19, 69–85.

Bialystok, E., Majumder, S., & Martin, M. M. (2003) Developing phonological awareness: is there a bilingual advantage? *Applied Psycholinguistics*, 24, 27–44.

Boutet, J., Gauthier, F., Saint-Pierre, M. (1983) Savoir dire sur la phrase. *Archives de Psychologie*, 51, 205–28.

Bradley, L. & Bryant, P. E. (1983) Categorizing sounds and learning to read: a causal connection. *Nature*, 310, 419–21.

Brown, H. D. (1994) *Principles of language learning and teaching*. Englewood Cliffs, NJ: Prentice Hall Regents.

Bruck, M. & Genesee, F. (1995) Phonological awareness in young second language learners. *Journal of Child Language*, 22, 307–24.

Burani, C. & Caramazza, A. (1987) Representation and processing of derived words. *Language and Cognitive Processes*, 2, 217–27.

Campbell, R. & Sais, E. (1995) Accelerated metalinguistic (phonological) awareness in bilingual children. *British Journal of Developmental Psychology*, 13, 61–8.

Caravolas, M. & Bruck, M. (1993) The effect of oral and written language input on children's phonological awareness: a cross-linguistic study. *Journal of Experimental Child Psychology*, 55, 1–30.

Carlisle, J. F. (1995) Morphological awareness and early reading achievement (pp. 189–209). In L. Feldman (ed.), *Morphological aspects of language processing*. Hillsdale, NJ: Lawrence Erlbaum Associates.

Carlisle, J. (2003). Morphology matters in learning to read: a commentary. *Reading Psychology*, 24, 291–322.

Cazden, C. B. (1976) Play with language and metalingusitic awareness: one dimension of language experience. In J. S. Bruner, A. Jolley, & K. Silva (eds.), *Play: its role in development and evolution*. New York: Basic Books.

Chen, X., Anderson, R. C., Li, W., Hao, M., Wu, X., & Shu, H. (2004) Phonological awareness of bilingual and monolingual Chinese children. *Journal of Educational Psychology*, 96, 142–51.

Chiappe, P. & Siegel, L. S. (1999) Phonological awareness and reading acquisition in English-and Punjabi-speaking Canadian children. *Journal of Educational Psychology*, 91, 20–8.

Chiappe, P., Siegel, L. S., & Gottardo, A. (2002) Reading-related skills of kindergarteners from diverse linguistic backgrounds. *Applied Psycholinguistics*, 23, 95–116.

Cisero, C. A. & Royer, J. M. (1995) The development of cross-language transfer of phonological awareness. *Contemporary Educational Psychology*, 20, 275–303.

Clahsen, H., Sonnenstuhl, I., & Blevins, J. (in press) Derivational morphology in the German mental lexicon: a dual mechanism account. In H. Baayen & R. Schreuder, (eds.), *Aspects of morphological processing*. Mouton de Gruyter.

Comeau, L., Cormier, P., Grandmaison, E., & Lacroix, D. (1999) A longitudinal study of phonological processing skills in children learning to read in a second language. *Journal of Educational Psychology*, 91(1), 29–43.

Cossu, F., Shankweiler, D., Liberman, I. Y., Toal, G., & Katz, L. (1988) Awareness of phonological segments and reading ability in Italian children. *Applied Psychology*, 9, 1–16.

Cromdal, J. (1999) Childhood bilingualism and metalinguistic skills: analysis and control in young Swedish–English bilinguals. *Applied Psycholinguistics*, 20, 1–20.

Cummins, J. (1978) Bilingualism and the development of metalinguistic awareness. *Journal of Cross-Cultural Psychology*, 9(2), 131–49.

Cummins, J. (1979). Linguistic interdependence and the educational development of bilingual children. *Review of Educational Research*, 49, 221–51.

Cummins, J. (1980) The cross-lingual dimensions of language proficiency: implications for bilingual education and the optimal age issue. *TESOL Quarterly*, 14, 175–87.

Cummins, J. (1981) The role of primary language development in promoting educational success for language minority students (pp. 3–49). In California State Department of Education (ed.), *Schooling and language minority students: a theoretical framework*. Los Angeles, California: Department of Education, Evaluation, Dissemination and Assessment Center.

Cummins, J. (1991) Interdependence of first- language second-language proficiency in bilingual children. In E. Bialystok (ed.), *Language processing in bilingual children*. New York, NY: Cambridge University Press.

Cummins, J. (1994) Primary language instruction and the education of language minority students (pp. 3–45). In California State Department of Education (ed.), *Schooling and language minority students: a theoretical framework*. Los Angeles, California: Department of Education, Evaluation, Dissemination and Assessment Center.

Cutler, A. & Butterfield, S. (1992). Rhythmic cues to speech segmentation: evidence from juncture misperception. *Journal of Memory and Language*, 31, 218–36.

D'Angiulli, A., Siegel, L. S., & Serra, E. (2001) The development of reading in English and Italian bilingual children. *Applied Psycholinguistics*, 22, 479–507.

Da Fontoura, H. A. & Siegel, L. S. (1995) Reading, syntactic, and working memory skills of bilingual Portuguese–English Canadian children. *Reading, & Writing*, 7 (1), 139–53.

Diaz, R. M. (1985) Bilingual cognitive development: addressing three gaps in current research. *Child Development*, 56, 1376–88.

Droop, M. & Verhoeven, L. (2003) Language proficiency and reading ability in first- and second-language learners. *Reading Research Quarterly*, 38, 78–103.

Durgunoglu, A. (2002) Cross-linguistic transfer in literacy and implications for language learners. *Annals of Dyslexia*, 52, 189–204.

Durgunoglu, A. Y., Nagy, W. E., & Hancin-Bhatt, B. J. (1993) Cross-language transfer of phonological awareness. *Journal of Educational Psychology*, 85, 453–65.

Durgunoglu, A., Peynircioglu, Z. F., & Mir, M. (2002) The role of formal definitions in reading comprehension of bilingual students. In R. R. Heredia, & J. Altarriba (eds.), *Bilingual sentence processing* (pp. 299–316). Amsterdam: Elsevier Science Publisher.

Galambos, S. J. & Hakuta, K. (1988) Subject-specific and task-specific characteristics of metalinguistic awareness in bilingual children. *Applied Psycholinguistics*, 9, 141–62.

Galambos, S. J. & Goldin-Meadow, S. G. (1990) The effects of learning two languages on levels of metalinguistic awareness. *Cognition*, 34, 1–56.

Garcia, G. E. (1991) Factors influencing the English reading test performance of Spanish-speaking Hispanic children. *Reading Research Quarterly*, 26 (4), 371–92.

Garcia, G. E. (2000) Bilingual children's reading. In M. L. Kamil, P. B. Mosenthal, P. D. Pearson, R. Barr (eds.), *Handbook of reading research*: Vol. III (pp. 813–34). Mahwah: NJ: Lawrence Erlbaum Associates.

Garcia, G. E., Jimenez, R. T., & Pearson, P. D. (1998) Metacognition, childhood bilingualism, and reading. In J. H. Douglas, & J. Dunlosky (eds.), *Metacognition in educational theory and practice*. Mahwah, NJ: Lawrence Erlbaum Associates.

Gass, S. M. & Selinker, L. (1994). *Second language acquisition*. Hillsdale, NJ: Lawrence Erlbaum Associates.

Gaustad, M. G. (2000) Morphographic analysis as a word identification strategy for deaf readers. *Journal of Deaf Studies & Deaf Education*, 5, 60–80.

Gaux, C. & Gombert, J. E. (1999). Implicit and explicit syntactic knowledge and reading in pre-adolescents. *British Journal of Developmental Psychology*, 17, 169–88.

Geva, E. & Siegel, L. S. (2000) Orthographic and cognitive factors in the concurrent development of basic reading skills in two languages. *Reading and Writing: An Interdisciplinary Journal*, 12, 1–30.

Gombert, J. E. (1992) *Metalinguistic development*. Chicago: University of Chicago Press.

Gomeau, L., Cormier, P., Grandmaison, E., & Lacroix, D. (1999) A longitudinal study of phonological processing skills in children learning to read in a second language. *Journal of Educational Psychology*, 91, 29–43.

Goswami, U. (1999) The relationship between phonological awareness and orthographic representation in different orthographies. In M. Harris, & G. Hatano (eds.), *Learning to read and write: a cross-linguistic perspective* (pp. 134–56). Cambridge: Cambridge University Press.

Gottardo, A., Stanovich, K. E., & Siegel, L. S. (1996) The relationship between phonological sensitivity, syntactic processing and verbal working memory in the reading performance of third-grade children. *Journal of Experimental Child Psychology*, 63, 563–82.

Gottardo, A., Yan, B., Siegel, L. S., & Wade-Woolley, L. (2001) Factors related to English reading performance in children with Chinese as a first language: more evidence of cross-language transfer of phonological processing. *Journal of Educational Psychology*, 93, 530–42.

Hakes, D. T. (1980) *The development of metalinguistic abilities in children*. Berlin: Springer-Verlag.

Hakuta, K. & Diaz, R. M. (1985) The relationship between degree of bilingualism and cognitive ability: a critical discussion and some new longitudinal data. In K. E. Nelson (ed.), *Children's language* (pp. 319–44). Hillsdale: Lawrence Erlbaum Associates.

Hancin-Bhatt, B. & Nagy, W. E. (1994) Lexical transfer and second language morphological development. *Applied Psycholinguistics*, 15, 289–310.

Harley, T. (2001) *The psychology of language*. New York: Psychology Press.

Ho, C., S.-H., Wong, W.-L., & Chan, W.-S. (1999) The use of orthographic analogies in learning to read Chinese. *Journal of Child Psychology*, 40, 393–403.

Ho, C., S.-H., Ng, T.-T., & Ng, W.-K. (in press) A "radical" approach to reading development in Chinese: the role of semantic radicals and phonetic radicals. *Journal of Literary Research*, 35(3), 849–78.

Holligan, C. & Johnston, R. S. (1988) The use of phonological information by good and poor readers in memory and reading tasks. *Memory and Cognition*, 16, 522–32.

Jannedy, S., Poletto, R., Weldon, T. L. (1991). *Language files*. Columbus, OH: Ohio State University.

Jimenez, R. T., Garcia, G. E., & Pearson, P. D. (1995) Three children, two languages, and strategic reading: case studies in bilingual/monolingual reading. *American Educational Research Journal*, 32, 67–97.

Johnson, E. K., Jusczyk, P. W., Cutler, A., & Norris, D. (2003) Lexical viability constraints on speech segmentation by infants. *Cognitive Psychology*, 46, 65–97.

Juel, C., Griffith, P. L., & Gough, P. B. (1986) Acquisition of literacy: a longitudinal study of children in first and second grade. *Journal of Educational Psychology*, 78, 243–55.

Jusczyk, P. W., Cutler, A., & Redanz, N. J. (1993) Infants' preference for the predominant stress patterns of English words. *Child Development*, 64, 675–87.

Ku, Y.-M. & Anderson, R. C. (2003) Development of morphological awareness in Chinese and English. *Reading and Writing: An Interdisciplinary Journal*, 16, 399–422.

Lado, R. (1957) *Linguistics across cultures*. Ann Arbor: University of Michigan Press.

Leong, C. K. (1999) Phonological and morphological processing in adult students with learning/reading disabilities. *Journal of Learning Disabilities*, 32, 224–38.

Lesaux, N. K. & Siegel, L. S. (2003) The developmental of reading in children who speak English as a second language. *Developmental Psychology*, 39, 1005–19.

Lesaux, N. K., Lipka, O., & Siegel, L. S. (2003) Syntactic awareness as the red herring? Reading comprehension skills of children from diverse linguistic backgrounds. Unpublished manuscript. The University of British Columbia.

Lesaux, N. K., Siegel, L. S., & Rupp, A. A. (2003) The developmental of reading skills in children from diverse linguistic backgrounds: findings from a 5-year longitudinal study. The University of British Columbia.

Lesaux, N.K., Lipka, O., & Siegel, L. S. (2006) Investigating congitive and linguistic abilities that influence the reading comprehension skills of children from diverse linguistic backgrounds. Reading and Writing, 19 (1), 99–131.

Li, W., Anderson, R. C. Nagy, W., & Zhang, H. (2002) Facets of metalinguistic awareness that contribute to Chinese literacy. In W. Li, J. S. Gaffney, J. L. Packard (eds.), *Chinese children's reading acquisition: theoretical and pedagogical issues* (pp. 87–106). Norwell, MA: Kluwer Academic Publishers.

Lindsey, K. A., Manis, F. R., & Bailey, C. E. (2003) Prediction of first-grade reading in Spanish-speaking English-language learners. *Journal of Educational Psychology*, 95, 482–94.

Liow, S. J. R. & Poon, K K. L. (1998) Phonological awareness in multilingual Chinese children. *Applied, Psycholinguistics*, 19, 339–62.

Lipka, O. & Siegel, L. S. (2003) The development of reading skills of children with English as a second language from different language backgrounds. Unpublished manuscript. The University of British Columbia.

Lipka, O. & Siegel, L. S. (2007) The development of reading skills in children with English as a second language. *Scientific Studies of Reading*, 11 (2), 105–31.

Luk, G. C.-M. (2003) Exploring the latent factors behind inter-language correlations in reading and phonological awareness. Master's thesis, York University, Toronto.

McQueen, J. M., Norris, D. G., & Cutler, A. (1994) Competition in spoken word recognition: spotting words in other words. *Journal of Experimental Psychology: Learning, Memory and Cognition*, 20, 621–38.

Mahony, D., Singson, M., & Mann, V. (2000) Reading ability and sensitivity to morphological relations. *Reading and Writing: An Interdisciplinary Journal*, 12, 191–218.

Mattingly, I. G. (1984) Reading, linguistic awareness, and language acquisition.

In J. Downing, & R. Valtin (eds.) *Language awareness and learning to read* (pp. 9–26). New York: Springer-Verlag.

Mattys, S. L. & Jusczyk, P. W. (2001) Phonotactic cues for segmentation of fluent speech by infants. *Cognition*, 78, 91–121.

Morgan, J. L. & Saffran, J. R. (1995) Emerging integration of sequential and suprasegmental information in preverbal speech segmentation. *Child Development*, 66, 911–36.

Mumtaz, S. & Humphreys, G. W. (2001) The effects of bilingualism on learning to read English: evidence from the contrast between Urdu–English bilingual and English monolingual children. *Journal of Research in Reading*, 24 (2), 113–34.

Muter, V. & Diethelm, K. (2001) The contribution of phonological skills and letter knowledge to early reading development in a multilingual population. *Language Learning*, 51 (2), 187–219.

Nagy, W. E. & Anderson, R. C. (1984) How many words are there in printed school English? *Reading Research Quarterly*, 19, 304–30.

Nagy, W. & Gentner, D. (1990) Semantic constraints on lexical categories. *Language and Cognitive Processes*, 5, 169–201.

Nagy, W. E. & Scott, J. A. (1990) Word schemas: expectations about the form and meaning of new words. *Cognition & Instruction*, 7, 105–27.

Nagy, W. E. & Anderson, R. C. (1998) Metalinguistic awareness and literacy acquisition in different languages. In D. Wagner, R. Venezy, & B. Street (eds.), *Literacy: an international handbook* (pp. 155–60). Boulder, CO: Westview Press.

Nagy, W. E. & Scott, J. A. (2000) Vocabulary processes. In M. L. Kamil, P. B. Mosenthal, P. D. Pearson, R. Barr (eds.), *Handbook of reading research*: Vol. III (pp. 269–84). Mahwah, NJ: Erlbaum.

Nagy, W. E., Anderson, R. C., Schommer, M., Scott, J. A., & Stallman, A. C. (1989) Morphological families in the internal lexicon. *Reading Research Quarterly*, 24, 263–82.

Nagy, W. E., Kuo-Kealoha, A., Wu, X., Li, W., Anderson, R. C., & Chen, X. (2002) The role of morphological awareness in learning to read Chinese. In W. Li, J. S. Gaffney, & J. L. Packard (eds.), *Chinese language acquisition: theoretical and pedagogical* issues (pp. 59–86). Norwell, MA: Kluwer Academic Publisher.

Napps, S. E. (1989) Morphemic relationships in the lexicon: are they distinct from semantic and formal relationships? *Memory and Cognition*, 17, 729–39.

Nation, K. & Snowling, M. J. (2000) Factors influencing syntactic awareness skills in normal readers and poor comprehenders. *Applied Psycholinguistcs*, 21, 229–41.

Niswander, E., Pollatsek, A., & Rayner, K. (2000) The processing of derived and inflected suffixed words during reading. *Language and Cognitive Processes*, 15: 4/5, 389–420.

Nunes, T., Bryant, P., & Olsson, J. (2003) Learning morphological and phonological spelling rules: an intervention study. *Scientific Studies of Reading*, 7, 289–307.

Porpodas, C. (1993) The relation between phonemic awareness and reading and spelling of Greek words in the first school years. In M. Carretero, M. Pope, R. J. Simons and J. I. Pozo (eds.), *Learning and instruction*, Vol. III, (pp. 203–17). Oxford: Pergamon Press.

Pratt, C. & Grieve, R. (1984) The development of metalinguistic awareness: an introduction. In W. E. Tunmer, C. Pratt, & M. L. Herriman (eds.), *Metalinguistic awareness in children*. Berlin: Springer-Verlag.

Ricciardelli, L. (1992) Bilingualism and cognitive development in relation to threshold theory. *Journal of Psycholinguistic Research*, 21, 301–16.

Sandra, D. (1994) The morphology of the mental lexicon: internal word structure viewed from psycholinguistic perspective. *Language and Cognitive Processes*, 9, 227–69.

Schneider, W. & Naslund, J. C. (1999) The impact of early phonological processing skills on reading and spelling in school: evidence from the Munich Longitudinal Study. In F. E. Weindert and W. Schneider (eds.), *Individual development from 3 to 12: findings from the Munich Longitudinal Study*. Cambridge: Cambridge University Press.

Shankweiler, D., Crain, S., Katz, L., Fowler, A. E., Liberman, A. E., Brady, S. A., Thornton, R., Lundquist, E., Dreyer, L., Fletcher, J. M., Stuebing, K. K., Shaywitz, S. E., & Shaywitz, B. A. (1995) Cognitive profiles of reading disabled children: comparisons of language skills in phonology, morphology and syntax. *Psychological Science*, 6, 149–56.

Shu, H. & Anderson, R. C. (1997) Role of radical awareness in the character and word acquisition of Chinese children. *Reading Research Quarterly*, 32, 78–89.

Siegel, L. (1993) Phonological processing deficits as the basis of a reading disability. *Developmental Review*, 13, 246–57.

Siegel, L. S. & Lipka, O. (2003) Syntactic awareness skills in English of children with English as a second language who speak Slavic or Chinese languages as a first language. Unpublished manuscript. The University of British Columbia.

Stanovich, K. E., Cunningham, A. E., & Cramer, B. B. (1984) Assessing phonological awareness in kindergarten children: issues of task comparability. *Journal of Experimental Child Psychology*, 38, 175–90.

Taft, M. (1991) *Reading and the mental lexicon*. Hillsdale, NJ: Earlbaum.

Tahta, S., Wood, M., & Lowenthal, K. (1981) Foreign accents: factors relation to transfer of accent from the first language to the second language. *Language and Speech*, 24, 265–72.

Treiman, R. and Zukowski, A. (1991). Levels of phonological awareness. In S. Brady and D. Shankweiler (eds.), *Phonological processes in literacy*. Hillsdale, NJ: Erlbaum.

Tunmer, W. E. & Nesdale, A. R. (1985) Phonemic segmentation skill and beginning reading. *Journal of Educational Psychology*, 77, 417–27.

Tunmer, W. E., Herriman, M., & Nesdale, A. (1988) Metalinguistic abilities and beginning reading. *Reading Research Quarterly*, 23, 134–58.

van Gelderen, A., Schoonen, R., de Glopper, K., Hulstijn, J., Simis, A., Snellings, P., & Stevenson, M. (2004) Linguistic knowledge, processing speed, and metacognitive knowledge in first- and second- language reading comprehension: a componential analysis. *Journal of Educational Psychology*, 96, 19–30.

Van Kleeck, A. (1982) The emergence of linguistic awareness: a cognitive framework, *Merrill-Palmer Quarterly*, 29, 237–65.

Vellutino, F. R. & Scanlon, D. M. (1987) Phonological coding, phonological awareness, and reading ability: evidence from a longitudinal and experimental study. *Merrill-Palmer Quarterly*, 33, 321–63.

Verhoeven, L. T. (1991) Predicting minority children's bilingual proficiency: child, family, and institutional factors. *Language Learning*, 41, 205–33.

Verhoeven, L. T. (1994) Transfer in bilingual development: the linguistic interdependency hypothesis revisited. *Language Learning*, 44, 381–415.

Verhoeven, L. T. (2000) Components in early second language reading and spelling. *Scientific Studies of Reading*, 4, 313–30.

Wimmer, H., Lander, K. & Schneider, W. (1994). The role of rime awareness in learning to read a regular orthography. *British Journal of Developmental Psychology*, 12(4), 469–84.

Zhou, X. & Marslen-Wilson, W. (1994) Words, morphemes, and syllables in the Chinese mental lexicon. *Language and Cognitive Processes*, 9, 393–422.

Zhou, X. & Marslen-Wilson, W. (1995) Morphological structure in the Chinese mental lexicon. *Language and Cognitive Processes*, 10, 545–600.

4 Impacts of prior literacy experience on second-language learning to read

Keiko Koda

During the past decade, unprecedented numbers of children and youth have undergone schooling in languages other than their native language. Although these numbers are continually growing, our understanding of how second-language reading skills develop is still limited. Since learning to read in a second language differs markedly from that in a first, it is essential that its unique characteristics be recognized and properly addressed in second-language literacy research. Dual-language involvement is one such distinction because learners bring their first-language linguistic knowledge, and possibly literacy skills, to the process of learning to read in a second language. In point of fact, one of the conclusions of a recent research synthesis is that oral proficiency and literacy in the first language can be used to promote literacy development in a second language (August & Shanahan, 2006).

Clearly, systematic explorations of how the two languages involved interact and impact upon one another in shaping second-language reading skills will shed substantial light on literacy development in bilingual readers. Consequently, the primary goal of this chapter is to explore principled approaches—both conceptual and methodological—in examining such cross-linguistic interactions, as well as the impacts of prior literacy experience in second-language reading development. The rationale underlying such explorations is simply that, despite the commonly held belief that first- and second-language reading abilities are closely related, little is known about the mechanisms conjoining literacy learning in two languages. The clarification of such mechanisms—leading to subsequent empirical examination—will yield important clues for explaining other critical issues in second-language literacy development, such as the optimal method for teaching literacy to second-language learners already literate in their first language; the functions of oral language proficiency in second-language literacy development; and possible variations in the developmental path in first- and second-language literacy acquisition.

In delving into such uncharted territory, brief summaries of relevant theories are useful. The chapter opens with a brief introduction of transfer. Although transfer has long been a major concern in the second-language literature, a clear consensus as to what "transfer" really involves has yet to emerge. In the absence of a well-articulated theory, many critical questions remain untackled. Little information is available, for example, as to what is actually transferred, under what conditions, how transferred competencies alter second-language reading development, and whether transfer occurs in the same manner—and to the same degree—among learners from diverse first-language backgrounds. It is thus important to clarify why the existing conceptualizations fail to address these vital questions.

A viable theory of transfer must incorporate accurate descriptions of what has been previously acquired and what must be learned in a new language. Lacking such information, it is virtually impossible to conceptualize what is readily available for transfer, how such availability differs among individual learners, and to what extent the transferred competencies facilitate second-language reading acquisition. Probing these issues demands a valid method of uncovering similarities and differences in learning-to-read experiences across languages. The concept of reading universals is crucial in this regard, because it specifies the learning-to-read requirements imposed on all learners in all languages, and thus, invariant across languages. Systematic comparisons of how the requisite tasks are accomplished in different languages should, therefore, permit us to determine the specific ways in which the universal demands are altered by the properties of a particular language and its writing system. Hence, theories of reading universals establish the basis for selecting focal constructs for analysis in identifying cross-linguistic variations in learning-to-read experiences in typologically diverse languages.

Metalinguistic awareness—the ability to identify, analyze and manipulate language forms—has been selected as the focal construct in the current exploration. The significance of this ability lies in its capacity for enabling the learner to analyze words into their phonological and morphological constituents. Since learning to read entails learning to map between spoken-language elements and the graphic symbols that encode those elements, metalinguistic awareness, emanating from oral-language development, substantially expedites the initial stages of reading acquisition. Therefore, systematic examinations of first-language metalinguistic contributions to second-language reading acquisition are likely to yield substantial insights into shared resources, across languages, available to second-language learners.

These formulations, as well as their corollary principles, collectively constitute the theoretical foundations for a unified framework through which the impacts of prior literacy experience on second-language reading development can be conceptualized and examined across diverse groups of second-language learners.

Transfer

Language transfer

Transfer has long been a major theoretical concept in second-language research. Despite its centrality, however, there is little agreement as to what constitutes transfer, partially because of the constantly shifting views of second-language learning—what is learned and how it is learned. Traditionally, for example, transfer has been viewed as the learners' reliance on first-language knowledge. Krashen (1983), for example, regards transfer as the resultant state stemming from the learner's falling back on old knowledge, or first-language rules, when new knowledge is not yet sufficiently developed. Gass and Selinker (1983) offer a similar, but somewhat more refined, view: "the learner is transferring prior linguistic knowledge resulting in IL (interlanguage) forms which, when compared by the researchers to the target language norms, can be termed 'positive,' 'negative,' or 'neutral' " (p. 6). Odlin (1989) reinforces the general thrust of this notion by stating, "transfer is the influence from similarities and differences between the target language and any other language that has been previously (and perhaps imperfectly) acquired" (p. 27). These views of transfer share two major assumptions. First, what is transferred is linguistic knowledge, conceived as a set of rules. Second, the reliance on first-language knowledge is, more or less, associated with an insufficient grasp of second-language rules. Consequently, these views further presume that transfer tends to cease when second-language linguistic knowledge has developed and, more critically, that once sufficient proficiency is attained, first-language knowledge plays no role in explaining individual differences in second-language learning.

Nonetheless, these contentions are no longer uniformly endorsed. As a case in point, in Functionalist theories, language is viewed as a set of relations between forms and functions (Van Valin, 1991), and its acquisition as the process of internalizing form-function relationships through cumulative use of language in communication (MacWhinney & Bates, 1989). Since such relationships do not embody closely matched, one-on-one correspondences, they are regarded as correlational, rather than absolute rules, and their acquisition is described in terms of probability, rather than an all-or-nothing state. Consequently, under the Functionalist assumptions, what is transferred is not a set of rules, as traditionally conceived, but the internalized form-function relationships and their mapping skills. Hence, this view of language regards linguistic knowledge as a continually developing, ever changing, entity, and as such, conceptualizes transfer as a dynamic process, rather than as a static end result.

Alternative conceptualizations of transfer have also been proposed. Recent syntheses of research on second-language literacy development suggest broader definitions of transfer (August & Shanahan, 2006; Riches & Genesee, 2006). For example, transfer is seen as the ability to learn new

language and literacy skills by drawing on the previously acqr
(Genesee *et al.*, 2006). Similarly, prior experience is regarde
of knowledge, skills, and abilities that is available when learning
a new language (Riches and Genesee, 2006). In these newer concepu.
tions, the investigative focus has shifted from characterizing first-languag.
influence either as negative or positive, to identifying the resources available
to second-language learners when learning a new language as well as literacy
skills in that language.

Reading skill transfer

In second-language reading, as in second-language learning, a clear consensus as to what actually transfers has yet to emerge, in part because of the
polarized views of reading. One faction perceives reading as an indivisible
whole, while another sees it as a constellation of separate components. Pro-
ponents of the former believe that language is acquired as a whole through
communication, and communicative use of language is intrinsic in reading.
As such, reading is indivisible and learned holistically as a meaning-
construction process (Goodman, 1967, 1969). Since the ultimate goal of
reading—text-meaning construction—is the same in all languages, there
should be little difference in the reading process across languages. The early
transfer research, based on the assumption that those with strong reading
skills in a first language should also read well in a second language, focused
on two primary issues: the interrelationship between first-language and
second-language reading competence (e.g. Cummins *et al.*, 1981; Legarretta,
1979; Skutnabb-Kangass & Toukomaa, 1976; Troike, 1978); and the
conditions either inhibiting, or facilitating, reading skill transfer from one
language to another (e.g. Clarke, 1979; Devine, 1987, 1988).

Studies addressing the first issue consistently showed that reading abilities
in the two languages correlated strongly, leading to the contention that first-
language reading ability is a primary determinant of second-language
reading achievement (Cummins, 1979, 1991). The research in the latter
cluster demonstrated that adult second-language learners who were highly
literate in their first-language exhibited reading behaviors typically associated with poor readers. The observations were interpreted as suggesting that
limited second-language knowledge inhibited highly literate learners from
transferring their well-developed first-language skills, thereby causing them
to behave like poor readers when reading in a second language (Clarke,
1979; Yorio, 1971).

The holistic view of reading, however, has been challenged regarding its
assumption that the reading process is similar across languages. Empirical
investigations involving skilled readers of a wide variety of languages uniformly suggest that different information-processing procedures—reflecting
distinct properties of the individual languages and their respective writing
systems—are used in typologically diverse languages (e.g. Katz & Frost,

1992; Mazuka & Itoh, 1995; Saito *et al.*, 1999; Taft & Zhu, 1995; Vaid, 1995). From the language-specific perspective, subsequent transfer studies have demonstrated (1) that second-language learners with typologically diverse first-language backgrounds use qualitatively different procedures when reading the same target (second) language (e.g. Akamatsu, 1999; Brown & Haynes, 1985; Green & Meara, 1987); (2) that such procedural diversity can be identified with structural variations in learners' respective first languages (e.g. Koda, 1989, 1990, 1993; Ryan & Meara, 1991); and most critically, (3) that transferred first-language competencies interact with second-language print input in complex yet predictable ways (Koda, 1998, 1999, 2000, 2002; Wang *et al.*, 2003). Viewed collectively, these findings indicate that first-language reading experience not only has lasting impacts on second-language reading development, but also systematically alters processing procedures for second-language print information. However, these studies were conducted with adult learners only. The question remains as to whether these insights can be generalized to school-age learners, that is, to those whose first-language literacy skills are still under development.

The holistic view of reading has also been criticized on yet another ground. By defining reading as a single, unitary construct, the early studies generally disregarded the component skills underlying efficient print information processing. The research also has given little attention to what is actually transferred from one language to another, and how transferred skills contribute to second-language reading development. In more recent studies, reading is seen as a constellation of closely related, yet separate, mental operations, each entailing a unique set of sub-skills (e.g. Carr & Levy, 1990). Since this view incorporates multiple skills in tandem, it allows the tracing of developmental relationships among component skills, as well as their functional interconnections, both within and across languages. Recent biliteracy studies, conducted under the componential view, consistently show close connections between first- and second-language phonological skills (e.g. Abu-Rabia, 1995; Da Fontoura & Siegel, 1995; Gholamain & Geva, 1999; Wang *et al.*, 2005) and their relation to second-language decoding skills (Durgunoglu *et al.*, 1993; Gholamain & Geva, 1999). Although the scope of the existing studies has been somewhat limited, focusing almost exclusively on phonological skills, the approach in itself holds high promise for advancing transfer research by allowing systematic examinations of the relative extent to which varying first-language skills contribute directly and indirectly to second-language reading development.

Reading universals

For a theory of transfer to inform second-language literacy development, it must clarify how prior literacy experience affects second-language learning to read. Such explication is only possible through systematic comparisons of literacy experiences across languages. The notion of reading universals is vital in this regard because it designates the learning-to-read requisites imposed on all readers in all languages. Therefore, careful analyses of how particular requisite tasks are achieved in diverse languages should allow reasonably accurate estimates of the extent and manner in which the universal demands are altered by the linguistic and orthographic properties specific to the languages under consideration. Accordingly, these comparisons will make it possible to identify variations in literacy-learning experiences systematically across languages. Hence, the significance of reading universals can be understood as the guiding principle for establishing the scope of such comparisons.

Since reading entails the extraction and integration of linguistic information printed in text, how meaning is linguistically coded, and how linguistic information is graphically represented, largely determines what must be acquired to be a competent reader in a particular language. However, identifying cross-linguistic variations in learning-to-read experience is not simple. Languages and writing systems vary in virtually all aspects, including the constituent elements, their functions, and principles governing their structural organization. For cross-linguistic analysis to be useful, there must be criteria for determining which properties, and variations therein, are relevant to reading acquisition. Theories of reading universals provide such criteria, as well as methodological guidance, in determining the variations to be included in the analysis.

According to the universal grammar of reading (Perfetti, 2003; Perfetti & Dunlap, this volume; Perfetti & Liu, 2005), reading is the dynamic pursuit embedded in two interrelated systems: languages and writing systems. Inevitably, reading acquisition requires a linkage of the two, entailing mapping between spoken language elements and the graphic symbols that encode them (e.g. Fowler & Liberman, 1995; Goswami & Bryant, 1992; Nagy & Anderson, 1999). Consequently, in learning to read in any language, children must first recognize which language elements are encoded in the writing system (the general mapping principle), and then deduce precisely how these elements are encoded (the mapping details). For example, children learning to read English must understand that each letter represents a distinct sound (the alphabetic principle), and then, gradually work out the details of sound–symbol correspondences (the mapping details) through repeated print decoding and encoding experience.

To successfully grasp general mapping principles, children must gain several basic insights: that print relates to speech; that speech can be segmented into a sequence of sounds; and most critically, that these segmented sounds systematically relate to the graphic symbols in the writing system. Since these insights do not involve language-specific details, once they are developed in one language, they should not only be readily available, but also fully functional, for subsequent literacy development in another language. This, however, is not necessarily the case for mapping details, because their acquisition requires substantial print input and experience in the language in which literacy is being learned. How mapping details are acquired, therefore, should vary systematically in diverse languages according to the extent that the representational properties of their writing systems differ. What is common across languages in this task lies only in the task itself. Prior literacy-learning experience fosters an explicit understanding of what is to be accomplished in the task, and this, in turn, may expedite the process by allowing learners to be more reflective and strategic.

The clear implication of all these considerations is that second-language literacy is a repeated process to the extent that the literacy experiences are similar between the languages involved. Such similarities should allow second-language learners to usefully exploit the resources accumulated through prior learning experience, thereby accelerating second-language reading development. Thus, in essence, the concept of reading universals, properly incorporated, significantly contributes to theories of reading transfer by providing bases for conceptualizing and examining the facilitation benefits stemming from prior literacy experience.

Metalinguistic awareness

Metalinguistic awareness is a multi-dimensional construct, and its facets can be defined in conjunction with various structural features of language (e.g. Adams, 1990; Stahl & Murray, 1994; Yopp, 1988). Bialystok (2001) describes metalinguistic awareness as an explicit representation of "the abstract structure that organizes sets of linguistic rules without being directly instantiated in any of them" (2001: p.123). Although such insights evolve through the result of learning and using a particular language, metalinguistic awareness is distinct from linguistic knowledge in that it implies an understanding of language in its most fundamental and generalized properties, independent of surface form variations. For example, among English-speaking children, syntactic awareness reflects the realization that the order in which words are presented determines sentence meaning, and change in the order in a sentence is likely to alter its meaning. An abstract notion of this sort contrasts with a more specific knowledge of the canonical word order (subject–verb–object) in English sentences.

Roles of metalinguistic awareness in literacy acquisition

Of late, interest in metalinguistic awareness has risen sharply among reading researchers. As noted above, reading is embedded in a spoken language and its writing system, and its acquisition entails establishing a linkage between the two. As such, the present consensus is that learning to read is fundamentally metalinguistic because it necessitates an understanding of how spoken language elements are partitioned and mapped onto graphic symbols (e.g. Fowler & Liberman, 1995; Goswami & Bryant, 1992; Kuo & Anderson, this volume; Nagy & Anderson, 1999). Since the primary unit of this mapping is either phonology or morphology, two specific facets are of vital significance to learning to read in any language: grapho-phonological (i.e. recognizing the relationship between graphic symbols and speech sounds); and grapho-morphological (i.e. recognizing the relationship between graphic symbols and morphological elements of spoken words).

The roles of metalinguistic awareness in literacy learning in English have been extensively studied over the past two decades. Evidence from research focusing on phonological awareness has led to the widely endorsed conviction that to master an alphabetic script, children not only must recognize that words can be divided into sequences of phonemes, but also acquire the ability to analyze a word's internal structure in order to identify its phonemic constituents. Early reading studies, in fact, show that children's sensitivity to the phonological structure of spoken words is directly related to their word reading and spelling abilities (e.g. Stahl & Murray, 1994; Stanovich, 2000; Stanovich *et al.*, 1984; Yopp, 1988); that phonological segmentation capability is a powerful predictor of reading success among early and middle-grade students (e.g. Bryant *et al.*, 1990; Juel *et al.*, 1986); and that reading progress is significantly enhanced by phonological awareness training (e.g. Bradley & Bryant, 1991). Importantly, moreover, phonological deficits are a common attribute of weak readers in typologically diverse languages, including Arabic (e.g. Abu Rabia, 1995), Portuguese (Da Fontoura & Siegel, 1995), Chinese (e.g. So & Siegel, 1997; Zhang & Perfetti, 1993), and Japanese (Kuhara-Kojima *et al.*, 1996).

The role of morphological awareness in reading development also has been examined. Independent of phonological awareness, morphological awareness makes a unique contribution to English literacy. It has been found that the skill to segment a word into its morphological constituents is a reliable predictor of reading achievement (e.g. Carlisle, 1995; Carlisle & Nomanbhoy, 1993; Fowler & Liberman, 1995); that considerably more omissions of inflectional and derivational morphemes occur in the writing and speaking of less-skilled readers (e.g. Duques, 1989; Henderson & Shores, 1982; Rubin, 1991); and that capability to use morphological information during sentence comprehension distinguishes skilled from less-skilled high-school readers (e.g. Tyler & Nagy, 1989, 1990). Reflecting its multidimensionality, morphological awareness evolves gradually over time, as its diverse facets mature according to their own timetables. The staged maturation is seen in relation to bound morphemes in English, for example. Children acquiring English as their first language are sensitized to inflectional morphemes in structurally transparent words well before schooling (Berko, 1958; Carlisle, 2003), but the productive use of inflectional information does not occur until grades two or three (Bear *et al.*, 1996). The awareness of derivational morphemes is a late-developing facet, emerging between grades four and eight (Ku & Anderson, 2003; Tyler & Nagy, 1989, 1990). Similar developmental disparities also have been reported in varying facets of Chinese morphological awareness (Ku & Anderson, 2003; Shu & Anderson 1999). Viewed collectively, findings from both phonological and morphological awareness studies make it plain that metalinguistic insights facilitate the initial stages of literacy learning in several distinct ways.

Cross-linguistic variations in metalinguistic awareness

Certain basic facets of metalinguistic insights are prerequisites to reading acquisition, enabling children to initiate the critical task of linking spoken-language elements and graphic symbols. It is important to note, however, that literacy and metalinguistic awareness are developmentally interdependent. Typically, children form sensitivity to structural regularities of the language they are acquiring well before formal literacy instruction commences (MacWhinney, 1987; Slobin, 1985). While the early phases of literacy acquisition are dependent on this rudimentary understanding acquired during oral-language development, such sensitivity is progressively refined and gradually becomes explicit through print decoding and encoding experience (e.g. Bowey & Francis, 1991; Perfetti *et al.*, 1987; Vellutino & Scanlon, 1987). In this respect, the ultimate form of metalinguistic awareness is an outcome of literacy.

Because of their reciprocity, one can argue that the specific metalinguistic facets directly related to print information extraction are shaped to accommodate the specific ways in which language elements are graphically represented in the writing system. Two implications arise: (1) lexical information—both phonological and morphological—is accessed through orthographic knowledge; and (2) the facets of metalinguistic awareness underlying efficient print information extraction are closely allied with the dominant orthographic properties. Therefore, it seems reasonable to suggest that literacy learning in diverse languages involves distinct facets of metalinguistic awareness. In fact, differential patterns of metalinguistic contribution to reading acquisition have been reported in a recent study involving native Mandarin-speaking children. Reflecting the prominence of grapheme-morpheme connections in Chinese characters, morphological awareness was found to be a stronger predictor than phonological awareness of literacy acquisition in Chinese (Li *et al.*, 2002).

There are several reasons why metalinguistic awareness should be the primary focus in the current exploration of reading skill transfer in second-language literacy development. First, metalinguistic awareness becomes more explicit and refined through print processing experience. As noted above, its resulting capabilities are assumed to reflect the specific ways phonological and morphological information are graphically represented. Hence, the awareness competencies likely to transfer can be identified through careful analyses of grapheme-to-phoneme and grapheme-to-morpheme relationships in a particular writing system, thereby allowing them to be measured empirically for subsequent examinations. Second, since the maturation of diverse awareness facets relies heavily on print input and exposure in a particular langue, specific awareness capabilities, available for transfer at given points in time, also can be predicted, based on the first-language literacy experience of a particular age group of second-language learners. Finally, metalinguistic awareness is a powerful enabling factor supporting many of the operations essential for initial reading acquisition. Therefore, linkages between this construct and reading sub-skills have causal implications. Presumably, systematic probing of their connections both within and across languages likely will yield significant new insights into possible contributions of prior literacy experience in second-language reading development.

The Transfer Facilitation Model

The theoretical formulations described above have yielded a number of significant implications directly relevant to the examination of the impacts stemming from prior literacy experience in second-language reading development. Listed below, they encapsulate the fundamental premises underlying the current conceptualization of reading skill transfer.

- Reading skills transfer across languages.
- Children form sensitivity to the regularities of spoken language during oral language development.
- Writing systems are structured to capture these regularities
- Learning to read involves learning to map spoken language elements onto graphic symbols in the writing system.
- Metalinguistic awareness precipitates the initial phases of learning to read by enabling the learner to analyze spoken words into their constituent elements.
- The awareness becomes increasingly explicit through cumulative print processing experience.
- The resulting metalinguistic awareness reflects the specific ways in which language elements are graphically encoded in the writing system, and therefore, varies systematically across languages.

In keeping with these postulations, the Transfer Facilitation Model represents an attempt to explain precisely how metalinguistic awareness developed in one language promotes learning to read in another among diverse groups of second-language learners. Given the strong probabilities that metalinguistic capabilities relate both causally and reciprocally to reading development, and also that they transfer across languages, it is essential to clarify the precise role of metalinguistic awareness in reading development both within and across languages.

In a sense, the model is a particular instantiation of the Functionalist approach to language learning. As described earlier, in this approach, language is seen as a set of relationships between forms and functions (Van

Valin, 1991), and language learning as the process of internalizing these relationships progressively through cumulative use of language in communication (MacWhinney & Bates, 1989). The core contention is that language learning is driven by communicative language use, thereby relating its outcomes to linguistic exposure and experience. As such, it additionally explains why systematic variations occur in the internalized relationships across languages as well as learners. This view, however, does not clarify how recurring form-function correspondences, implicit in input, are detected, abstracted, and internalized.

In order to clarify how form-function mappings are learned and assimilated, an additional theory is necessary. Since reading acquisition, as repeatedly noted, involves establishing mappings between language elements and graphic symbols, such clarification is equally useful in conceptualizing reading skill development. Since, by extension, learning to read in a second language can be regarded as the process of forming additional mapping relationships in a new language, the clarification is also vital in explaining how the formation of new mapping patterns can be altered, via transfer, by the previously-established mapping patterns.

Connectionism is one such theory, offering plausible explanations of how form-function relationships emerge. Its main contention is that the internalization of form-function relationships can occur through cumulative experience of mapping forms onto corresponding functions and vice versa. The more frequently particular patterns of form-function mappings are experienced, the stronger the links holding the relevant elements together. As such, the theory describes knowledge acquisition as a gradual transition from deliberate efforts to automatic execution, rather than as an all-or-nothing process, and knowledge as a dynamic, ever-changing state, rather than a static entity. It should be underscored, moreover, that Connectionist theories make no distinction between language learning and other domains of learning, as well as knowledge acquisition and skills development. Consequently, the internalization of a particular form-function relationship can be recognized as such when its mapping becomes "automated"—that is, non-deliberate, non-volitional, activation initiated through input (Logan, 1988).

By extending these contentions, transfer can be defined as an automatic activation of well-established first-language competencies, triggered by second-language input. Although this definition is restrictive in that it limits the model's scope only to those operations wherein automaticity is attainable, such a restriction is advantageous and perhaps even necessary in theory formation because the restriction enables the model to address a range of critical issues in a theoretically coherent fashion. Several assumptions underlie the proposed model of transfer. First, for transfer to occur, the competencies to be transferred must be well rehearsed—to the point of automaticity—in the first language. Second, transfer is not likely to cease at any given point in second-language development. Third, transferred competencies will continuously mature through processing experience with second-language input. Evidently, these assumptions are distinct from those underlying the earlier views of transfer.

Given the non-volitional, non-selective, nature of first-language involvement, a critical issue remains as to how transferred capabilities facilitate second-language reading development. As noted above, the proposed view of transfer presupposes that second-language competencies evolve from continuous interplay between transferred first-language competencies and second-language print input; that the emerging competencies continue to evolve through further experience with second-language print input; and that these competencies gradually reach optimal utility as they accommodate the linguistic and orthographic properties specific to the second language. Although cross-language transfer presumably occurs for any competence, the proposed model centers on metalinguistic awareness, as its focal construct, for the reasons outlined in the previous section. In what follows, the model's central claims and related hypotheses are presented.

Shared metalinguistic awareness

Second-language reading acquisition is presumed to impose the same initial requisites as those for first-language learning to read. However, actual demands may differ among first- and second-language learners because the latter group of learners has access to the metalinguistic awareness developed in the first language. Since, as noted above, the initial task of learning to read either in first or second language, involves learning the general manner in which the writing system encodes language elements, the metalinguistic insights necessitated for this task do not involve language-specific details. Therefore, the language-independent metalinguistic facets, already available to second-language learners, should facilitate reading acquisition in a new language. Hence, the model posits that prior literacy experience provides all learners, regardless of their first-language background, with direct and equal facilitation in learning the general mapping principle in any new language. Since underdeveloped capabilities are unlikely to transfer, success in first-language learning to read, as an index of the availability of the requisite metalinguistic capabilities, should be a reliable predictor of initial reading development in a second language. We can hypothesize, therefore, that a strong relationship exists between first-language metalinguistic awareness and second-language decoding skills; and also that such cross-linguistic connections are particularly obvious among school-age learners whose first-language metalinguistic awareness is at different levels of maturation.

First-language metalinguistic sophistication

Beyond the initial phase, however, establishing mapping details requires the metalinguistic facets that are closely attuned to the linguistic and orthographic properties of the second language. Since the formation of such language-specific acumen entails the detection of recurring grapheme-phoneme and grapheme-morpheme correspondences, it requires substantially more input than the awareness facets that underlie general mapping principles. The proposed model thus postulates that amounts of second-language print input and experience are dominant factors determining how well language-specific awareness facets develop in a second language.

Presumably, first-language metalinguistic awareness is also available in this phase of learning to read. However, the transferred facets are not directly serviceable in learning the mapping details in a new writing system because they are closely attuned to the first-language orthographic properties. Their contribution lies in the fact that learners have undergone the same task once before because prior experience promotes reflection on what the task is about and how it can be achieved. As such, the transferred awareness should provide indirect, but useful, assistance, guiding the process of learning mapping details. With such top-down assistance, the task becomes more deductive in a second language, requiring less input for its completion than that required in the first language. Insofar as a high-level of maturation is a precondition for transfer, first-language metalinguistic sophistication—particularly, those facets closely attuned to the first-language properties—should be a reliable indicator of how well one can develop corresponding metalinguistic awareness through second-language print processing experience. Accordingly, the second hypothesis is that first-language metalinguistic sophistication and second-language print experience are both strong predictors of the rate at which corresponding metalinguistic awareness matures in a second language.

Language distance

Under the Connectionist premises, the model also presumes that second-language metalinguistic awareness emerges from continuous interactions between transferred first-language metalinguistic awareness and second-language print input. It is also assumed that the transferred awareness gradually transforms itself into optimal utility in the second language. Logically, then, such transformation is achieved more easily and with less input when the two languages share similar linguistic and orthographic properties, simply because less adjustment is necessary in such a case. On the premise that the evolving second-language awareness serves as a foundation through which second-language decoding skills are shaped, the model predicts that linguistic/orthographic distance (degrees of similarity) between the languages involved should play a significant role in explaining individual differences in the rate in which second-language metalinguistic awareness and related reading sub-skills develop. In particular, when the two languages share similar structural properties, what is required for extracting phonological and morphological information is also likely to be analogous—if not identical. This being the case, transferred first-language metalinguistic awareness should contribute to the formation of second-language decoding skills. In contrast, when the two are distinct, the transferred competencies must be reshaped to accommodate the second-language properties. Put simply, language distance essentially determines the extent of modification and adjustment on the transferred competencies, as well as the amount of second-language print input and experience necessary for such fine-tuning. The model thus offers a plausible explanation of why decoding competence is acquired more rapidly by learners with some first-language backgrounds than those with others. Consequently, a third hypothesis can be formulated: the distance between the two languages accounts for the differential rates in which second-language metalinguistic awareness and related reading sub-skills develop among learners with diverse first-language backgrounds.

Cross-linguistic variations

Finally, the model assumes that continual cross-linguistic interactions involved in second-language reading development typically induce sustained assimilation of processing experiences in the two languages. Under this assumption, the model posits that the resulting second-language competencies reflect major properties of both languages, and thus, vary systematically across learners with diverse first-language backgrounds. Hence, the fourth, and final, hypothesis is that variations in second-language processing procedures are attributable, in part, to differential processing requirements imposed by both first- and second-language writing systems.

Preliminary evaluations

The proposed model of transfer has generated four major claims and related hypotheses regarding how transferred first-language competencies are incorporated in second-language reading development. In the sections below, their predictive validity is examined through a review of relevant empirical studies.

Facilitation from shared metalinguistic awareness

Given the well-documented contributions of metalinguistic awareness to first-language reading development, the primary question is to what extent second-language reading development, particularly among school-age learners, benefits from the previously acquired metalinguistic awareness. Since the initial task of learning to read is uniformly constrained by the universal properties of reading, what is required in this task should be the same between a first and a second language. The proposed model predicts, therefore, that the language independent facets of metalinguistic awareness, once developed in one language, are readily available and similarly functional in learning to read in another language.

A growing number of studies involving young cohorts of second-language learners have provided considerable support for this prediction. Earlier studies investigated whether phonological awareness in either first or second language relates to second-language word-reading ability among school-age learners. Cisero and colleagues (1992), for example, contrasted English monolingual and Spanish-dominant bilingual first grade children in phoneme detection performance, and concluded that in both groups competent readers were superior in phonemic analysis to their less competent counterparts. Similarly, in a study on Spanish dominant bilingual first graders, Durgunoglu *et al.* (1993) determined that first-language phonological awareness is a powerful predictor of subsequent word recognition skills in both languages.

Subsequent studies, employing a large battery of tasks in both first and second languages, focused on the cross-linguistic connections among a wide range of component skills. Collectively, their findings suggest that significant relationships exist in a variety of corresponding skills between the languages involved; that poor readers are uniformly weak in phonological skills in both languages; and that their deficiencies usually are domain-specific and not attributable to non-phonological factors (e.g. Abu-Rabia, 1995; August *et al.*, 2001; Carlisle & Beeman, 2000; Cormier & Kelson, 2000; Da Fontoura & Siegel, 1995; Gholamain & Geva, 1999; Verhoeven, 2000; Wade-Woolley & Geva, 2000). Da Fontoura and Siegel (1995), for instance, examined literacy development among Portuguese-English bilingual children in each of their two languages. Measuring and comparing phonological skills, syntactic knowledge and working memory, the researchers found high correlations between corresponding skills in the two languages. They also determined that reading problems in both languages were associated with phonological skill deficits.

In a study with second grade children who were simultaneously learning to read English and Hebrew, Wade-Woolley and Geva (2000) also acquired evidence of cross-linguistic relations between phonological skills and word-reading ability. Findings from a more recent study (Wang *et al.*, 2005) involving second and third grade children learning to read English and Chinese are also illuminating. While phonological awareness was strongly related across the two unrelated languages, no such relationship was found for orthographic knowledge. Similarly, biliteracy studies incorporating oral language measures show that oral language proficiency is not a good predictor of decoding skills in a second language (August *et al.*, 2001; August & Shanahan, 2006; Durgunoglu *et al.*, 1993; Gholamain & Geva, 1999).

Taken as a whole, these findings make it clear that, as in first-language learning to read, second-language reading acquisition is dependent on phonological awareness, and such dependency occurs both within and across languages. Thus, as predicted, phonological awareness developed in one language seems available and serviceable in learning to read in another language. Further, the initial phase of second-language reading development may be independent of other aspects of linguistic knowledge. Such independence, also as predicted, allows the previously acquired phonological awareness to be equally facilitative to all learners possessing it in learning the basic grapheme-phoneme mappings. Hence, it seems reasonable to suggest that phonological awareness serves as a shared resource, enhancing the initial stage of second-language reading development.

Contributions of first-language metalinguistic sophistication

Once children achieve general mapping principles, they must then deduce the specific way in which language elements are graphically encoded. Morphological awareness contributes to this phase of reading development through its capacity for enabling learners to analyze a word's internal structure according to its morphological constituents. The proposed model posits that, when transferred, first-language metalinguistic insights—morphological awareness, in particular—serve as a filter through which second-language print input is analyzed and categorized, thus assisting learners in gaining a functional understanding of the specific mapping details in the new language.

It should be noted, however, that developing morphological awareness in a second language poses a serious challenge to school-age learners. For one thing, deducing grapheme-morpheme relationships with underdeveloped linguistic knowledge is highly demanding because symbol-to-morpheme mappings are far more diverse and language-specific than symbol-to-sound mappings. And, unlike adults, school-age learners have yet to refine morphological awareness in their first language. Lacking morphological sophistication, they are less capable of either segmenting linguistic input into its morphological components, or linking the segmented elements with corresponding graphic units. Without sufficiently developed morphological awareness in either language, these learners are not likely to benefit from linguistic input—oral or print—howsoever accumulated.

Despite its potential significance, to date, the role of morphological awareness in second-language literacy development remains largely unexplored. One recent study of children in grades three, four and five who were learning to read English and Korean (Park, 2004) has yielded illuminating findings. The researcher found that while second-language reading comprehension and oral proficiency were closely related among metalinguistically sophisticated learners (i.e. those who scored high on a metalinguistic awareness test), no such relationship existed among their metalinguistically less sophisticated counterparts. The findings were interpreted as suggesting that first-language morphological awareness mediates the extent that second-language input contributes to reading development among school-age learners. In other words, without sufficiently developed first-language metalinguistic sophistication, young second-language learners are unable to benefit from linguistic input in detecting recurring grapheme-morpheme mapping patterns in the new language.

Studies exploring morphological awareness among adult learners offer a completely different picture. Within the proposed model, it has been predicted that morphological awareness, once developed in one language, is readily available in learning to read in another language, providing top-down, deductive, assistance in the formation of corresponding awareness in a second language. Consequently, metalinguistically "trained" adult learners should be more adept than younger cohorts at uncovering how language elements correspond with graphic symbols in a new language. With the growing interest in logographic literacy, an increasing number of studies have begun to address character-knowledge development in second-language learners of Chinese and Japanese.

Ke (1998), for example, examined how college-level learners of Chinese develop sensitivity to the functional properties of character-internal components, or radicals. He found that after one year of Chinese study, his participants became aware of the utility of radicals in building character knowledge; and that such awareness was directly related to the participants' character-recognition ability. Using a think-aloud protocol analysis, Everson and Ke (1997) determined that while intermediate learners depended on rote-memorization approaches to character identification, advanced learners were more analytical, invoking character segmentation and radical information retrieval.

Wang *et al.* (2003) explored how adult learners of Chinese acquire sensitivity to the second-language orthographic structure. Using two experimental tasks (lexical decision and naming), the researchers found that character processing among American learners of Chinese was considerably impaired by structural complexity, radical combination violations, and radical misplacement. These results corroborate those from the studies described above, suggesting that beginning learners of Chinese, despite their limited print exposure, become sensitized to the internal structure of Chinese characters. Even more critically, such sensitivity—an understanding of the visual-orthographic constraints—appears to guide character information extraction among adult learners of Chinese with alphabetic first-language backgrounds.

In a psycholinguistic experiment, Koda and Takahashi (2007) compared radical awareness among native and non-native Kanji users through semantic category judgment (deciding whether a given character belongs to a specific semantic category, such as "female" and "metal"). Their data demonstrated that both native and non-native participants benefited similarly when radical information was semantically consistent with the whole-character meaning. The groups' responses differed, however, when radical information conflicted with the character meaning. While native Japanese readers responded more slowly but accurately when dealing with such conflicts, their non-native counterparts made far more errors by disregarding the

conflicts. The researchers interpreted these findings as indicating tha
ond-language learners are sensitized to the primary function of sem
radicals and attentive to their information during Kanji processing. F
ever, the basic understanding is hardly sufficient for differentiating valid
from invalid radical information and incorporating valid information select-
ively in Kanji meaning extraction.

In sum, the studies involving adult learners of Chinese and Japanese
repeatedly suggest that these learners are progressively sensitized to the
functional and structural properties of characters' morphological components, and gradually rely on this sensitivity both in learning new
characters and retrieving stored character information. Of perhaps greatest
significance, however, is the finding that such sensitivity readily develops, as
the model predicts, with somewhat restricted exposure (usually 250–400
characters) among metalinguistically adroit adult learners. This contrasts
sharply with children learning to read Chinese as their first language, who
require knowledge of roughly 1,500–2,000 characters to develop similar
metalinguistic insights (Shu & Anderson, 1999).

Language distance effects

On the assumption that literacy-related competencies, once established in
one language, transfer to another, the model further postulates that the
aspects of transferred awareness, which are attuned to dominant first-
language properties, are gradually adjusted to those unique to the second
language. Because amounts of adjustment are determined essentially by
degrees of structural similarity between the languages involved, facilitation
benefits from transferred metalinguistic awareness will vary among learners
with various first-language backgrounds.

Hence, the model predicts that language distance is responsible, in
part, for the rate at which second-language metalinguistic awareness and
related reading sub-skills evolve among learners with diverse first-language
backgrounds. This, in turn, would explain differences in learners' print
information extraction efficiency at a given point in their second-language
reading development. Although systematic probing of the relationship
between language distance and second-language metalinguistic awareness
has yet to occur, initial inquiries into the distance effects are currently
underway. Studies involving ESL learners demonstrate that more accurate
and rapid performance is found for learners from alphabetic, as compared
to non-alphabetic, first-language backgrounds (e.g. Dhanesschayakupta,
2003; Green & Meara, 1987; Koda, 2000; Muljani et al., 1998). The
critical question in this research, therefore, is how shared properties between
the two languages accelerate second-language print information extraction.

Muljani and colleagues (1998) shed significant light on the issue by testing
orthographic distance effects on second-language intraword structural sensitivity. Comparing lexical-decision performance (deciding whether or not a

given string of letters is a real word) among proficiency-matched adult ESL learners with related (Indonesian employing a Roman-alphabetic script) and unrelated (Chinese using a logographic system) orthographic backgrounds, the study revealed that only Indonesian participants benefited from intra-word structural congruity (i.e. spelling-pattern consistency) between English and Indonesian. Their superiority, however, was far less pronounced on those stimuli with spelling patterns unique to English. Collectively, these findings seem to suggest that although related orthographic backgrounds induce general facilitation in lexical processing, accelerated efficiency occurs only at the operations posing identical processing demands between the two languages. Hence, orthographic distance, as predicted, appears to explain overall performance differences among learners with related and unrelated first-language backgrounds. Critically, moreover, it also underscores the precise way in which first-language experience expedites second-language lexical processing.

Cross-linguistic variations

Given that the metalinguistic capabilities underlying print information extraction are adjusted to the linguistic and orthographic properties specific to the language in which literacy is first learned, a critical question in second-language research is how and to what extent these transferred metalinguistic capabilities nevertheless contribute to the formation of corresponding second-language awareness and reading sub-skills. On the assumption that second-language competencies emerge through continual interplay between transferred metalinguistic awareness and second-language print input, the proposed model postulates that newly acquired competencies, reflecting both first- and second-language properties, vary systematically across learners with diverse first-language backgrounds.

Despite its centrality and significance, such variation has attracted far less attention than it deserves among second-language researchers. More recently, however, empirical explorations have been initiated in the form of systematic comparisons of second-language metalinguistic awareness. In a series of studies, Koda and associates (Koda, 2000; Koda *et al.*, 1998) have shown that processing experiences in both first and second languages are associated with second-language morphological awareness among proficiency-matched ESL learners with contrasting first-language backgrounds (agglutinative Korean and isolating Chinese). Using a morphological segmentation task (deciding whether a given word can be morphologically divided), the researchers found that Korean participants outperformed the Chinese only when the stimulus English words were structurally similar to Korean words. The two groups did not differ when the stimuli were structurally unique to English. Instead, performance on these items was correlated with English proficiency for both Chinese and Korean participants. The findings thus lend support to the model's prediction that the morphological insights specific to the target language are gained mainly through second-language print experience, and their acquisition appears to be relatively unaffected by qualitative differences in first-language experience.

In related studies, Koda (1998) compared phonological awareness and decoding among proficiency-matched Korean and Chinese adult ESL learners. While intraword segmentation is central to phonological processing in alphabetic systems, it is not mandatory in logographic orthographies. It was hypothesized, therefore, that intraword analysis experience among Korean participants in their first language would accelerate their phonological segmentation and decoding development in the second language. The results of the study, however, showed that the two ESL groups did not differ in either phonological segmentation or decoding.

Although the findings did not confirm the study's hypothesis, they provide partial support for the model's prediction that the development of second-language phonological awareness and early decoding depend on shared metalinguistic insights, and thus, are minimally affected by first-language orthographic experiences. Interestingly, however, a clear contrast existed in the extent to which the two variables were related with reading comprehension. In the Korean data, phonological awareness and decoding were closely interconnected, and the two variables were both highly correlated with reading comprehension, but there were no systematic relationships among the three variables in the Chinese data. These results seem to indicate that the two groups utilize letter-by-letter decoding during reading comprehension to differential degrees. Hence, first-language orthographic experience may have induced different procedural approaches in second-language decoding during text comprehension.

First-language influences were also examined through semantic category judgment (Wang, *et al.*, 2003). In the study, participants were first presented with a category descriptor, such as "flower" and then with a target word. The task was to decide whether the word was a member of the given category. The task would have been simple if real category-member words, such as "rose," had appeared. Instead, target words were manipulated either phonologically or graphically. Phonologically manipulated targets were homophones of category-member words. Using the above example, instead of showing the word "rose," its homophone "rows" was presented. Graphically manipulated targets were non-homophonic but visually similar to category-member words (e.g. "fees" for "feet"). The primary hypothesis was that the two ESL groups would respond differently to the two types of manipulation. Korean participants would be more likely to accept homophonic targets as category members, while Chinese would make more false positive responses to graphically similar targets.

The data demonstrated that phonological and graphic similarity both significantly interfered with category judgment performance of both ESL groups. However, the magnitude of interference stemming from each type of manipulation varied considerably between the groups. Korean learners made significantly more errors by accepting homophonic items, whereas Chinese participants responded positively but erroneously to graphically similar targets. These results seem to indicate that although the two groups use both phonological and graphic information during second-language lexical processing, each relies more on its preferred information sources. More critically, the groups' preferences are directly associated with their respective first-language orthographic experience. Taken together, their results seem to suggest that prior literacy experiences in the two languages are both operative during second-language reading, jointly shaping print information extraction skills.

All in all, the results from these pioneer studies are informative. However, for any generalizations to occur regarding cross-linguistic variations in second-language metalinguistic awareness and reading sub-skills, the research base must be substantially expanded. Here again, however, the available data, although limited in quantity, lend initial support to the model, suggesting that prior literacy experience has lasting impacts, and when transferred, first-language literacy-related competencies interact with second-language print input.

Summary and future research directions

In an attempt to explain how literacy experience in one language is incorporated in reading development in another, the Transfer Facilitation model has been proposed through systematic deductions. The model's major contentions can be summarized as follows:

- Facilitation from shared metalinguistic awareness competencies: inasmuch as the initial task of learning to read is universally constrained, necessitating similar, language-independent, metalinguistic insights, the awareness facets underlying this task, once developed in one language, are readily available in learning to read in another language.
- Contribution of first-language metalinguistic sophistication: when transferred, language-specific awareness facets, closely attuned to first-language properties, promote reflective and strategic approaches in developing corresponding awareness facets and reading sub-skills in a second language. With such top-down assistance, deducing the specific details of grapheme-phoneme and grapheme-morpheme mappings can be achieved with far less input and print experience in a second language than those required in first-language learning to read.
- Language distance effects: when transferred, first-language meatalinguistic awareness competencies, reflecting the dominant properties of the first language, are adjusted through print experience in the second language. Because degree of adjustment is determined essentially by how closely the two languages are related, the development of

second-language metalinguistic awareness and related reading sub-skills requires different amounts of print input and experience for learners with similar, and dissimilar, first-language backgrounds.

• Cross-linguistic variations: second-language competencies are formed through complex interactions between transferred first-language competencies and second-language print input. As a result, the emerging competencies, reflecting both first- and second-language properties, vary systematically across learners with diverse first-language backgrounds.

Although these contentions receive reasonable support from the research currently available in the literature, the model has yet to be tested empirically. As a logical step forward, future research could build purposefully on the four hypotheses the model generated.

Future research directions

The model's first hypothesis deals with a relationship between first-language metalinguistic awareness—particularly, phonological awareness—and initial reading development in a second language. The relation has been examined in well-designed biliteracy studies, comparing phonological awareness in first and second languages (Cisero & Royer, 1995; Durgunogulu *et al.*, 1993; Gholamain & Geva, 1999; Wang, *et al.*, 2005), as well as its relation to second-language decoding (Durgunoglu *et al.*, 1993; Gholamain & Geva, 1999). Although the findings generally converge on reliable cross-linguistic connections among the constructs, the correlational nature of the studies does not permit causal inferences regarding their relationships.

Stronger evidence relating to the facilitation attributable to transfer, however, may be possible through longitudinal studies assessing developmental changes in the connections between metalinguistic awareness and decoding skills both within and across languages during early reading development in a second language. Even more convincing evidence of transfer-induced facilitation should stem from training studies designed to analyze how explicit metalinguistic awareness instruction in one language accelerates initial reading development in another. Properly established, the cross-linguistic linkages—both developmental and causal—between phonological awareness and decoding will provide substantial clues to effective instructional interventions for language minority students.

The second hypothesis relates to assistance stemming from first-language metalinguistic sophistication in shaping metalinguistic acumen specifically attuned to the second language. The proposed model suggests that the acquisition of such acumen requires sufficiently developed first-language metalinguistic awareness, as well as ample print exposure and experience in the second language. The absence of first-language metalinguistic sophistication, however, is likely to prevent school-age learners from exploiting linguistic input in either language, howsoever accumulated. Although such deficits are often alluded to in scholarly debates (e.g. Cummins, 1979), their underlying causes neither have been clarified, nor examined empirically. Given the potential for yielding significant implications for literacy education, future studies should profit from methodical examinations of the three-way interactions among first-language metalinguistic sophistication, second-language print exposure/experience, and second-language linguistic knowledge, in shaping second-language metalinguistic awareness and related reading sub-skills.

The third hypothesis concerns differential facilitation attributable to linguistic/orthographic distance between the languages involved. Current data suggest that orthographic distance is a strong predictor of the rate at which second-language decoding skills develop. To date, however, the hypothesized role of metalinguistic awareness as a factor mediating the observed connection between orthographic distance and second-language decoding efficiency has yet to be empirically tested. In view of the explanatory potential of this factor, future research should directly address the relationship between orthographic distance and second-language metalinguistic awareness, as well as that between second-language metalinguistic awareness and decoding efficiency among learners with diverse first-language orthographic backgrounds.

The final hypothesis generated by the model pertains to systematic variations in second-language competencies among learners with diverse first-language backgrounds. Inasmuch as these variations are attributable to transferred first-language metalinguistic awareness, empirical testing of the hypothesis is essential in clarifying the long-term impacts of prior literacy experience on the formation of reading sub-skills in another language. Since successful comprehension relies on well-developed information extraction skills, systematic exploration of cross-linguistic variations in developmental paths and the resulting reading competencies are extremely vital in isolating comprehension problems associated with inefficient or inaccurate text information extraction among learners with diverse prior literacy experiences.

To sum up, dual-language involvement is the foremost attribute highlighting the unique characteristic of second-language reading. A clearer understanding of how literacy experiences in two languages interact and coalesce in the formation of second-language reading skills, should take primacy in second-language reading research. In an attempt to clarify such cross-linguistic interplay, the proposed model of transfer seeks to offer systematic explanations of how literacy experience in one language alters reading development in another. Future research, consequently, should concentrate on its empirical validations, as well as practical applications of their implications.

References

Abu-Rabia, S. (1995) Learning to read in Arabic: reading, syntactic, orthographic and working memory skills in normally achieving and poor Arabic readers. *Reading Psychology* 16, 351–94.

Adams, M. J. (1990) *Beginning to read.* Cambridge, MA: MIT Press.

Akamatsu, N. (1999) The effects of first language orthographic features on word recognition processing in English as a second language. *Reading and Writing* 11(4). 381–403.

August, D. & Shanahan, T. (eds.) (2006) *Executive summary: developing literacy in second-language learners: report of the National Literacy Panel on Language-Minority Children and Youth.* Mahwah, NJ: Lawrence Erlbaum.

Bear, D. R., Invernizzi, M., Templeton, S., & Johnston, F. (1996) *Words their way: word study for phonics vocabulary, and spelling instruction.* Upper Saddle River, NJ: Merrill.

Berko, J. (1958) The child's learning of English morphology. *Word*, 14, 150–77.

Bialystock, E. (2001) *Bilingualism in development.* Cambridge: Cambridge University Press.

Bowey, J.A. and Francis, J. (1991) Phonological analysis as a function of age and exposure to reading instruction. *Applied Psycholinguistics* 12, 91–121.

Bradley, L. & Bryant, P. E. (1983) Categorizing sounds and learning to read: a causal connection. *Nature*, 301, 419–21.

Bradley, L. & Bryant, P. (1991) Phonological skills before and after learning to read. In S. A. Brady & D. P. Shankweiler (eds.) *Phonological processing in literacy* (pp. 37–45). Hillsdale, NJ: Erlbaum.

Brown, T. & Haynes, M. (1985) Literacy background and reading development in a second language (pp. 19–34). In T. H. Carr (ed.), *The development of reading skills.* San Francisco, CA: Jossey-Bass.

Bryant, P. E., MacLean, M., & Bradley, L. L. (1990) Rhyme, language, and children's reading. *Applied Psycholinguistics*, 11, 237–51.

Carlisle, J. (1995) Morphological awareness and early reading achievement (pp.189–209). In L. Feldman (ed.), *Morphological aspects of language processing.* Hillsdale, NJ: Lawrence Erlbaum Associates.

Carlisle, J. F. (2003) Morphology matters in learning to read: a commentary. *Reading Psychology*, 24, 291–322.

Carlisle, J. F. & Nomanbhoy, D. (1993) Phonological and morphological development. *Applied Psycholinguistics*, 14, 177–95.

Carlisle, J. F. & Beeman, M. M. (2000) The effects of language of instruction on the reading and writing achievement of first-grade Hispanic children. *Scientific Studies of Reading*, 4, 331–53.

Carr, T. H. & Levy, B. A. (eds.). (1990) *Reading and its development: component skills approaches.* San Diego: Academic Press.

Cisero, C. A. & Royer, James M. (1995) The development and cross-language transfer of phonological awareness. *Contemporary Educational Psychology*, 20, 3, 275–303.

Cisero, C.A., Carlo, M.S. and Royer, J.M. (1992) Can a child raised as English speaking be phonemically aware in another language? Paper presented at the annual meeting of the American Educational Research Association, San Francisco, CA.

Clarke, M. A. (1979) The short circuit hypothesis of ESL reading or when language competence interferes with reading performance. *Modern Language Journal*, 64, 203–9.

Cormier, P. & Kelson, S. (2000) The roles of phonological and syntactic awareness in the use of plural morphemes among children in French immersion. *Scientific Studies of Reading* 4, 267–94.

Cummins, J. (1979) Linguistic interdependence and educational development of bilingual children. *Review of Educational Research*, 49, 222–51.

Cummins, J. (1991) Interdependence of first- and second-language proficiency in bilingual children (pp. 70–89). In E. Bialystok (ed.), *Language processing in bilingual children*. New York: Cambridge University Press.

Cummins, J., Swain, M., Nakajima, K., Handscombe, J. & Green, D. (1981) Linguistic interdependence in Japanese and Vietnamese students. Report prepared for the Inter-America Research Associates, June. Toronto: Ontario Institute for Studies in Education.

Da Fontoura, H. A. & Siegel, L. S. (1995) Reading syntactic and memory skills of Portuguese–English Canadian children. *Reading and Writing: An International Journal*, 7, 139–53.

Devine, J. (1987) General language competence and adult second language reading (pp. 73–86). In J. Devine, P. L. Carrell, & D. E, Eskey (eds.), *Research on reading English as a second language*. Washington, DC: Teachers of English to Speakers of Other Languages.

Devine, J. (1988) A case study of two readers: models of reading and reading performance (pp. 127–30). In J. Devine, P. L. Carrell, & D. E. Eskey (eds.), *Interactive approach to second language reading*. New York: Cambridge University Press.

Dhanesschayakupta, U. (2003) Transfer of cognitive skills among Chinese and Thai ESL readers. Unpublished doctoral dissertation, University of Pittsburgh.

Duques, S. (1989) Grammatical deficiency in writing: an investigation of learning disabled college students. *Reading and Writing*, 2, 1–17.

Durgunoglu, A. Y., Nagy, W. E. & Hancin, B. J. (1993) Cross-language transfer of phonemic awareness. *Journal of Educational Psychology*, 85, 453–65.

Everson, M. E. and Ke, C. (1997) An inquiry into the reading strategies of intermediate and advanced learners of Chinese as a Foreign Language. *Journal of the Chinese Language Teachers Association* 32, 1–20.

Fowler, A. E. & Liberman, I. Y. (1995) The role of phonology and orthography in morphological awareness (pp. 157–88). In L. B. Feldman (ed.), *Morphological aspects of language processing*. Hillsdale, NJ: Lawrence Erlbaum Associates.

Gass, S. & Selinker, L. (eds.) (1983) *Language transfer in language learning*. Rowley, MA: Newbury House.

Genesee, F., Geva, E., Dressler, C., Kamil, M. L. (2006) Synthesis: cross-linguistic relationships. In D. August & T. Shanahan (eds.), *Developing literacy in second-language learners: report of the National Literacy Panel on Language-Minority Children and Youth*. Mahwah, NJ: Lawrence Erlbaum.

Gholamain, M. & Geva, E. (1999) Orthographic and cognitive factors in the concurrent development of basic reading skills in English and Persian. *Language Learning* 49, 183–217.

Goodman, K. S. (1967) Reading: a psycholinguistic guessing game. *Journal of the Reading Specialist*, 6, 126–35.

Goodman, K. S. (1969) Analysis of oral language miscues: applied psycholinguistics. *Reading Research Quarterly*, 5, 9–30.

Goswami, U. & Bryant, P. (1990) *Phonological skills and learning to read.* Hove, UK: Erlbaum.

Green, D. W. & Meara, P. (1987) The effects of script on visual search. *Second Language Research*, 3, 102–17.

Henderson, A. J. & Shores, R. E. (1982) How learning disabled students' failure to attend to suffixes affects their oral reading performance. *Journal of Learning Disabilities*, 15, 178–82.

Juel, C., Griffith, P. L. & Gough, P. B. (1986) Acquisition of literacy: a longitudinal study of children in first and second grade. *Journal of Educational Psychology*, 78, 243–55.

Katz, L. & Frost, R. (1992) Reading in different orthographies: the orthographic depth hypothesis (pp. 67–84). In R. Frost & L. Katz (eds.), *Orthography, phonology, morphology, and meaning.* Amsterdam: Elsevier.

Ke, C. (1998) Effects of language background on the learning of Chinese characters among foreign language students. *Foreign Language Annals*, 31, 91–100.

Koda, K. (1989) The effects of transferred vocabulary knowledge on the development of L2 reading proficiency. *Foreign Language Annals*, 22, 529–42.

Koda, K. (1990) The use of L1 reading strategies in L2 reading. *Studies in Second Language Acquisition*, 12, 393–410.

Koda, K. (1993) Transferred L1 strategies and L2 syntactic structure during L2 sentence comprehension. *Modern Language Journal*, 77, 490–500.

Koda, K. (1998) The role of phonemic awareness in L2 reading. *Second Language Research*, 14, 194–215.

Koda, K. (1999) Development of L2 intraword structural sensitivity and decoding skills. *Modern Language Journal*, 83, 51–64.

Koda, K. (2000) Cross-linguistic variations in L2 morphological awareness. *Applied Psycholinguistics*, 21, 297–320.

Koda, K. (2002) Writing systems and learning to read in a second language (pp. 225–48). In W. Li, J. S. Gaffney, & J. L. Packard (eds.), *Chinese children's reading acquisition: theoretical and pedagogical issues.* Boston: Kluwer Academic.

Koda, K. & Takahashi, T. (2007) Role of radical awareness in lexical inference in Kanji. Manuscript submitted for publication.

Koda, K., Takahashi, E. and Fender, M. (1998) Effects of L1 processing experience on L2 morphological awareness. *Ilha do Desterro*, 35, 59–87.

Krashen, S. (1983) Newmark's "Ignorance Hypothesis" and current second language acquisition theory. In In S. Gass & L. Selinker (eds.), *Language transfer in language learning.* Rowley, MA: Newbury House.

Ku, Y-M. & Anderson, R. C. (2003) Development of morphological awareness in Chinese and English. *Reading and Writing: An Interdisciplinary Journal*, 16, 399–422.

Kuo, L., & Anderson, R. C. (this volume) Conceptual and methodological issues in comparing metalingustics awareness across languages. In K. Koda & A. M. Zehler (eds.), *Learning to read across languages: cross-linguistic relationships in first and second language literacy development.* New York: Routledge.

Kuhara-Kojima, K., Hatano, G., Saito, H. & Haebara, T. (1996) Vocalization latencies of skilled and less skilled comprehenders for words written in hiragana and kanji. *Reading Research Quarterly*, 31, 158–71.

Legarretta, D. (1979) The effects of program models on language acquisition of Spanish speaking children. *TESOL Quarterly*, 13, 521–34.

Li, W., Anderson, R. C., Nagy, W. & Zhang, H. (2002) Facets of metalinguistic awareness that contribute to Chinese literacy. In W. Li, J. S. Gaffney, & J. L. Packard (eds.), *Chinese children's reading acquisition: theoretical and pedagogical issues* (pp. 87–106). Boston: Kluwer Academic.

Logan, G. D. (1988) Toward an instance theory of automatization. *Psychological Review*, 95, 492–527.

MacWhinney, B. (1987) The competition model. In B. MacWhinney (ed.), *Mechanisms of language acquisition* (pp. 249–308). Hillsdale, NJ: Erlbaum.

MacWhinney, B. & Bates, E. (eds.) (1989) *The crosslinguistic study of sentence processing*. New York: Cambridge University Press.

Mazuka, R. & Itoh, K. (1995) Can Japanese speakers be led down the garden path (pp. 295–330)? In R. Mazuka & N. Nagai (eds.), *Japanese sentence processing*. Hillsdale, NJ: Erlbaum.

Muljani, M., Koda, K. & Moates, D. (1998) Development of L2 word recognition: a connectionist approach. *Applied Psycholinguistics*, 19, 99–114.

Nagy, W. E. & Anderson, R. C. (1999) Metalinguistic awareness and literacy acquisition in different languages (pp. 155–60). In D. Wagner, R. Venezky, & B. Street (eds.), *Literacy: an international handbook*. New York: Garland.

Odlin, T. (1989) *Language transfer*. New York: Cambridge University Press.

Park, E. C. (2004) The relationship between morphological awareness and lexical inference skills for English language learning with Korean first-language background, doctoral dissertation. Dissertation Abstracts International, 65 (05), 1761, (UMI No. 3131518).

Perfetti, C. A. (2003) The universal grammar of reading. *Scientific Studies of Reading*, 7, 3–24.

Perfetti, C. A. & Liu, Y. (2005) Orthography to phonology and meaning: comparisons across and within writing systems. *Reading and Writing*, 18, 193–210.

Perfetti, C. A. & Dunlap, S. (this volume) Learning to read: general principles and writing system variations. In K. Koda & A. M. Zehler (eds.), Learning to read across languages: *cross-linguistic relationships in first and second-language literacy development*. New York: Routledge.

Perfetti, C. A., Beck, I., Bell, L. C. & Hughes, C. (1987) Phonemic knowledge and learning to read are reciprocal: a longitudinal study of first grade children. *Merrill-Palmer Quarterly*, 33, 283–319.

Riches, C. & Genesee, F. (2006) Crosslanguage and crossmodal influences. In F. Genesee, K. Lindholm-Leary, W. Saunders, & D. Christian (eds.), *Educating English language learners: a synthesis of research evidence*. New York: Cambridge University Press.

Rubin, H. (1991) Morphological knowledge and writing ability. In R. M. Joshi (ed.), *Written language disorders* (pp. 43–69). Boston: Kluwer Academic.

Ryan, A. & Meara, P. (1991) The case of invisible vowels: Arabic speakers reading English words. *Reading in a Foreign Language*, 7, 531–40.

Saito, H., Masuda, H. & Kawakami, M. (1999) Subword activation in reading Japanese single Kanji character words. *Brain & Language*, 68, 75–81.

Shu, H. & Anderson, R. C. (1999) Learning to read Chinese: the development of metalinguistic awareness. In A. Inhuff, J. Wang, & H. C. Chen (eds.),

Reading Chinese scripts: a cognitive analysis (pp. 1–18). Mahwah, NJ: Lawrence Erlbaum.

Skutnabb-Kangass, T. & Toukomaa, P. (1976) *Teaching migrant children's mother tongue and learning the language of the host country in the context of socio-cultural situation of the migrant family*. Helsinki: the Finnish National Commission for UNESCO.

Slobin, D. I. (1985) (ed.) *The crosslinguistic study of language acquisition*, Volume 2. Hillsdale, NJ: Lawrence Erlbaum.

Snow, C. (2006) Cross-cutting themes and future research directions. In D. August & T. Shanahan (eds.), *Developing literacy in second-language learners: report of the National Literacy Panel on Language-Minority Children and Youth*. Mahwah, NJ: Lawrence Erlbaum.

So, D. & Siegel, L. S. (1997) Learning to read Chinese: semantic, syntactic, phonological and short-term memory skills in normally achieving and poor Chinese readers. *Reading and Writing: An International Journal*, 9, 1–21.

Stahl, S. A. & Murray, B. A. (1994) Defining phonological awareness and its relationship to early reading. *Journal of Educational Psychology*, 86, 221–34.

Stanovitch, K. E. (2000) *Progress in understanding reading: scientific foundations and new frontiers*. New York: Guilford.

Stanovich, K. E., Cunningham, A. E. & Cramer, B. B. (1984) Assessing phonological awareness of kindergarten children: issues of task comparability. *Journal of Experimental Psychology*, 38, 175–90.

Taft, M. & Zhu, X. P. (1995) The representation of bound morphemes in the lexicon: a Chinese study (pp. 109–29). In L. B. Feldman (ed.), *Morphological aspects of language processing*. Hillsdale, NJ: Lawrence Erlbaum.

Troike, R. C. (1978) Research evidence for the effectiveness of bilingual education. *NABE Journal*, 3, 13–24.

Tyler, A. & Nagy, W. (1989) The acquisition of English derivational morphology. *Journal of Memory and Language*, 28, 649–67.

Tyler, A. & Nagy, W. (1990) Use of derivational morphology during reading. *Cognition*, 36, 17–34.

Vaid, J. (1995) Effect of reading and writing directions on nonlinguistic perception and performance: Hindi and Urdu data (pp. 295–310). In I. Taylor & D. R. Olson (eds.), *Scripts and literacy: reading and learning to read the world's scripts*. Dordrecht: Kluwer Academic.

Van Valin, R. D. (1991) Functionalist linguistic theory and language acquisition. *First Language*, 11, 7–40.

Vellutino, F. R. & Scanlon, D. M. (1987) Phonological coding, phonological awareness, and reading ability: evidence from a longitudinal and experimental study. *Merrill-Palmer Quarterly*, 33, 321–63.

Verhoeven, L. (2000) Components in early second language reading and spelling. *Scientific Studies of Reading*, 4, 313–30.

Wade-Woolley, L. and Geva, E. (2000) Processing novel phonemic contrasts in the acquisition of L2 word reading. *Scientific Studies of Reading* 4, 295–311.

Wang, M., Koda, K., Perfetti, C. A. (2003a) Alphabetic and non-alphabetic L1 effects in English semantic processing: a comparison of Korean and Chinese English L2 learners. *Cognition*, 87, 129–49.

Wang, M., Perfetti, C. A., and Liu, Y. (2003b) Alphabetic readers quickly acquire orthographic structure in learning to read Chinese. *Scientific Studies of Reading* 7, 183–208.

Wang, M., Perfetti, C. A. & Liu, Y. (2005) Chinese–English biliteracy acquisition: cross-language and writing system transfer. *Cognition*, 97, 67–88.

Yopp, H. K. (1988) The validity and reliability of phonemic awareness tests. *Reading Research Quarterly*, 23, 159–77.

Yorio, C. A. (1971) Some sources of reading problems in foreign language learners. *Language Learning*, 21, 107–15.

Zhang, S. & Perfetti, C. A. (1993) The tongue-twister effect in reading Chinese. *Journal of Experimental Psychology: Learning, Memory and Cognition*, 19, 1–12.

Part II

Languages, writing systems and learning to read

Part II Introduction and glossary

The chapters in Part II provide descriptions of five typologically diverse languages together with their respective writing systems: Arabic, Chinese, Hebrew, Khmer, Korean. Based on these descriptions, each chapter demonstrates how linguistic and orthographic properties influence learning to read in the language at hand. The terms relevant to the linguistic and orthographic descriptions, as well as learning to read competencies, are listed below.

Metalinguistic competencies related to learning to read

Segmental understanding	Recognizing that speech can be divided into word, and words can be segmented into smaller, functionally identifiable, elements
Symbolic awareness	Understanding the separation between word form and word meaning—that is, recognizing that words do not embody the properties of their referents, and thus perceiving the arbitrary nature of meaning assignment in language
Phonological awareness	Understanding the phonological structure of spoken words; as well as the ability to analyze and manipulate phonological information
Morphological awareness	Grasping the morphological structure of spoken words; as well as the ability to analyze and manipulate morphological information
Syntactic awareness	Recognizing that the specific ways of linking words (and/or modifying word forms) change sentence meaning
Grapho-phonological awareness	Understanding how phonological information is graphically represented in the writing system

Grapho-morphological awareness	Understanding how morphological information is graphically represented in the writing system
Concept of print	Awareness that print relates to speech
Mapping principle	Understanding what information is conveyed through each graphic symbol
Alphabetic principle	Understanding that each alphabetic letter represents a phoneme
Logographic principle	Awareness that each logographic character represents a whole word or morpheme (and its corresponding sound and meaning)

Linguistic knowledge directly related to learning to read

Spoken language competence	Understanding what is being communicated in contextually supportive oral interaction; it entails knowledge of oral vocabulary, basic sentence structure and grammar
Symbol knowledge	Understanding what specific linguistic (phonological and/or morphological) information is represented by each graphic symbol (letter or character) in the writing system
Orthographic knowledge	Recognizing how graphic symbols are combined to form words (e.g. spelling patterns)

Reading sub-skills

Decoding	Extracting phonological information directly from printed words
Orthographic processing	Identifying words through the analysis of spelling patterns (or patterns of symbol combinations) of printed words
Morphological processing	Identifying either grammatical properties or word meanings based on a word's morphological information
Word identification	Retrieving stored word meanings
Sentence processing	Determining overall sentence meanings by incrementally integrating word meanings based on syntactic and pragmatic rules
Main idea detection	Identifying the significant ideas of a text by selectively integrating the information relevant to its main theme
Lexical inference	Inferring context-appropriate meanings of unknown words based on word-part analysis and/or contextual information

Coherence building	Connecting information across sentences through explicit linguistic devices (connectives and other discourse signals specifically used to connect sentential information), lexical overlaps (identifying the same word or synonyms in other sentences), as well as coreferences (identifying the referent of pronouns)
Text-based inference	Inferring information not explicitly stated in order to bridge voids in explicitly stated text elements

5 Arabic literacy development and cross-linguistic effects in subsequent L2 literacy development

Michael Fender

Arabic presents a case in which reading is first learned in a form of the language that is different from the everyday language spoken in the home and community. Children learn to speak a colloquial dialect of Arabic as their first language, but then learn to read and write using literary Arabic, or Modern Standard Arabic (MSA). MSA is quite distinct from the colloquial Arabic in vocabulary and in some aspects of phonology and grammar; consequently, children learn to read in what is in some respects a second language.

Description of the Arabic language and its writing system

Characteristics of the Arabic orthography

Modern Standard Arabic (MSA) or Classical Arabic (CA) utilizes an alphabetic orthography comprised of 28 letters. These represent primarily consonants but also include three letters that correspond to long vowel phonemes: aleph /aa/, yeh /ii/, and wow /uu/. In addition, there are three short vowel forms that are written as diacritics placed above or below the consonant letters. There are also diacritics that indicate no vowel, and consonant and vowel lengthening (Bauer, 1996; Fischer, 1998).

Arabic is written from right to left in cursive form, and letters within words must be combined when possible. There are six letters that cannot be joined to a following letter and there are spaces within words when these letters appear. Therefore, a reader must learn to distinguish word boundaries from those breaks in the cursive script that occur when a letter is of the type that does not connect. Some letters have different forms for word-initial, word-medial, and word-final positions, and thus learning to read the letters in the Arabic orthography requires knowledge of the writing rules in conjunction with the different word positions of the letters (Abu Rabia, 2001; Bauer, 1996).

More significantly, Arabic can be characterized as a "deep" or opaque orthography in that the written from of the language does not include representation of all vowels (Abu-Rabia & Siegel, 2003; Frost *et al.* 1987). In the orthography, short vowels are not represented, and thus words are under-specified. As a result, words that have similar spellings and only differ on the basis of short vowels are represented as homographs that share the same spelling. The reader must determine the intended word through use of the context, that is, by processing morphological, syntactic and semantic information in the text to form a judgment about the appropriate reading of the word. However, such complex processing of the deep orthography is not required of children who are beginning to learn to read.

Children initially learn to read Arabic through use of a fully vowelized orthography in which all the consonants and vowels are represented in the script. In this "shallow" orthography the short vowels are included in the form of diacritic markings above and below the consonants. Thus, beginning readers learn through a phonologically transparent writing system in which each letter or symbol corresponds to one phoneme. These texts are easy to phonologically decode or "sound-out" since the letters and diacritics have highly consistent and reliable grapheme-to-phoneme (letter to sound) correspondences. Children generally begin the transition to reading a deeper orthography in the third or fourth grade, when they begin to read texts in which the short vowel diacritics are not included. It should be noted that the fully vowelized, shallow orthography is not only used for children's books; the shallow orthography is also used in certain formal texts such as the Koran and poetry.

The deep orthography (without vowel diacritics) is the standard form of Arabic used for texts for skilled readers, including newspapers, magazines, and textbooks. Arabic uses a root-plus-affix structure to form words and so the reader must infer the short vowels associated with the consonant roots to identify the intended words represented within the deep unvowelized texts. For example, the English words "sing," "song," and "sang" would all be represented in an unvowelized text in the same way, i.e. as the consonant root 'SNG' (Shimron, 1999). The reader would need to use the context information, including both sentence and pragmatic context (Abu-Rabia, 2001) to determine the correct reading. However, the short vowel phonemes are at least in part predictable because of the relatively limited number of syllable patterns within MSA. These patterns are CV, CVC, CVCC, CVV, and CVVC, with the latter two patterns including long vowels (Al-Ani, 1970). The system is complicated further because short vowel suffixes at the ends of nouns carry case-marking or sentence function information (e.g. subject/agent or object/theme of the sentence), and these suffixed vowels are not represented in the deep or unvowelized texts. However, the case or noun markers have mostly been dropped from the colloquial dialects as well.

Characteristics of Arabic phonology

The phoneme inventory of MSA corresponds more or less to the orthography; that is, there are 28 letters and 28 phonemes (Bateson, 1967; Fischer,

1998). However, it is important to keep in mind that MSA is the formal or literary language, and that the phoneme inventories of colloquial Arabic vary from MSA (Saiegh-Haddad, 2003). There are other differences between MSA and colloquial Arabic that are important to note. For example, colloquial Arabic dialects allow word-initial consonant clusters, while none are permitted within MSA; also, while word-final consonant clusters are rare in colloquial Arabic dialects, they are common in monosyllabic MSA words (Nasr, 1967; Saiegh-Haddad, 2003).

Characteristics of Arabic morphology

Arabic words are generated from root morphemes that must then be combined with specific patterns of affixes, i.e. vowels and consonants added to the root in specific patterns. That is to say, Arabic words are composed of two abstract morphemes: the root morpheme, and the affix pattern that provides phonological and morphosyntactic information (e.g. part of speech). A root is composed of typically three or four consonants that represent an abstract concept or meaning, sometimes referred to as a semantic field. For example, the root consonant morpheme KTB, (ك ت ب) is associated with the concept "to write." According to Bees (1999), there are about 5,000 root morphemes in MSA. The root morphemes are not pronounceable by themselves and are pronounced only in combination with an affix pattern. The affix pattern not only provides vowels and phonological information, but also derives the morphosyntactic features that specify noun, verb or adjective forms (for experimental evidence of both root and affix pattern representations, see Boudelaa & Marslen-Wilson, 2004; 2005).

The affix word patterns essentially incorporate vowels (and sometimes consonants) in positions before, between, and after the root morpheme consonants. For example, the root KTB is mapped onto different affix patterns or affix frames to generate verb forms such as كَتَبَ /kataba/, "he wrote"; يَكْتُب /yaktub/, "he writes," or other parts of speech, e.g. the nouns كِتاب /kitaab/, "book," and مَكْتَب /maktab/, "office."

More specifically, when the root morphemes in Arabic are mounted onto an affix pattern, the root morphemes undergo both non-concatenative and concatenative processes to derive verb, noun, and adjective forms with specific phonetic, syntactic, and semantic information. In the non-concatenative processes, the affix patterns involve the infixing of vowels and sometimes consonants within the root consonants to derive and inflect words. Concatenative processes involve the attachment of prefixes or suffixes to a word form. For verbs, these affix patterns mark person, gender and number distinctions, and for nouns, affix patterns are applied to feminine and masculine nouns to mark case (with suffix vowels), dual plurals and, to a certain extent, plurals (more than two) (Beesley, 1999; Plunkett and Nakisa, 1997).

Thus, root morphemes such as KTB are mounted on word affix patterns that can be described in terms of a three-tier system in which non-concatenative processes (infixes) and concatenative processes (prefixes/ suffixes) are applied to the lexical root to create words (Bees, 1999; Goldsmith, 1990; McCarthy, 1985). As an example, the inflected verb form, كَتَبَ /kataba/, "he wrote", is the result of the root morpheme undergoing both non-concatenative vowel infixing and concatenative suffix attachment in the integration of three grammatical elements or tiers (Beesely, 1999; for similar proposals see Goldsmith, 1990; McCarthy, 1985).

Vocalic tier (active voice)	a a
Lexical root tier:	K T B
Syllable pattern and affix tier:	C V C V C a

As shown above, /kataba/ is the result of integrating: (1) the lexical root morpheme KTB which conveys the concept "to write"; (2) the vocalic tier or vocalic melody involving vowel infixing to express active/passive voice; and (3) the syllable template tier representing the consonant (C) and vowel (V) word pattern and affix pattern on which the root morpheme and vocalic melody are mapped (Boudelaa & Marslen-Wilson, 2004; McCarthy, 1979). The CV or syllable template is an abstract morpheme with no phonological information, yet it provides key structural information about the affix word pattern, including prefixes and suffixes. Thus, in the example above, the suffix vowel "a" at the end of the verb, which conveys gender and person, is part of the overall syllable pattern (Beesley, 1999).

The affix word patterns deriving verb forms include infixing vowel patterns that express tense and voice (see Bateson, 1967). For example, each root morpheme is associated with a specific vowel to indicate the perfect tense on a verb. The root morpheme KTB requires the short vowel /a/ as the perfective stem vowel infix in the root, while QBL, (ق ب ل) which means "to accept," requires the short vowels /a/ and /i/ as the perfective stem vowel infixes between the second and third root consonants, respectively (قَبِل /qabila/, "he accepted"). Separate infix vowels need to be specified for the imperfect tense (i.e. present and future tense/aspect) forms (Bateson, 1967; Beesley, 1999). For example, KTB takes a short vowel /u/ infix to generate the imperfect tense (يَكتُب /yaktub/, "he writes").

The CV or syllable template further specifies the verb through use of vowel or consonant lengthening to distinguish between reciprocal/reflexive verb forms and perfect verb forms (Bateson, 1967). Where there is no vowel or consonant lengthening, the verb is perfect (i.e. finished or completed action). Vowel lengthening (VV) in the syllable template indicates a reciprocal verb (i.e. a verb with action involving a mutual exchange); and consonant lengthening (CC) marks extensive action (i.e. action continuing over a period of time or with violence). In the /kataba/ example above, there is no consonant or vowel lengthening (i.e. no CC or VV is included), indicating that the verb is in the past or perfect form (Boudelaa & Marslen-Wilson, 2004).

For derivations involving nouns, consonants (e.g. م, /m-/, and ت, /t-/) are used as part of the affix pattern to derive nouns from root morphemes. For example, the prefix consonant /m-/ is used to derive the nouns مَكتَب /maktab/, "office," and مَكتَبَة /maktabah/, "library," from the root KTB, "to write." The prefix /t-/ can be used to transform the root morpheme RTB (ب ت ر) which means "to arrange", into the noun تَرتيب /tartiib/, which means "arrangement" or "organization." There are word-final forms e.g. ا /-an/, and ين /-iy/, that are part of the affix pattern that derive different word forms. For example, شُكراً /shukran/ is a verbal noun derived from "to thank", and nationalities like مَصري /misriy/, "Egyptian" are derived from country names like مَصر /misr/, "Egypt" (Bateson, 1967).

Arabic nouns are inflected for case, gender (masculine, feminine) and number (singular, dual, plural). Feminine nouns often end with the suffixes, ة /ʔh/ or ى /a/. Many nouns which are not formally feminine (i.e. do not include the above word endings) function as such grammatically; these nouns include words for the body, names of countries, and cities, among other categories of noun. Gender and number are obligatory; feminine nouns are modified by adjectives with feminine marking and must agree with feminine verb endings (i.e. gender is part of the verb morphology).

Plural nouns are derived through concatenative and non-concatenative morphological processes in a complex system. Suffixes such as ات /-aat/ and ين /-uun/ (the double vowels indicate long vowels) are used to indicate regular or "sound" plurals. For example, the feminine plural is created by adding the suffix, ات to the singular form, e.g. سليمة سليم /salim/, /salimʔh/, "sound," becomes سليمات /salimat/, "sounds." The masculine plural is created by adding the suffixes, ون ين /-uun/, /-iin/. However, regular or sound plurals represent only approximately 25 percent of Arabic noun plural forms (Plunkett & Nakisa, 1997). The vast majority of nouns have "broken" plurals in which the root consonants of the noun are rearranged with new vowels, consonantal elements may be added, and feminine endings to singular nouns are lost. There are at least 30 possible distinct patterns for broken plurals. It appears that the broken plural noun forms are determined more by the syllabic structure than by the phonology of the singular noun forms (McCarthy and Prince, 1990; Plunkett and Nakisa, 1997). That is, singular nouns that share similar syllabic and vowel melody patterns tend to share the same broken plural patterns, whereas nouns with similar phonetic information (i.e. phonetic neighbors) generally do not share the same broken plural pattern.

Arabic syntactic structure

Although Arabic is a highly inflected language that utilizes case-marking possibilities, there is a tendency in MSA and in the colloquial dialects to indicate grammatical relationships through word order. Verb-Subject-Object (VSO) order is common in MSA (Bateson, 1967; Mohammad, 2000; Kaye & Rosenhouse, 1997; Saiegh-Haddad, 2003), and Subject-Verb-Object (SVO) sentences are common in the colloquial Arabic. The reliance on word order may be attributed to the fact that case-marking inflections are not encoded in unvowelized texts in MSA (Bauer, 1996) and are not commonly used in the colloquial dialects of Arabic (Saiegh-Haddad, 2003). Thus word order appears important for conveying grammatical function of noun phrases. Even so, word order can be variable. For example, although declarative clauses in MSA predominantly utilize VSO word order, SVO word order is also utilized (and other word orders are utilized as well, e.g. object initial sentences with passive voice).

Questions in Arabic are formed by the use of question words at the beginning of a sentence. For example, مَن /men/, which means "who," appears at the beginning of the sentence من كتب الدرس /men kataba ad'dars/, which is translated as "who wrote the lesson". Likewise, relative pronouns appear in clause-initial positions of relative clauses just as in English. Finally, Arabic allows a range of complex sentence types, such as adverbial clauses of time and conditional clauses. In the latter, the subordinated clause may either precede or follow the independent clause (Schulz *et al.*, 1996)

From the perspective of formal syntax, MSA and the colloquial forms of Arabic are head-initial languages in which the head of a phrase precedes its complements and modifiers. In other words, verbs generally appear in the sentence before verb complements such as direct objects, and always before sentential complements (see below). Nouns appear before adjectives and relative clauses, and prepositions appear before noun phrases in the prepositional phrase. The clearest indicator of the head-initial structure of Arabic is that verbs with sentential complements (e.g. يعرف /ya?rIf/, "know") require that the verb appear before the that-clause or sentential complement, e.g. هو يعرف بأن البقر تأكل عشبا /hUw? ya?rIf bi?n ?lbaqar t?kUl ?Ishban/, "He knows that all cows eat grass" (see Homeidi, 1994; Mohammad, 2000).

Arabic discourse structure

There is very little systematic information about text or discourse structures in Arabic, though there are some descriptive studies. Mohamed and Omar (1999) examined the sentence structures in two Arabic texts and two English texts. They found that there were more compound sentence structures in Arabic than in English while, in contrast, the English texts had more complex sentences with subordinate clauses than did the Arabic texts. They concluded that Arabic texts utilize coordination more extensively than English texts, and that English texts tend to utilize more subordinate clause structures compared to Arabic. In other descriptive work, researchers have found that Arabic utilizes more repetition and restatement than English texts (Al-Jubouri, 1984). Also, Ostler (1987) found that Arabic-language writers of English as a Second Language use more compound sentence structures when they write in English compared to native English speakers. Ostler attributes this to rhetorical pattern transfer from Arabic.

Conner (1996) provides a brief review of some of the contrastive rhetoric research on Arabic and English. Most of the studies she cites are descriptive in nature and indicate that Arabic texts exhibit general principles of coordination. That is, Arabic discourse blocks typically contain ideas that develop through patterns of repetition and parallelism. These patterns include use of exact co-reference of the theme, repeated in sentence after sentence, and also repetition of words.

Thus, while much of the descriptive research on Arabic text and discourse structures offers characterizations that are syntactic in nature, the studies also indicate some of the cohesive devices and patterns in Arabic discourse. However, much more work needs to be done to gain a better understanding of Arabic discourse patterns, particularly since most of the descriptive research has been conducted on small samples of text.

Metalinguistic and other requisite competencies in learning to read in Arabic

Oral language competence

Children acquire a colloquial Arabic as their first language, and then sub-sequently learn to read in MSA. Given this situation of diglossia, oral language competence with MSA is likely to be a significant factor in Arabic literacy acquisition (Abu Rabia, 1995, 2001; Ayari, 1996; Feitelson *et al.*, 1993). MSA is substantially different from the colloquial forms of Arabic, particularly in some grammatical aspects such as negation, but perhaps more importantly in terms of vocabulary. For that reason, oral competence in terms of MSA vocabulary knowledge is likely to be an important factor in the acquisition of Arabic literacy skills.

Orthographic knowledge and processing skills

In learning to read Arabic, children must acquire segmental awareness by developing the concept of letter and word segments. Wagner (1993) and Wagner & Spratt (1993) examined the development of these segmental skills among preschool children by assessing their Arabic letter and word bound-ary knowledge. The children were given tasks in which they had to dis-tinguish letter and non-letter symbols, distinguish words from strings of non-letter symbols, distinguish between correctly connected cursive spell-ings and incorrectly connected cursive spellings, and distinguish between intra-word cursive breaks and word boundaries (i.e. be able to distinguish between graphic displays with one word and two words). They also assessed the children's letter knowledge in tasks that involved identifying letters in words, naming letters, and pronouncing sounds associated with letters. They found strong correlations between the tasks measuring letter concept, word concept, and letter knowledge on one hand, and a strong correlation between letter knowledge and word decoding on the other. These findings indicate that letter and word awareness correspond to an awareness of some rudimentary orthographic rules associated with letter forms in initial, medial, and final positions. As found in other alphabetic literacy research, letter knowledge was strongly related to word decoding in the findings. Among first graders, Wagner *et al.* (1989) found very strong correlations for letter knowledge and word decoding, and letter knowledge and word-picture naming (a task in which children matched words to corresponding picture representations). Not surprisingly, these results indicate that awareness and knowledge of orthographic forms correspond to word decoding skills.

A study done by Taouk and Coltheart (2004) examined the word recognition skills of native-speaking Arabic children in Australia who were developing Arabic literacy skills in a heritage language program. They constructed a task in which the subjects read words written solely with the medial forms of the letters, rather than with the appropriate initial, medial, and final letter forms. They found that sixth grade children were significantly faster than skilled adult readers of Arabic in reading these words. The findings suggest that the sixth graders may have been less affected by the use of all medial forms because they were still at a phonological decoding stage, whereas the adults may have been relying more on orthographic representations or on spelling knowledge that was disrupted by the graphic violations of the spellings.

Another study, conducted by Abu Rabia *et al.* (2003), showed that children with L1 Arabic reading disabilities exhibit deficits in phonological processing skills, but do not exhibit corresponding deficits in orthographic knowledge and orthographic processing skills. Orthographic knowledge in Arabic, as in English, seems to develop with print experience, regardless of phonological deficits (Siegal *et al.*, 1995). Together, these studies suggest that native readers of Arabic acquire and master more detailed orthographic knowledge representations of words over time. Taouk and Coltheart (2004) claim that mature and fluent readers of Arabic rely less on a phonological processing route and more on a whole-word orthographic processing route in which words are recognized as whole chunks.

In general, children developing reading skills in Arabic acquire the basic orthographic constraints associated with the word initial, medial, and final forms of the letters in words (Abu Rabia, 2001). With print experience, Arabic readers acquire the letter knowledge and permissible spelling patterns of the orthography that help facilitate word recognition during reading.

Grapho-phonological awareness

As native Arabic-speaking children in kindergarten and first grade develop a basic awareness of letters and their corresponding sounds, they also develop phonemic awareness and consequent phonological processing skills (Saiegh-Haddad, 2003). Parallel findings have also been found for kindergarten and first grade children learning to read Hebrew (Bentin *et al.*, 1991). It is clear that phonological processing skills are instrumental in learning to read in Arabic (Abu Rabia, 1995, 1997a; Taouk & Coltheart, 2004; Wagner, 1993), which is due to the fact that children make extensive use of letter-sound conversion rules as they learn to read in a fully-vowelized (i.e. shallow) alphabetic orthography. However, research also shows that phonological processing skills continue to account for word recognition and reading skills in the unvowelized, deep orthography as well (Abu-Rabia & Siegel, 2003). In fact, evidence suggests that phonological processing is mandatory and conducted at the earliest stages of word recognition among fluent, mature adult readers of Arabic (Bentin & Ibrahim, 1996).

Grapho-morphological awareness

As mentioned previously, Arabic content words such as nouns, verbs, and adjectives (as opposed to function words such as determiners and preposi-tions) are composed of an abstract root morpheme and a word affix pattern of co-occurring prefix, infix, and suffix forms. The affix word pattern incorporates two types of information, the vocalic melody and the larger CV word structure. The vocalic melody provides the vowels that indicate voice and tense information. The CV word structure is the morphemic level that specifies the syllable structure, (i.e. specifying whether the vowels in each syl-lable are short or long, whether the consonants are lengthened, and whether prefixes or suffixes are added). The CV word structure incorporates the root morpheme and vocalic melody, and provides derivational information through the prefix, infix, and suffix additions that are necessary to generate the specific verb, noun, and adjective forms.

Words written in the deep orthography, while they do not include diacrit-ics marking the short vowels in the affix word pattern, still include other inflectional or derivational affix information. This includes information such as that represented by long vowels (e.g. "aa" in /kitaab/, "book") and consonants (e.g. "t" in /taktub/, "he writes"), which encode a substantial amount of a word's morphosyntactic information (Boudelaa & Marslen-Wilson, 2004). Nonetheless, without the short vowel diacritics, words printed in the deep orthography are underspecified and potentially ambigu-ous (Abu Rabia, 2002), particularly since some root morpheme forms (e.g. QBL) are homographs and represent more than one meaning. Such forms are usually distinguished by their short vowels. For example, QBL with no short vowel diacritics can spell "before" or the perfect verb form of "to wait." Since these two words differ with respect to short vowels, they are differentiated by vowel diacritics in the shallow orthography but not in the deep orthography. Hence, in reading the deep orthography, readers need to use their morphological knowledge of the homographs in conjunction with syntactic and semantic context information to infer the correct vowels and determine the correct reading (Abu Rabia, 2002; Abu Rabia *et al.*, 2003).

Since morphologically complex words are root morphemes merged with prefix, infix, and suffix forms (i.e. affix word pattern), readers need to develop grapho-morphological awareness that enables them to perceive and distinguish root morphemes from the long vowels and consonants in the affix word pattern. There is evidence that skilled readers of Arabic and Hebrew are sensitive to both root morphemes and affix patterns in morphologically complex words, and can utilize root and word pattern knowledge to facilitate word recognition (Abu Rabia, 2002; Bentin & Feldman, 1990; Boudelaa & Marslen-Wilson, 2004, 2005; Feldman & Bentin, 1994). In fact, an explicit morphological awareness of roots and word patterns distinguishes children with grade-appropriate reading skills from age-matched children with reading disabilities. Studies in both Arabic and Hebrew have shown that children in the upper elementary grades with reading disabilities have significantly weaker morphological awareness than age-matched controls (Abu Rabia *et al.*, 2003; Ben-Dror *et al.*, 1995). Interestingly, both the Arabic and Hebrew studies measured morphological awareness through an oral production task as well as a morphological judgment task with print stimuli. Though limited in number, such studies indicate that morphological awareness distinguishes children with age-appropriate reading abilities and poor readers with disabilities, and that skilled readers perceive and process root morphemes and affix patterns while reading morphologically complex words.

Grapho-morphological awareness may be particularly important in the acquisition of unfamiliar MSA vocabulary (Badry, 1984). Once a sensitivity to the root morphemes and derivational/inflectional affix patterns in MSA is developed, then the reader can utilize that information to identify the syntactic and semantic functions of unknown MSA words, and this information in turn can help the reader to figure out meanings of unfamiliar words in context. In this way, grapho-morphological awareness can facilitate vocabulary-learning processes.

Syntactic awareness and sentence processing skills

In Arabic, syntactic knowledge and sentence processing skills may be particularly important in reading and comprehending sentences, given the use of the deep orthography for most texts intended for mature readers. In these texts, syntactic awareness will assist the reader in identifying the appropriate word, particularly where the omission of short vowels in the orthography results in a number of possible homographs. Thus, syntactic awareness and knowledge of MSA is particularly important for developing reading fluency at the word- and sentence-levels. This seems generally true with MSA and Hebrew where word-level processing skills must operate at two levels: at the word recognition level, in order to recognize the root word morpheme forms and affix patterns that they are mounted on; and at a phrase or clause level, in order to be able to utilize the morphosyntactic information of the affix pattern to integrate the word into phrase and clause structures. Thus, morphosyntax and syntactic parsing are closely tied to fluent reading, as is true of most if not all languages. However, given that the affix patterns of words encode both phonological and morphosyntactic information, both of which are necessary for word (lexical) processing and sentence processing, there is a tight interactive connection between word recognition processes and syntactic parsing processes.

There have been very few studies that examine syntactic awareness skills among children learning to read in Arabic. A study by Abu Rabia and colleagues (2003) compared phonemic, morphemic, and syntactic awareness skills among fifth grade children who were normal and reading disabled readers, as well as a group of third grade normal readers. They found that the fifth grade reading disabled readers had significantly lower phonemic, morphemic, and syntactic awareness skills than the third and fifth grade normal readers. In the study, syntactic awareness was examined in a task that involved reading sentences with syntactic errors and correcting the errors. In this task, the reading disabled children exhibited significantly lower syntactic awareness compared to both the third and fifth grade normal readers. However, in performance on an oral cloze task, the fifth grade reading disabled group was comparable to the third grade normal readers. A similar study on syntactic awareness was conducted in Hebrew by Bentin *et al.* (1990), using tasks that required the children to detect and correct syntactic errors. In this study, reading disabled fourth graders showed significantly lower syntactic awareness than a group of fourth grade skilled readers. The study also compared the fourth grade skilled readers with fourth grade poor readers without specific reading disabilities. While there were no differences found between the two groups in ability to detect syntactic errors, the good readers were significantly better in correcting the syntactic errors they identified. These studies suggest that syntactic awareness skills are weaker among disabled readers, and among poor decoders with poor comprehension skills. However, more research is necessary for anything more than tentative conclusions to be made about syntactic metalinguistic skills.

There has not been any on-line sentence reading research[1] conducted on how Arabic is processed. However, research with a variety of other languages indicates that the syntactic structure of a language shapes the sentence-processing routines that emerge during language acquisition. Since Arabic under-utilizes its case-marking system, word order information in conjunction with the head-initial phrase and clause structures of Arabic (in both colloquial Arabic and MSA) can be expected to play an important role in shaping the development of sentence-processing skills. Evidence to date shows that head-initial languages utilize similar sentence-processing routines, and that these routines contrast considerably with the sentence processing observed for head-final languages such as Japanese and Korean (see Frenck-Mestre & Pynte, 1997; Konieczny *et al.*, 1997; Mazuka, 1998; Miyamoto, 2002). As a consequence of the head-initial phrase structures, Arabic word-integration or sentence-parsing procedures utilize a set of right-branching word-integration processes in which the head of a phrase (e.g. the noun in a noun phrase or the verb in a verb phrase) guides and constrains how subsequent words (such as modifiers or complements) are attached or integrated into the preposition, noun, and verb phrase structures. For example, noun phrases must remain open after the head noun is processed in order for post-position modifiers such as adjectives, prepositions, or relative clauses to be attached and interpreted on-line. Likewise, the verb in the verb phrase signals to the reader/listener important verb complement information that must be integrated into the verb phrase. For example, transitive verbs in declarative sentences signal that a direct object complement is in the text or speech stream, whereas Arabic psyche verbs, e.g. the verbs meaning "to know" and "to believe," often signal a sentence as a verb complement (e.g. as in "believe that the answer is correct"). This type of head-initial structure fosters a top-down set of sentence processing skills in which the head of the phrase projects syntactic and semantic information to help integrate the words that follow.

Differences and similarities in learning to read in Arabic and English

There are many similarities in the development of basic literacy skills in Arabic and English. First, beginning readers of Arabic and of English must acquire the ability to read alphabetic orthographies. This requires learning the specific letter-to-phoneme correspondences, learning to blend letters and phonemes to decode or sound out words, and learning some of the spelling patterns of the writing system.

However, there are considerable differences in literacy acquisition for English- and Arabic-speaking children. Most notably, Arabic-speaking children must learn to read in MSA, the literary form of the language, which is considerably different from the colloquial languages Arabic children acquire as their first languages. Thus, Arabic-speaking children may in many cases be learning to read in a second language. As a consequence, they may experience considerable difficulties in comprehending texts due to their unfamiliarity with the formal literary language (MSA), that is, due to the differences in phonology, morphology, syntax, and semantics (i.e. vocabulary) between the colloquial Arabic that is the children's first language and MSA.

In addition, children acquiring Arabic literacy skills must eventually learn to read unvowelized texts, texts in which the vowel diacritics are not provided. As noted earlier, beginning readers first learn to read with fully vowelized texts that are phonologically "shallow," i.e. they provide one-to-one letter-to-phoneme connections with all vowels included. However, in the third and fourth grades of primary school, children begin to read texts written without the vowel diacritics. To read these texts, the children need to learn to use their morphological knowledge, knowledge of sentence syntax, and the context, to identify words that are ambiguous due to the incomplete vowel spellings (Abu Rabia, 2001). Some researchers have suggested that Arabic literacy development includes fluent word identification skills that incorporate both a word's spelling and the word's context information (Abu Rabia, 1997a, 1997b, 1998). Therefore, initial literacy development in Arabic is like English in that it involves the establishment of phonological decoding skills to drive word-level reading. However, beyond this, literacy skills in Arabic also require the development of morphological and sentence processing skills that enable the reader to read unvowelized texts (Abu-Rabia, 2001; Azzam, 1993; see Shimron, 1999, for parallel comments on Hebrew).

In contrast to this, native readers of English must acquire the word-specific spelling forms or graphemic spelling patterns of words that deviate from letter-to-sound correspondences (e.g. make, great, bread) in order to develop word-level reading proficiency. This requires the acquisition of orthographic (i.e. spelling) knowledge that is in many ways independent of simple letter-to-phoneme correspondences and corresponding processing skills (Barker *et al.*, 1992; Ehri & Snowling, 2004; Perfetti, 1991; Stanovich & West, 1989). In short, fluent readers of English develop automatic, context-free word recognition skills that involve orthographic or spelling representations independent of letter-phoneme correspondences. Fluent readers in Arabic develop automatic word recognition skills that are based on reliable letter-sound correspondences and that may be more sensitive to the sentence context information (e.g. syntax and semantics) necessary to infer fully realized morphosyntactic word forms with the correct part of speech.

Research on literacy learning and processing involving Arabic speakers

Research on skilled readers

How do basic phrase- and sentence-level structure patterns shape Arabic sentence-processing skills?

Although there has not been any on-line research conducted on how Arabic is processed, as noted earlier, research with a variety of other languages indicates that the syntactic structure of the language shapes sentence processing routines as they emerge during language acquisition (Fender, 2001;

Frank & Vijay-Shanker, 2000; Juffs, 1998; Mazuka, 1998). Since both colloquial and MSA dialects underutilize their case-marking system, word order shapes sentence-processing skills (Mohammad, 2000). The word order is determined by the head-initial phrase structure and the SVO and VSO clause structures of Arabic (colloquial and MSA dialects, respectively). As words are taken in from a written or spoken text, the heads of phrases signal attachment and interpretation possibilities for subsequent words in the phrase. That is, head-initial phrase structures foster a top-down set of sentence-processing skills in which the head of the phrase provides the structural information that can be used to integrate subsequent words into open phrase or clause units. Thus, Arabic is likely to employ a set of top-down phrase- and sentence-processing routines typical of other head-initial phrase languages, including English (Fender, 2001, 2003).

Research on beginning readers

How does the orthographic structure shape Arabic decoding (both phonological and morphological mapping) skills?

In general, since the Arabic orthography is highly reliable and consistent, beginning and fluent readers of Arabic rely as much as possible on their phonological processing skills (Abu Rabia, 1997a, 1997b, 1997c; Bentin & Ibrahim, 1996). This seems to be especially the case since native readers of Arabic learn to read with a phonologically shallow script, and thus develop word recognition skills that rely on phonological decoding (Abu Rabia, 1997a, 1997b, 1997c; Wagner, 1993).

Unfortunately, little is understood about the morphological processing skills involved in first-language Arabic literacy development. Badry (1984) found that native Arabic-speaking children learn to infer morphological patterns and then apply them to novel stimuli. However, this was found to be true more for older children 8–9 years of age than for younger children 5–7 years of age.

It seems very likely that morphological knowledge and processing skills facilitate word-level and sentence-level processing in MSA. Since children will encounter MSA words that are unfamiliar or partially familiar, the ability to infer morphological patterns would help them identify root morphemes and semantically related words (see Shimron, 1999, for similar comments on Hebrew morphology and word recognition).

How do Arabic-speaking children develop phonological mapping skills?

Beginning native Arabic-language readers first must learn that letters correspond to phonemes, i.e. they must develop phonemic awareness in learning to map letters to sounds (Abu Rabia, 1999; Eviatar & Ibrahim, 2001). Once children develop this basic mapping principle and learn the letter-to-phoneme connections of the Arabic orthography, they can begin to map print to oral language and begin to comprehend texts. Entailed in this process are the specifics of learning letter-to-phoneme or letter-to-sound correspondences, learning to blend letters and phonemes to decode or sound out words, and learning some of the spelling patterns of the writing system. Initial literacy development with the fully vowelized orthography involves the development of word recognition skills that rely on phonological decoding processes. As children gain more experience in decoding words, word forms become more and more familiar and require less effort devoted to phonological decoding processes.

With the exception of Wagner (1993) and colleagues (Wagner *et al.*, 1989), there has been very little empirical research examining how Arabic language children develop phonological mapping skills over time. Wagner and colleagues found that children developed basic pre-literacy competency skills such as distinguishing letters and letter sequences from other symbols and symbol sequences (e.g. numbers, nonsense shapes), and developed skills in segmenting and identifying letters. Also, as found for other alphabetic orthographies, Arabic-speaking children develop phonemic awareness during the earliest stages of literacy development; this phonemic awareness then helps them learn to decode and map printed words to speech (Eviatar & Ibrahim, 2000; Wagner, 1993). Phonological decoding skills develop in conjunction with phonemic awareness as children acquire the Arabic letter-to-phoneme correspondences through experience with the phonologically shallow (i.e. fully-vowelized) orthography that is used for beginning readers.

How do Arabic-speaking children develop morphological mapping skills?

Very little research has been conducted in the area of morphological processing by Arabic language children. An exception is a developmental study by Badry (1984) that examined how native Arabic language children develop morphological knowledge and processing skills during language acquisition. Badry found that children first learn morphological stems as static forms, and that with time they begin to discover word families that share the same root morphemes. That is, the children begin to recognize root morphemes and their derived patterns by way of semantics. Gradually, children acquire the ability to derive morphologically complex words from novel stems, a process that is likely facilitated as they begin to learn to decode unfamiliar MSA forms. Thus, according to Badry, they develop an abstract knowledge of the morphological patterns associated with root morphemes and use that knowledge to derive word forms for novel root stems.

Some researchers have argued that Arabic-speaking children must learn to rely on morphological mapping skills to help them read unvowelized texts

(Azzam, 1993; Shimron, 1999). For example, Azzam (1993) states that, until they have acquired the morpheme root and pattern system, Arabic-speaking children will have difficulty in learning to read unvowelized scripts and in developing spelling skills that are grammatically accurate. However, as Shimron (1999) notes, knowledge of how children develop and utilize morphological mapping skills is a completely new area in literacy research with Semitic languages (see also Abu Rabia, 2001).

How do Arabic-speaking children develop sentence-processing skills?

Arabic-speaking children develop the ability to integrate words into phrases and clauses when they acquire their native language, the colloquial Arabic (Abu Rabia, 1995; Ayari, 1996; Feitelson *et al.*, 1993). Despite the many differences between the colloquial first language, and MSA, children are likely to utilize both structural and semantic/conceptual information to process sentences as they learn to read in MSA. It is likely that the key to developing fluent and accurate MSA sentence-processing skills and hence comprehension is the ability to utilize both the phrase-structure knowledge and the morphological knowledge required to integrate words into clauses and process their meaning (Abu Rabia, 1995, 1997a, 1997b, 1997c, 2001; Azzam, 1993; Badry, 1984; Wagner, 1993).

How does the diglossic nature of Arabic affect the development of Arabic reading fluency?

As native Arabic-speaking children learn to read, they must learn MSA, essentially a second language for them (Abu-Rabia, 1995, 2001; Ayari, 1996). Given this situation of diglossia, as noted above, native-speaking Arabic children may experience considerable difficulty learning to read Arabic since, among other differences, MSA presents them with a vocabulary that is significantly different from the colloquial Arabic they learn as a first language (Badry, 1984). Interestingly, Eviatar and Ibrahim (2000) found that Arabic children who had learned to read MSA exhibited metalinguistic language skills more akin to Russian-Hebrew bilingual children than to monolingual Hebrew speakers, and related this finding to the differences in grammatical and morphological structures of colloquial Arabic and MSA. Thus, given the differences that exist between MSA and their first language, reading for Arabic-speaking children is a labor-intensive activity, and it may take a considerable amount of time for children to become comfortable and proficient in working with MSA. Research evidence (Abu Rabia, 2000; Feitelson *et al.*, 1993) suggests that children with some early exposure to MSA (i.e. oral storytelling in MSA in kindergarten) do significantly better in comprehending stories in first grade than do children who have not had such early exposure to MSA. However, most children are exposed to very little MSA prior to first grade. Thus, the difficulties that the situation of diglossia presents for children in early literacy learning may be a factor in producing low literacy rates within the Arab world (Ayari, 1996).

How are Arabic-speaking children taught to read?

This is a very difficult question to answer since there are many countries (approximately 20) in which MSA is the standard language. Wagner (1993) describes the use of a highly structured and drill-based approach to instruction in some of these countries (Wagner, 1993), and this same approach may be characteristic of most of the educational systems where MSA is the standard language. Wagner describes early primary school classes in which children write letters and words that a teacher dictates, and then write these on the board to check their accuracy. At the earliest stages of literacy development, children may also work on copying letters and words. Later, children read and write larger texts. In some cases, children may be presented with an unvowelized text and asked to write the text with the correct vowel diacritics. These lessons may be typically accompanied by lessons on spelling and grammar (Wagner, 1993). Unfortunately, there is very little information available overall on Arabic literacy instruction.

Learning to read in a second language

Transfer of phonological processing skills

There is now some research evidence to indicate that native Arabic speakers rely as much as possible on phonological processing skills to recognize words (Abu Rabia, 1996a, 1997b; Abu-Rabia & Siegel, 1995; Bentin & Ibrahim, 1996). This does not seem surprising since (1) native-readers of Arabic spend the first two and sometimes three years of school learning how to read and write with phonologically shallow (fully-vowelized) texts that represent all the phonemic information in the text, and (2) the grapheme-phoneme correspondences in Arabic are highly reliable and not as irregular and variable as in the English spelling system. In fact, Abu-Rabia (2001) has argued that unvowelized texts are read by utilizing phonological processing skills in conjunction with context cues.

In terms of transfer, there is evidence that child and adult native-readers of Arabic transfer these phonological processing skills to the learning of a second alphabetic language (Abu-Rabia & Siegel, 2003; Wagner *et al.*, 1989; Brown and Haynes, 1985). Brown and Haynes (1985) found that native speakers of Arabic were better able to sound out pseudo-English words than a proficiency-matched group of Japanese, English as a second language (ESL) readers, even though the Japanese readers were faster at recognizing geometric shapes, non-words, and words. This finding indicates that native-Arabic speakers and readers rely on their phonological process-ing skills as much as possible during English word recognition, at least as they are in the process of acquiring English.

However, an over-reliance on phonological processing skills while devel-oping reading skills in English as a second language is likely to prove prob-lematic given the irregularities in English spelling, and this may be the case particularly for words in which there are unstressed vowels. Ryan and Meara (1991) found that a group of intermediate-level Arabic-speaking ESL students performed significantly less quickly and less accurately compared to other proficiency-matched ESL students on a same-different word recog-nition task involving longer words with both stressed and unstressed vowels. Fender (2003) found that adult Arabic-speaking, high-intermediate level ESL learners were significantly slower at recognizing English words than a proficiency-matched group of Japanese ESL students. Such findings indicate that native-Arabic speakers transfer phonological processing skills to read-ing in English as a second language, with the result that they experience reading difficulties at the word level. It may be that Arabic language readers develop functional reading skills with less precise or specific spelling know-ledge, and that this leads to less automatic word-recognition skills. That is, the native-Arabic readers may develop imprecise orthographic representa-tions of words particularly when the grapheme-phoneme relationships devi-ate or are irregular or inconsistent (e.g. the vowel "o" in phone, gone, done). Consequently, they may have more difficulties in accurate spelling of English words, and this may be the case particularly when vowels encode a large portion of the word.

Transfer of morphological processing skills

It is not clear to what extent Arabic morphology, morphological awareness, and morphological mapping skills will transfer, especially since English and Arabic utilize such different morphological decomposition and composition processes (McCarthy, 1985; Badry, 1984; Goldsmith, 1990). However, the notion of word families and root words should help native-Arabic speakers to begin to decompose morphologically complex English words and learn word families.

Transfer of sentence-processing skills

There has not been much research in Arabic on the transfer of sentence-processing skills. However, there is mounting evidence that first-language sentence-processing skills interact with and shape the development of second-language sentence-processing skills (Fender, 2001; Hoover & Dwivedi, 1998; Juffs, 1998). Hence, it is important to pay particular attention to the struc-tural properties of a language since these will ultimately shape the underlying processing skills. Since both Arabic and English are head-initial languages, it would be expected that both languages would require similar sentence processing skills. In short, the head-initial phrase structure of Arabic overlaps considerably with English, and this may facilitate the English word integration and sentence processing skills of Arab ESL learners.

There is some preliminary evidence that, compared to proficiency-matched Japanese ESL learners, adult Arabic ESL learners are better able to process on-line and comprehend English sentences (Fender, 2001, 2003). This finding suggests that Arabic ESL learners utilize their first-language (Arabic) sentence processing skills in processing similarly structured English sentences.

If this is the case, then Arabic-speaking ESL speakers may be able to utilize their first-language word-integration skills to guide their development of ESL word-integration processes, particularly for English verb phrases. If so, then this would indicate the influence of a general first language-ESL interaction in terms of ESL word integration that is not just limited to Japanese and Arabic ESL situations. Namely, it is plausible that a verb's grammatical constraints (i.e. argument or complement requirements) that guide subsequent word attachment and integration procedures in constructing phrases in the first-language, Arabic, may also facilitate word integration procedures in the second-language. More specifically, lexical information in verbs that specify verb projection and attachment possibilities can be employed to facilitate word integration processes. These first-language word integration effects should be apparent in ESL word integration reading times and/or comprehension outcomes of Arabic and Japanese ESL students.

Social/cultural factors affecting Arabic literacy development

There are two social/cultural factors that affect literacy development among Arabic-speaking children: diglossia and lack of early exposure to MSA. First, there is a situation of diglossia, in which children speak a colloquial or vernacular language but learn to read in another, MSA. MSA is sufficiently different from the colloquial Arabic languages that it is viewed as nearly a second language for children (Abu Rabia, 2000, 2001; Ayari, 1996; Feitelson *et al.*, 1993). MSA is widely used as the literary or educated form of Arabic, and is used in formal situations such as political speeches, religious sermons, lectures and news broadcasts. Though MSA is acquired during formal schooling and is understood by educated Arabs, it is not used in everyday life, and there is often a mixture of colloquial and MSA forms used among educated Arabs. Ayari (1996) reports that literate Arabic speakers who master MSA still state ". . . that they are not able to engage in reading and writing processes with any degree of pleasure, confidence, or skill." Thus students may lack confidence or interest in engaging in reading and writing.

Second, children are not exposed to MSA before formal schooling in the first grade. Parents and kindergarten teachers tell stories to children in the colloquial Arabic believing that the children will not be able to understand the stories in MSA (Ayari, 1996; Feitelson, *et al.*, 1993). The consequence is that children lack both exposure to MSA and also to pre-literate print experiences. However, recent research has shown an advantage in early literacy learning for children who have been exposed to MSA in oral storytelling in kindergarten (Abu Rabia, 2000; Feitelson *et al.*, 1993).

Note

1 On-line language research examines the cognitive/linguistic processes involved in parsing a sentence (e.g. research examining the word-by-word reading times involved in recognizing words and integrating them into larger phrase and clause units of meaning). On-line research typically utilizes response times or reading times that reflect the underlying processing skills in fluent or semi-fluent sentence processing (usually at the word or phrase level). In contrast, off-line research examines the products or results of on-line processing and usually focuses on accuracy or comprehension. Thus, making some sort of judgment or decision about a sentence after reading a sentence is an example of off-line research.

References

Abu-Rabia, S. (1995). Learning to read in Arabic: reading, syntactic, orthographic and working memory skills in normally achieving and poor Arabic readers. *Reading Psychology*, 16(4), 351–94.

Abu-Rabia, S. (1996) The role of vowels and context in the reading of highly skilled native Arabic readers. *Journal of Psycholinguistic Research*, 25(6), 629–41.

Abu-Rabia, S. (1997a) Reading in Arabic orthography: the effect of vowels and context on reading accuracy of poor and skilled native Arabic readers. *Reading and Writing*, 9(1), 65–78.

Abu-Rabia, S. (1997b) Reading in Arabic orthography: the effect of vowels and context on reading accuracy of poor and skilled native Arabic readers in reading paragraphs, sentences, and isolated words. *Journal of Psycholinguistic Research*, 26(4), 465–82.

Abu-Rabia, S. (1997c) The need for cross-cultural considerations in reading theory: the effects of Arabic sentence context in skilled and poor readers. *Journal of Research in Reading*, 20(2), 137–47.

Abu-Rabia, S. (1998) Reading Arabic texts: effects of text type, reader type and vowelization. *Reading and Writing*, 10(2), 105–19.

Abu-Rabia, S. (1999) The effect of Arabic vowels on the reading comprehension of second- and sixth-grade native Arab children. *Journal of Psycholinguistic Research*, 28(1), 93–101.

Abu-Rabia, S. (2000) Effects of exposure to literary Arabic on reading comprehension in a diglossic situation. *Reading and Writing*, 13(1–2), 147–57.

Abu-Rabia, S. (2001) The role of vowels in reading Semitic scripts: data from Arabic and Hebrew. *Reading and Writing*, 14(1–2), 39–59.

Abu-Rabia, S. (2002) Reading in a root-based morphology language: the case of Arabic. *Journal of Research in Reading*, 25, 3, 299–309.

Abu-Rabia, S. & Siegel, L. (1995) Different orthographies different context effects: the effects of Arabic sentence context in skilled and poor readers. *Reading Psychology*, 16(1), 1–19.

Abu-Rabia, S. & Siegel, L. (2003) Reading skills in three orthographies: the case of trilingual Arabic–Hebrew–English speaking Arab children. *Reading and Writing: An Interdisciplinary Journal*, 16, 611–34.

Abu-Rabia, S., Share, D., & Monsour, M. (2003) Word recognition and basic cognitive processes among reading-disabled and normal readers in Arabic. *Reading and Writing: An Interdisciplinary Journal*, 16, 423–42.

Al-Ani, S. (1970) *Arabic phonology*. The Hague, Netherlands: Mouton & Co.

Al-Jubouri, A. (1984) The role of repetition in Arabic argumentative discourse. In J. Swales & H. Mustafa (eds.), *English for specific purposes in the Arab world*. Birmingham, UK: Language Studies Unit, University of Aston in Birmingham.

Ayari, S. (1996) Diglossia and illiteracy in the Arab world. *Language Culture and Curriculum*, 9(3), 243–53.

Azzam, R. (1993) The nature of Arabic reading and spelling errors of young children: a descriptive study. *Reading and Writing: An Interdisciplinary Journal*, 5(4), 355–85.

Badry, F. (1984) Acquisition of lexical derivational rules in Moroccan Arabic: implications for the development of Standard Arabic as a second language through literacy. Unpublished dissertation manuscript, University of California, Berkeley.

Barker, T., Torgesen, J., & Wagner, R. (1992) The role of orthographic processing skills on five different reading tasks. *Reading Research Quarterly*, 27(4), 334–45.

Bateson, M. C. (1967) *Arabic language handbook*. Washington DC: Center for Applied Linguistics.

Bauer, T. (1996). Arabic writing. In P. Daniels & P. Bright (eds.), *The world's writing systems*. New York, NY: Oxford University Press. 559–64.

Beesley, K. (1999) Arabic stem morphotactics via finite-state intersection. In E. Benmamoun, (ed.), *Perspectives on Arabic linguistics XII: papers from the Twelfth Annual Symposium on Arabic Linguistics*. Amsterdam: John Benjamins.

Ben-Dror, I., Frost, R., & Bentin, S. (1995) Orthographic representation and phonemic segmentation in skilled readers: a cross-language comparison. *Psychological Science*, 6(3), 176–81.

Bentin, S. & Feldman, L. (1990) The contribution of morphological and semantic relatedness to repetition priming and short and long logs: evidence from Hebrew. *The Quarterly Journal of Experimental Psychology*, 42A(4) 693–711.

Bentin, S. & Ibrahim, R. (1996) New evidence for phonological processing during visual word recognition: the case of Arabic. *Journal of Experimental Psychology: Learning, Memory, and Cognition*, 22(2), 309–23.

Bentin, S., Deutsch A., & Liberman, I. (1990) Syntactic competence and reading ability in children. *Journal of Experimental Child Psychology*, 48, 147–72.

Bentin, S., Hammer, R., & Cohen, S. (1991) The effects of aging and first grade schooling on the development of phonological awareness. *Psychological Science*, 2(4), 271–4.

Boudelaa, S. & Marslen-Wilson, W. (2004) Abstract morphemes and lexical representation: the CV-skeleton in Arabic. *Cognition*, 92, 3, 271–303.

Boudelaa, S. & Marslen-Wilson, W. (2005) Discontinuous morphology in time: incremental masked priming in Arabic. *Language and Cognitive Processes*, 20, 207–60.

Brown, T. L. & Haynes, M. (1985) Literacy background and reading development in a second language. In T. H. Carr (ed.), *The development of reading skills*. San Francisco, CA: Jossey-Bass.

Brustaad, K., Al-Batal, M., & Al-Tonsi, A. (1995) *Al-kittab fii taʔallum al-ʔarabiyya: a textbook for beginning Arabic*, Part One. Washington, DC: Georgetown University Press.

Brustaad, K., Al-Batal, M., & Al-Tonsi, A. (1997) *Al-kittab fii taʔallum al-ʔarabiyya: a textbook for beginning Arabic*, Part Two. Washington, DC: Georgetown University Press.

Connor, U. (1996) *Contrastive rhetoric: cross-cultural aspects of second-language writing*. New York: Cambridge University Press.

Ehri, L. & Snowling, M. (2004) Developmental variation in word recognition. In B. Shulman, K. Apel, B. Ahren, E. Silliman, & C. Stone (eds.), *Handbook of language and literacy: development and disorders*. New York: Guilford Press.

Eviatar, Z. & Ibrahim, R. (2000) Bilingual is as bilingual does: metalinguistic abilities of Arabic-speaking children. *Applied Psycholinguistics*, 21(4), 451–71.

Fakhri, A. (1995) Topical structure in Arabic–English interlanguage. In *Pragmatics and language learning*. Monograph Series, Volume 6.

Feitelson, D., Goldstein, Z., Iraqi, J., & Share, D. (1993) Effects of listening to story reading on aspects of literacy acquisition in a diglossic situation. *Reading Research Quarterly*, 28(1), 70–9.

Feldman, L. & Bentin, S. (1994) Morphological analysis of disruptive morphemes: evidence from the brew. *Quarterly Journal of Experimental Psychology*, 47, 407–35.

Fender, M. (2001) A review of L1 and L2/ESL word integration skills and the nature of L2/ESL word integration development involved in lower-level text processing. *Language Learning*, 51(2), 319–96.

Fender, M. (2003) English word recognition and word integration skills of native Arabic-and Japanese-speaking ESL learners. *Applied Psycholinguistics*, 24(2).

Fischer, W. (1998) Classical Arabic. In R. Hetzron (ed.), *The Semitic languages*. New York, NY: Routledge.

Frank, R. & Vijay-Shanker, K. (2000) Lowering across languages. In M. De Vincenzi & V. Lombardo (eds.), *Cross-linguistic perspectives on language processing*. Netherlands: Kluwer Academic Press.

Frencke-Mestre, C. & Pynte, J. (1997) Syntactic ambiguity resolution while reading in a second and native language. *Quarterly Journal of Experimental Psychology*, 50A(1), 119–48.

Frost, R., Katz, L., & Bentin, S. (1987) Strategies for visual word recognition and orthographic depth: a multilingual comparison. *Journal of Experimental Psychology: Human Perception and Performance*, 13, 104–15.

Goldsmith, J. (1990) *Autosegmental and metrical phonology*. New York, NY: Blackwell.

Homeidi, M. (1994) Government and binding and case assignment in modern standard Arabic. In J. Fisiak (ed.), *Papers and studies in contrastive linguistics*. Adam Mickiewicz University, Poznan.

Hoover, M. & Dwivedi, V. (1998) Syntactic processing in skilled bilinguals. *Language Learning*, 48(1), 1–29.

Juffs, A. (1998) Some effects of first language argument structure and morphosyntax on second language sentence processing. *Second Language Research*, 12(4), 406–24.

Kaye, A. S., & Rosenhouse, J. (1997) Arabic dialects and Maltese. In R. Hetzron (ed.), *The Semitic languages*. New York, NY: Routledge.

Konieczny, L., Hemforth, B., Scheepers, C., & Strube, G. (1997) The role of lexical heads in parsing: evidence from German. *Language and Cognitive Processes,* 12(2/3), 307–48.

McCarthy, J. (1979) Formal problems in Semitic phonology and morphology. Doctoral dissertation. Cambridge, MA: MIT.

McCarthy, J. (1985) *Formal problems in Semitic phonology and morphology.* New York, NY: Garland Publishing, Inc.

McCarthy, J. & Prince, A. (1990) Foot and word in prosodic morphology: the Arabic broken plural. *Natural Language and Linguistic Theory,* 8, 2, 209–83.

Mazuka, R. (1998) *The development of language processing strategies: a cross-linguistic study between Japanese and English.* Mahwah, NJ: Lawrence Erlbaum Associates.

Miyamoto, E. (2002) Case markers as clause boundary inducers in Japanese. *Journal of Psycholinguistic Research,* 31(4), 307–447.

Mohamed, A. H. & Omer, M. R. (1999) Syntax as a marker of rhetorical organization in written texts: Arabic and English. *IRAL,* 37(4), 291–305.

Mohammad, M. (2000) *Word order, agreement and pronominalization in standard and Palestinian Arabic.* Philadelphia, PA: John Benjamins Publishing Company.

Nasr, R. (1967) *Structure of Arabic: from sound to sentence.* Beirut: Librairie du Liban.

Ostler, S. (1987) English in parallels: a comparison of English and Arabic prose. In U. Conner & R. Kaplan (eds.), *Writing across languages: analysis of L2 text.* Reading, MA: Addison-Wesley.

Perfetti, C. (1991) Representations and awareness in the acquisition of reading competence. In L. Rieben and C. Perfetti (eds.), *Learning to read: basic research and its applications.* Hillsdale, NJ: Lawrence Earlbaum Associates.

Plunkett, B. (1993) The position of subjects in Modern Standard Arabic. In E. Mushira. & C. Holes (eds.), *Perspectives on Arabic linguistics V: papers from the Fifth Annual Symposium on Arabic Linguistics.* Amsterdam, The Netherlands: John Benjamins Publishing Company.

Plunkett, K. & Nakisa, R. (1997) A connectionist model of Arabic plural system. *Language and Cognitive Processes,* 12(5–6), 807–36.

Ryan, A. & Meara, P. (1991) The case of the invisible vowels: Arabic speakers reading English words. *Reading in a Foreign Language,* 7(2), 531–40.

Saiegh-Haddad, E. (2003) Linguistic distance and initial reading acquisition: the case of Arabic diglossia. *Applied Psycholinguistics,* 24, 3, 431–51.

Shimron, J. (1999) The role of vowel signs in Hebrew: beyond word recognition. *Reading and Writing,* 11(4), 301–19.

Shimron, J. & Sivan, T. (1994) Reading proficiency and orthography: evidence from Hebrew and English. *Language Learning,* 44(1), 5–27.

Siegel, L., Share, D., & Geva, H. (1995) Evidence for superior orthographic skills in dyslexics. *Psychological Science,* 6(4), 250–4.

Spratt, J. E., Seckinger, B., & Wagner, D. A. (1991) Functional literacy in Moroccan school children. *Reading Research Quarterly,* 26(2), 178–95.

Stanovich, K. & West, R. (1989) Exposure to print and orthographic processing. *Reading Research Quarterly,* 24, 402–33.

Taouk, M. & Coltheart, M. (2004) Learning to read in Arabic. *Reading and Writing,* 17, 27–57.

Wagner, D. A. (1993) *Literacy, culture, and development: becoming literate in Morocco*. New York, NY: Cambridge University Press.

Wagner, D. A. & Spratt, J. E. (1993) Arabic orthography and reading acquisition. In J. Altarriba (ed.), *Cognition and culture: a cross-cultural approach to cognitive psychology*. Advances in Psychology, 103. Amsterdam, Netherlands: North-Holland/Elsevier Science Publishers.

Wagner, D. A., Spratt, J. E., & Ezzaki, A. (1989) Does learning to read in a second language always put the child at a disadvantage? Some counterevidence from Morocco. *Applied Psycholinguistics*, 10(1), 31–48.

6 Learning to read Chinese

Cognitive consequences of cross-language and writing system differences

Min Wang and Chin-lung Yang

The Chinese language includes a number of varieties or dialects of the language. Mandarin, the most widely spoken Chinese language, forms the basis for Standard Mandarin, or Putonghua. Putonghua serves as the national lingua franca in China and is the official form of Chinese that is used as the language of instruction in schools in the People's Republic of China (PRC). As such, it is also a second language for the many speakers of Chinese dialects other than Mandarin. Therefore, the language described as Chinese in this chapter is Mandarin unless otherwise noted.

Chinese employs a logographic writing system (DeFrancis, 1989; Mattingly, 1992; Perfetti & Zhang, 1995) in which the basic grapheme is a character, a symbol that represents a morpheme. Each character maps onto a syllable that is a morpheme or word. Since the characters correspond to morphemes rather than the individual sounds of the spoken language, speakers of different Chinese languages may understand the script, even though the spoken languages are not mutually intelligible. Chinese is also a tonal language in which tones distinguish meaning. There are four tones in Mandarin (high-level, high-rising, falling-rising, and high falling); the number of tones varies by dialect.

Description of the language and its writing system

Characteristics of the Chinese orthography

Each Chinese character is composed of basic strokes, the smallest building materials for characters. There are 24 basic strokes, and sets of specified strokes are combined to form radicals, the basic components of Chinese characters. The combination of strokes must follow certain stroke-positional constraints, and random combinations of strokes that do not follow these constraints produce illegal radical forms.

According to the Chinese Radical Position Frequency Dictionary (1984), there are 541 radicals. Of these, many are themselves characters, that is, morphemes or words with unique pronunciations and meanings. For example, 子 has a meaning of "son," and is pronounced as /zi/3 (The number associated with the sound indicates the tone used). However, many other radicals (in fact, 238 radicals) are not independent characters. These radicals must be combined with other radicals to form characters, and they have no corresponding individual pronunciation associated with them.

Chinese characters can be classified into two categories based upon their structural complexity: single-component characters and multiple-component characters. Single-component characters are those that cannot be further divided into separate radicals. In other words, they comprise one radical; for example, 工, "work," pronounced as /gong/1. Compound characters are those that contain two or more radicals. An example of a compound character is 江, "river," pronounced as /jiang/1. More than 80 percent of Chinese characters are compound characters (Zhu, 1988).

The radicals in compound characters take specified positions within the character. For example, a two-radical character is normally configured into one of three structures, either left-right structure, top-bottom structure, or circular/semi-circular structure. Individual radicals have fixed, or legal, positions, requiring that a particular radical is always located in the same position, either left, right, top, or bottom, within any compound character. For example, the radical for "water" 氵 always occurs in the left position of the character, and appears in characters such as "river," "lake," "sea" and "stream" 江 湖 海 溪 (pronounced as /jiang/1, /hu/2, /hai/3, /xi/1, respectively). If this radical is written in the right position of a character, it violates its positional constraint, and creates an illegal character.

Individual radicals within a compound character can provide information on the meaning (semantic radical) or the pronunciation (phonetic radical) of the whole character. However, this correspondence between the radical and the whole character is not always transparent or reliable (e.g. Shu & Anderson, 1997; Shu, *et al.*, 2000). Also, the level of reliability differs for meaning versus sound relationships, and it differs for high frequency versus low-frequency compound characters (Shu & Anderson, 1999).

In the PRC, in recent years there have been efforts by the government to simplify the characters, and simplified forms have been created for many of the most common characters. There is now in use both a simplified orthography and a traditional orthography. The simplified orthography is used in the PRC while the traditional orthography is maintained in Taiwan and Hong Kong.

Characteristics of Chinese phonology

The phonological structure of spoken Chinese is relatively simple. The syllable is the basic speech unit of Chinese and there are four types of syllable structure: V (vowel), CV (consonant-vowel), VC (vowel-consonant), and CVC (consonant-vowel-consonant). Each syllable is traditionally divided into two parts: the onset and the rime. For example, /m/ is the onset and /a/ is the rime for the Chinese syllable /ma/. The onset of a Chinese syllable is always a single consonant, and for most syllables, the rime segments consist of vowels only. Only two consonants, /n/ and /ŋ/ (Siok & Fletcher, 2001) appear at the end of a rime in Mandarin. There are no consonant clusters in Chinese syllables and this is true for all Chinese dialects.

Given this relatively simple syllable structure, the Chinese language, including its various dialects, has a much smaller number of unique syllables than spoken English (Hanley *et al.*, 1999), resulting in a large number of homophones in spoken Chinese. The number of homophones is reduced somewhat by the use of tone in the language, since a change in the tone of a syllable indicates a change in meaning. For example, the syllable /ma/ with tone 1 means "mother," with tone 2 means "linen," with tone 3 means "horse," and with tone 4 means "blame." Tone in spoken Chinese is supra-segmental and is superimposed on words; more specifically, tones are attached to the rime of a word. The number of tones used in the Chinese language varies from one dialect to another. For instance, there are four tones in Mandarin (high-level, high-rising, falling-rising, and high falling), and nine tones in Cantonese (Hoosain, 1991).

Some compound characters include a phonetic radical that indicates the sound for the whole character; in other cases, the phonetic radical provides only partial information about the sound for the character. For example, the whole character may use the same syllable as indicated by the phonetic radical but may employ a different tone, or the whole character may share the same rime but have a different onset.

Characteristics of Chinese morphology

Written Chinese has two levels of morphological structure, the radical level and the compound character, or word, level (Shu & Anderson, 1997). At the first level, within an individual character, there are semantic components, referred to as semantic radicals, which provide information on the meaning of the whole character. There are about 200 semantic radicals in Chinese, and each is part of approximately 20 multiple-component, or compound, characters (characters that consist of more than one radical). In general, the mapping between the information provided by a semantic radical and the meaning of the whole character is more systematic and reliable than the mapping between a phonetic radical and the pronunciation of the whole character. Semantic radicals that provide reliable information relevant to the meaning of the whole character are referred to as "transparent semantic radicals." Cases in which the semantic radical does not indicate the meaning of the whole character occur more often for high-frequency characters than for low-frequency characters (Shu & Anderson, 1999). Many of the semantic radicals cannot stand alone as individual characters and therefore do not have pronunciations associated with them.

The second level of morphological structure is at the word level. For words that consist of two characters, each character represents an independent meaning that contributes to the meaning of the word. For example, the two-character word, 牛肉 "beef," is the result of the two separate meanings contributed by the characters 牛 "cattle" and 肉 "meat." Words that share a character share a similar meaning, as in for example, 牛奶 "cattle milk", 牛肉 "cattle meat", 牛油 "cattle oil".

Therefore, a single morpheme represented by a radical/character in Chinese can map onto multiple linguistic levels. Specifically, a single morpheme can be:

- A radical that is also a character (e.g. the single-component character, 木 "wood," /mu/4);
- A radical that is a component of a compound character (e.g. 树 "tree," /shu/4);
- An independent character that is a component of a multiple-character word (e.g. 木头 "wood," /mu/4 /tou/3); and,
- A radical of a character within a multiple-character word (e.g. 树丛 "forest", /shu/4 /cong/2).

Characters are combined to form multiple-character words through several principled ways. For example, one type of compounding is called syntactic compounding (e.g. 读书, "reading" consists of two characters, 读 "read" and 书 "book"). Another type of compounding is synonym compounding (e.g. 巨大, "very big," contains two synonymous characters, 巨 "huge" and 大 "big"). Antonym compounding combines two antonymous characters (e.g. 大小, "size" contains 大 "big" and 小 "small").

Chinese syntactic structure

At the morphosyntactic level, Chinese has a far simpler system compared to Indo-European languages. For example, there is no subject-verb agreement, or case marking or other grammatical inflections (Li & Thompson, 1981). As a result, Chinese words remain constant in form and do not generally undergo morphological transformation. However, there are several morphemes that signal such information as tense and plurality. For example, 了 (/le/) indicates "past action," and 着 (/zhe/), signifies "durative action." Thus, "walked" is represented in Chinese with the two-character word, 走了 (走 "walk" + 了 "past action"), while "walking" is denoted with 走着 (走 "walk" + 着 "durative action").

Similarly, plurality generally is not marked, and thus a word can be interpreted as either singular or plural. For example, 牛 (/niu/) can refer to either "cow" or "cows" in Chinese depending on the context. When plurality needs to be explicitly indicated, it is typically expressed by separate words such as 一些 (/yi xie/, "some"), or 许多 (/xu duo/, "many"). Thus, plurality marking in Chinese involves no morphological alteration within the word. However, Chinese does have plural forms for pronominal expressions, such as "I" and "he". These plural forms are created by combining the pronominal expression with a post-pronominal plural maker, 們 (/men/). Thus, "we" in Chinese is 我們 (/wo men/), which is a combination of 我 (/wo/, "I") and 們 (/men/, "plural marker"), and the third person plural is 他們 (/ta men/), which is formed by combining 他 (/ta/, "he") and 們 (/men/, "plural marker").

Without grammatical inflections providing information such as tense and number, the reader of Chinese must focus on the individual word meanings and their semantic relations in order to uncover the meaning of a sentence. Also, word boundaries are not marked in Chinese written texts since there is no space between words. The reader must examine the syntactic and semantic relations among neighboring characters in segmenting a character string into words (Hoosain, 1991). According to traditional linguistic analysis, listeners/readers of Chinese rely more upon semantic analysis of the constituent words in a sentence than upon structural mapping during sentence and discourse comprehension (Chao, 1968; Li & Thompson, 1981).

Traditional linguistic analysis also claims that Chinese listeners/readers use word order and pseudowords (a category of Chinese words, whose function is similar to that of prepositions) to retrieve syntactic information during sentence processing (Li & Thompson, 1981; Wang, 1955). This view further proposes that an important language-specific sentence/discourse property is the notion of Subject/Topic (Chao, 1968; Li & Thompson, 1981). Subject is a syntactic notion, and as such, it has a direct relationship with the verb; that is, the semantic scope of the subject is mostly constrained to its predicate within the sentence (Li & Thompson, 1981; Tsao, 1977). In contrast, topic is a discourse notion, characterizing what a sentence is about, but it does not necessarily have a direct relationship with the subsequent verb(s). Also, a topic, once set up, can extend across successive sentences to form a "topic chain" in the discourse.

Some aspects of linguistic analysis suggest that syntactic and semantic relations are parallel in English and Chinese. For example, in Chinese as in English, the sentence, /Gou yao ren/, 狗咬人, "Dog bites man" is different in meaning from /Ren yao gou, 人咬狗, "Man bites dog." In both Chinese and English, the syntactic and corresponding thematic mappings of the two sentences are quite distinct (Taylor & Taylor, 1995). In both languages, word order is important in determining these mappings. English is an SVO (subject-verb-object) language. Although word order is more flexible in Chinese than in English, the canonical word order in Chinese is also SVO. Because of this flexibility, the special markers 把/Ba/ and 被/Bei/ are required in sentences with non-SVO word order in Chinese (Sun & Givon, 1985).

In Chinese, non-canonical word orders occur often, especially in the spoken language. For example, the following sentences illustrate five distinct word orders to express "have written two letters." The constituent words that appear in common across all five of the sentences below are: 我 (/wo/, "I"), 寫完了 (寫 /xie/, "write" + 完了 /wan le/, "perfect past action"), and 兩封信 (兩 /liang/, "two" + 封信 /feng xin/, "letter").

(1)   我寫完了兩封信。
    Wo xie wan le liang feng xin.
    (I write complete two letter. SVO)

(2)   我把兩封信寫完了。
    Wo BA liang feng xin xie wan le.
    (I BA two letter write complete. SOV)

(3)   兩封信被我寫完了。
    Liang feng xin BEI wo xie wan le.
    (two letter BEI I write complete. OSV)

(4)   兩封信我寫完了。
    Liang feng xin wo xie wan le.
    (Two letter I write complete. OSV)

(5)   兩封信寫完了我。
    Liang feng xin xie wan le wo.
    (Two letter write complete I. OVS)

Sentence (1) represents the canonical word order SVO. Among the four non-canonical word orders in sentences (2) to (5), the two most common are the SOV with BA (把) construction shown in sentence (2) and the OSV with BEI (被) construction shown in sentence (3). In both of these constructions, the verb is placed after the object. The two syntactic markers, BA and BEI, signal different relationships between the semantic role and the syntactic role of the NPs they mark. More specifically, in sentence (2), the marker BA indicates that the subsequent NP (兩封信, "two letters") is the object both semantically and syntactically. In contrast, in sentence (3), the marker BEI indicates that the subsequent NP (兩封信 "two letter") is the object semantically, but the subject syntactically. Thus, the BEI construction is analogous to the passive voice in English. The other non-canonical word orders shown in sentences (4) and (5) are possible, but they are rarely used. They tend to occur more often in spoken Chinese and usually they are directly related to the topic-comment structure of the discourse. In this case, the initial NP (兩封信) would influence the interpretation of the sentences that follow in order to create a "topic chain" related to the theme of 兩封信.

In summary, the word order of Chinese sentences is quite flexible. Traditional linguists have argued that Chinese text comprehension is driven primarily by a semantically based process. They have thus contrasted the comprehension process in Chinese with the structural-mapping process used in comprehension of other languages, such as English, in which there is use of rigid word order and redundant morphosyntactic signals. Chinese is also described as a topic-prominent language, in which the notion of topic is important for processing sentences in a discourse efficiently. More detailed discussion of this notion is provided in the following section.

Chinese discourse structure

The comprehension of a discourse is not simply the adding together of the meanings of the constituent sentences. Rather, discourse comprehension entails building local and global coherence through a process in which the reader/listener is guided by information from various linguistic devices and by the structural organization of the discourse. Linguistic studies have indicated that discourse structure and referential overlap (anaphora) are two major elements in a coherent discourse. In this section, we will first discuss discourse structure within the theoretical frameworks offered by traditional linguistic analysis and by the discourse grammars put forward by psychologists. We will then briefly discuss the linguistic properties of referential overlap in Chinese discourse.

As noted above, linguistic analysis has suggested that Chinese is a topic-prominent language, in contrast to subject-prominent languages such as English. That is, in comprehending a text, Chinese readers tend to rely upon the semantic relationships among the constituent words in a sentence more than upon the structural mapping of these constituents. This reliance on semantic relationships is necessary given the very simple, impoverished morphosyntactic system and the use of flexible word order in Chinese.

The function of a topic is to set the semantic frame in a reader's memory representation; this frame serves to connect the extracted meanings of the sentences that follow. Thus, a topic, once set up, can extend to successive sentences that together form a "topic chain." This is in contrast to a subject, which is a syntactic entity and which has a scope that is far more limited than that of a topic. The meaning of a subject is predominantly related to the verb phrase within a single sentence. In topic-prominent Chinese, the sentence-initial noun phrase is not necessarily a subject; it can be a topic, a subject, or both, depending on the preceding context of the sentence. Therefore, linguists argue that the subject in a Chinese sentence tends to be determined semantically, rather than structurally. However, experimental research suggests otherwise.

Psycholinguistic studies examining how the referent of pronouns is detected have demonstrated that both the syntactic structure of a sentence and the sequential organization of sentences within a discourse influence comprehension of a local discourse segment in Chinese (Yang *et al.*, 1999; Yang *et al.*, 2003). Yang and his colleagues suggest that the syntactic and sequential structure of Chinese sentences plays a more important role than has been assumed, and that it guides the mapping of linguistic elements into mental representation. Other semantic factors (e.g. topic and pragmatics) are taken into account subsequently, as part of discourse-level processing during text comprehension.

The story grammars that have been developed to describe narrative texts in English (van den Broek, 1994) have been found to also account quite well for the basic components of Chinese narratives, that is, for components such as the setting, initial event, goal path, attempt, outcome, and ending. Despite this similarity, the story grammars do not capture certain traditional features of Chinese narratives. These include features such as the prominent presence of the storyteller's voice, the arrival of a moral exhortation, and the necessary resolution of conflicts at the end of the story. However, from the beginning of the twentieth century, Western influences on Chinese rhetoric have been introduced through the writings of pioneering authors and through translations of Western novels. As a result, the old way of telling a story has given way to newer forms and currently there are many more similarities than differences in the text structures of Chinese and English narratives.

Similarly, as in the case of narratives, the extensive Western influence has changed how Chinese expository texts are organized. Even so, Chinese and English differ in the linguistic devices used to build text coherence. Britton (1994) specifies four types of linguistic devices used to build coherence in English expository texts: overlap clues, syntactic prominence, given-new information sequence, and signaling phrases. Chinese and English texts can be compared and contrasted in terms of their use of these devices.

First, in Chinese a common overlap clue (anaphora, in particular) is repetition of the noun phrase. Since Chinese is a pro-drop language, omitting the second mention of the noun phrase is common when the sentence meaning can be constructed based on the context. In other words, subject anaphora can be omitted (zero-pronoun) providing that there is clear contextual information that can be used to resolve the identity of the intended referent (Huang, 1984; Li & Thompson, 1981, 1984; Tai, 1978). This requirement is important since, unlike other pro-drop languages such as Italian or Spanish, Chinese does not use morphosyntactic signals such as verb agreement and case marking to redundantly encode the information of the zero pronoun. Thus, it is commonly assumed that Chinese listeners and readers rely upon the preceding context and pragmatic knowledge in order to interpret zero pronouns, rather than upon the intrinsic meaning of the local sentence in which the zero pronoun appears (Chen, 1984; Li & Thompson, 1981, 1984).

Chinese also includes explicit subject anaphora (an overt pronoun). In spoken Chinese, the pronoun is encoded with information on number only; it does not encode information on gender, humanness, or animacy. For example, /ta/ can mean "he," "she," or "it" and /taman/ means "they" (Chao, 1968; Li & Thompson, 1981). However, in written Chinese, gender is distinguished in the written form of the character used to represent the pronouns. The male pronominal /ta/ is written as 他, a character in which the phonetic radical on the right indicates its pronunciation /ta/, and the semantic radical 人 /ren/ on the left denotes "person." In contrast, the female pronominal /ta/ is written as 她 which is composed of the same phonetic radical, but the semantic radical 女 /nu/ on the left indicates "female."

Second, syntactic prominence functions in a similar way in both English and Chinese. This has been shown in both linguistic analyses and in psycholinguistic research. Using Britton's example (1994), linguistic analysis of the title of a news story "The 1965 Air War in North Vietnam" shows that it is composed of one noun phrase with "war" as its head. Therefore, the syntactically most prominent word in the title is "war," which is also the topic of the text. Thus, in English, the modifiers of the head noun can either be placed in front of ("the 1965 Air") or after ("in North Vietnam") the head noun. Although Chinese is a modifier-modified structure language (Scollon *et al.*, 2000), wherein the head noun always appears at the end of the noun phrase, the phrase structure becomes similar to that of English when the modifier is too long. With a long modifier, the head noun can become buried and lose its prominence. Should this occur, Chinese can switch from the "modifier-modified" structure into a "head-predicate" structure to maintain a better given-new sequence chain. In psycholinguistic studies of the role of syntactic prominence in Chinese discourse comprehension, Yang and his colleagues (Yang *et al.*, 1999; Yang *et al.*, 2001; Yang *et al.*, 2003) have demonstrated that the syntactic prominence of a noun phrase affects the ease of retrieving the intended referent during the comprehension of subsequent text materials.

Third, the given-new structure seems to be a universal discourse feature across languages. As Britton (1994) points out, the canonical position of new information is typically closer to the end, rather than at the beginning of a sentence. The "subordinate-main" sequence (Scollon *et al.*, 2000), the prototypical structure of complex Chinese sentences, matches well with this kind of given-new information flow. Typically, the subordinate clause presents old information, while the new information is found in the main clause.

Fourth, signaling phrases that support discourse coherence are also generally similar in Chinese and English. However, some differences occur in the use of such phrases in Chinese that reflect the predominant subordinate-main structure of Chinese sentences. For example, adverbial connectives, such as "however" and "therefore," can always be used in the beginning of a new sentence or paragraph in English, but in Chinese, 可是 (/keshi/, "but"), 但是 (/danshi/, "but"), and 然而 (/ran'er/, "however") are rarely used in the beginning positions, probably because these call for the subordinate clause to precede. Similar constraints apply to 所以 (/su oyi/, "consequently," "accordingly"), 那麼 (/na me/, "therefore," "thus"), and other connectives which usually occur with their subordinate partners of 因為 (/yinwen/, "because"), and 如果 (/ruguo/, "if").

Metalinguistic and other requisite competencies in learning to read Chinese

Orthographic knowledge

In order to master the Chinese writing system, one must understand several basic aspects of the writing system. First, strokes have to be organized in precise ways to form correct graphic components of characters. Second, an individual character can often be divided into radicals. Children must be aware of the basic rules for combining these components in order to form correct characters. One of the basic rules is the positional rule. Each radical must appear in its designated position. For example, 扌 always occurs in the left position of a character, as in 打, 拍, 挑, and 拣 (meaning "hit," "pat," "choose" and "pick," pronounced /da/3, /pai/1, /tiao/1, /jian/3, respectively). The presence of this radical on the right side of the character would violate its positional constraint, and the character would be considered illegal. Thus Chinese learners need to internalize this and other basic rules so that they can detect orthographic violations. In addition, it is necessary to understand that distinct functions are assigned to different radicals. Semantic radicals in general appear in certain designated locations within a compound character, and so semantic radical locations are systematically related to their specific functions inside the whole character. Awareness of these requirements and skills in working with these are crucial to learning and remembering characters.

Grapho-phonological awareness

For a reader to process the phonological information of Chinese characters, he or she needs to be able to identify onset, rime, and tone in the character syllables. In addition, the reader must differentiate the onsets, rimes, and tones among different characters. In the PRC, initial literacy instruction includes use of an alphabetic system, Pinyin, to help children learn characters. The use of Pinyin fosters an awareness of the individual sounds that comprise syllables; thus, an intra-syllabic sensitivity is developed for monosyllabic characters. This sensitivity to the intra-syllabic structure promotes children's ability to segment individual characters.

Readers of Chinese must also recognize the information conveyed by individual radicals within a compound character, i.e. a character that includes multiple radicals. They must understand that some of the radicals within compound characters will provide phonological information, and that these phonetic radicals will normally occur on the right side of right-left formation characters (characters with two radicals side by side). Yet they must also be aware that the phonetic radicals do not always provide reliable information. Furthermore, the information provided by the phonetic radicals conforms with Mandarin (the school language), but not necessarily with the dialect spoken at home and/or in the community.

Grapho-morphological awareness

The requisite metalinguistic understanding underlying morphological processing in Chinese is that certain radicals may provide a clue to the meaning of individual characters. For example, the left or top radical in a compound character often provides semantic information, although it may not always be related to the meaning of the whole character. Even so, for many characters, those that share the same left or top (semantic) radical are generally semantically related. Similarly, multi-character words that share the same component character often share related meanings.

Sentence processing skills

In order to achieve adequate comprehension of a Chinese sentence, it is important for a learner to master those Chinese characters that carry morphosyntactic information such as number, tense, aspect and degree. The learner must also acquire knowledge of the constraints of different word orders and of the sentential transformations that allow the same meaning to be represented in different sentence structures. For example, children must learn that different word orders in Chinese can be used to derive the same meaning. They must also acquire the skills to appropriately interpret an initial noun phrase in a sentence as either a topic or subject, and to detect and process the topic-comment structure in a discourse for its appropriate semantic scope. Children also must acquire the skills to use/understand different kinds of referential expressions that highlight specific information embedded in the text, as well as to understand/be able to resolve the intended referents when there are missing noun phrases within a text.

Differences and similarities in learning to read in Chinese and English

As the above discussion has indicated, there are significant differences in learning to read in Chinese and English. First, as a holistic morpho-syllabic system, the Chinese orthography contrasts sharply with the linear structure of words in alphabetic languages. Second, the Chinese writing system contrasts with English in the print-to-speech mapping principle. The characters in Chinese do not map onto phonemes; instead, they map primarily onto morphemes or words. Third, Chinese phonology is distinct from English in its use of tone. Although onset and rime units are common to both Chinese and English, syllable structures are simpler in Chinese. For example, there are no initial consonant clusters in Chinese. Fourth, grammatical affixation (inflectional and derivational processes) plays a minor role in Chinese morphology. However, and last, semantic compounding is more prominent in Chinese than in English.

Based on these differences, learning to read in alphabetic English and logographic Chinese can vary in several major ways. First, English decoding involves systematic letter-to-phoneme mappings, whereas the lack of such sound-symbol systematicity in Chinese characters does not permit a similar type of mapping procedure. Second, in English, individual word-internal components in morphologically complex words (e.g. "uncreative") contribute collectively, though in varying degrees, to forming word meanings and therefore, morphological decomposition is integral to word identification. In contrast, in Chinese, a distinct function is assigned to each character-internal component, or radical. While the phonetic radical can provide a phonological code for the whole character, the semantic radical supplies information related, in one way or another, to the character's meaning. Efficiency in identifying the specific function assigned to each radical, therefore, greatly facilitates information extraction in Chinese character recognition. Third, since each letter in English carries a segment of speech sound, subsequent integration of letter segments is vital to phonological processing. In Chinese, however, both phonological and semantic information is associated holistically and independently with each character, both at the whole-character and radical levels. Chinese children, therefore, are required to attend to both whole-character and individual radical information, rather than conducting intraword segmentation and subsequent information integration.

Reading/information processing among skilled readers in Chinese as a first language

Word recognition skills

Until recently, phonological information was not considered to be an important element in reading in non-alphabetic languages such as Chinese. This view was based largely on the assumption that Chinese orthography is a "deep" orthography with little correspondence between sound and symbol. Learning to read Chinese or Japanese characters was thought to be primarily a product of visual memory and that learning to read involved the direct connection of orthographic units with semantic information in memory. However, there is now strong evidence for a generalized role of phonology not only in alphabetic languages but also in non-alphabetic writing systems such as Chinese. Studies have demonstrated that phonological processes not only play a role in recall and comprehension of sentences in Chinese (Hung & Tzeng, 1981; Tzeng *et al.*, 1977), but also in recognizing Chinese characters (e.g. Perfetti & Tan, 1998; Perfetti & Zhang, 1991, 1992, 1995; Seidenberg, 1985; Tan *et al.*, 1996). Findings from a number of experimental studies have demonstrated that there is early, rapid, and automatic phonological activation during visual Chinese character identification (e.g. Chua, 1999; Tan & Perfetti, 1998; see Perfetti *et al.*, in press for a detailed review). Research also has found that the phonetic components of compound characters are decomposed automatically and that phonological and semantic representations are both accessed by a reader when identifying a compound Chinese character (e.g. Zhou & Marslen-Wilson, 1999).

Compared to the relatively large volume of research on phonological processing involved in reading Chinese characters, there are only a limited number of studies to date that examine the role of morphological processing in Chinese word recognition. Feldman and Siok (1999a, 1999b) found that semantic transparency plays an important role in character identification. Semantic transparency refers to the extent to which the semantic radical contributes to the meaning of the whole character. A transparent semantic radical provides direct or indirect meaning information for the whole character, whereas an opaque radical has an inconsistent meaning relationship with the whole character. In Feldman and Siok's findings, transparent semantic radicals facilitated whole character identification, while opaque radicals inhibited character recognition. Zhou and Marslen-Wilson (1999) found similar results in a study of sublexical processing in Chinese, and their findings provide further support for the role of semantic radicals in Chinese word identification. In sum, the general consensus is that the semantic radical is decomposed from the whole character, and that its information is accessed while the whole character is being processed.

Sentence processing skills

Miao (1981) and Miao *et al.*, (1984) investigated Chinese speakers' reliance on word order versus word meaning in processing simple Chinese sentences. The results showed that the subjects predominantly assigned the agent to the animate noun in a sentence, regardless of its position, when sentences included only one animate noun. Also, when there was a conflict between word order and semantic information, semantic information was a stronger cue for Chinese native speakers. Thus, although Chinese speakers use both word order and semantic information for sentence understanding, they rely more heavily on semantic factors than on word order. Li *et al.* (1992; 1993) also claim that Chinese speakers predominantly rely on the use of word meaning in Chinese sentences. The observed sensitivity to the semantic information of the constituent words in a sentence can be attributed to features of Chinese morphosyntax, such as the fact that there are no inflections, and that there is a flexible word order.

Learning to read Chinese as a first language

Phonological processing skills

Research has shown that early phonological skills are useful in predicting accurate word recognition for Chinese children in primary grades (Ho & Bryant, 1997a, 1997b, 1997c; Hu & Catts, 1998; McBride-Chang & Ho, 2000; Shu, Anderson, & Wu, 2000). Ho and Bryant (1997a, 1997c) examined the development of phonological awareness and its relationship to later success in reading among Chinese children. In this research, they found that pre-reading phonological skills predicted a child's reading performance two and three years later, even after controlling for the effects of age, IQ, and the mother's education (Ho & Bryant, 1997c). The authors suggest that the main reason for this relationship is that phonological knowledge helps children to use the phonetic radicals in Chinese characters. Related to this finding, in more recent research, Anderson and his colleagues (Anderson *et al.*, 2003) have demonstrated that children in grades two and four are able to make use of the phonetic radical information in learning new characters. More specifically, the findings showed that the children were able to use the partial information provided in "tone-different" phonetic radicals, that is, radicals that share the same syllable (onset and rime) with the whole character but differ in tone. Also, to a limited degree, children were able to use the phonetic information in onset-different radicals, that is, radicals that share the same rime as the whole character but use a different onset, and thus represent a different syllable.

Hu and Catts (1993) found that young Chinese readers in grades two and three recognize phonologically similar characters less accurately than phonologically dissimilar ones. The phonological confusion effect varied with the degree of phonological similarity among the characters that were read. While characters with different rimes and different tones were recognized most accurately, characters with the same rimes but different tones were not recognized as well, and characters with the same rimes and same tones were the least recognized. These results suggest that Chinese characters are represented phonologically in working memory among beginning readers of Chinese. Furthermore, in other research, Chinese dyslexic children have been shown to have deficits in processing phonological information just like their counterparts who learn to read in alphabetic languages (Ho *et al.* 1998; So & Siegel, 1997). Interestingly, Ho and Ma (1999) have demonstrated that training in phonological skills is effective in helping Chinese children who have reading difficulties.

Ho and Bryant (1997a) found that Chinese children, like English-speaking children, initially detect relatively large sound segments (e.g. partial homophones, such as Chinese syllables that share the same onset and rime but have a different tone), and that they only gradually develop the ability to manipulate smaller units (e.g. to segment out rimes and tones within a syllable). More specifically, they found that Cantonese three-year-old children were not able to detect rime and tone separately but that five-year-olds were able to independently process rime and tone.

In the same study, cross-linguistic comparisons indicated that Chinese children develop an awareness of initial consonants and rimes later than do their English-speaking counterparts. The authors argued that differences in the oral and written language features of Chinese and English impact the children's rate of development of phonological awareness. For example, final consonants in English are more noticeable than they are in Chinese. Furthermore, learning to read Chinese does not encourage attention to the individual phonemes, including initial consonants in morphemes, whereas learning to read English does.

However, the role of phonology in reading Chinese characters is a controversial issue. The findings of at least two studies have indicated that phonology does not play a role in accessing character meaning. In one study (Chen *et al.*, 1995), the tasks involved single-component characters; in the second study (Zhou & Marslen-Wilson, 1996), the tasks involved words comprised of two characters. Based on their findings, the authors of the two studies conclude that graphic information plays an important role in processing Chinese characters. The findings in these studies suggest that reading for meaning is different in Chinese and English, given that phonology is less prevalent in the Chinese orthography. A more recent study by Chen and Shu (2001) provides further support for this view. Huang and Hanley (1994) showed that performance on a test involving visual paired-associate learning was significantly correlated with reading performance for young children in Hong Kong and Taiwan, but not for British children. In contrast, the reading performance of British children was predicted by their performance on phonological awareness tasks, even after controlling for the effects of IQ and vocabulary.

Despite the controversy surrounding the role of phonology in reading Chinese, some researchers believe that the important point is not whether phonology is useful in reading Chinese, but rather at what level phonological information is activated in reading Chinese. Perfetti and his colleagues have argued (see Perfetti *et al.*, in press; Kao *et al.*, 2002, for a detailed discussion), that in reading Chinese characters, phonological information is activated immediately after the whole character has been visually processed as a word rather than before the word has been recognized. Phonological processing in Chinese character recognition is reminiscent of Perfetti *et al.*'s (1992) idea of "at-lexical phonology." The characteristic of "at-lexical phonology" is that phonological information in Chinese becomes available at the word or lexical level, whereas phonological information in English word reading is available at the sub-word or letter/letter-cluster level. Thus, this concept characterizes the fundamental difference between the Chinese and English writing systems in terms of the timing of phonological involvement.

Morphological processing skills

Semantic radicals have been shown to play an important role in reading Chinese characters for skilled adult readers (e.g. Chen, 1993; Chen & Allport, 1995; Fang *et al.*, 1986; Seidenberg, 1985). Thus, it is important for children to acquire knowledge about the semantic radicals in order to learn new characters rapidly. Shu & Anderson (1997) showed that by grade three Chinese children who are good readers are able to use the information in semantic radicals to assist them in learning and remembering new characters, particularly when the characters are less frequent or less familiar. Chan and Nunes (1998) used a creative spelling task to test Chinese children's use of semantic and phonetic radicals to infer meaning and generate pronunciation of the character. The children were invited to help a Chinese boy create new characters to name unfamiliar objects. They were asked to select stroke patterns that represented either semantic or phonetic radicals. The results showed that children develop the understanding and ability to use semantic radicals earlier than they develop use of phonetic radicals. The findings also showed that in reading invented characters, children of six years of age were able to systematically employ the information provided by high frequency semantic radicals. In contrast, it was only starting at about age nine that the children were able to use the information provided by the phonetic radicals.

In a study with first- and fourth- grade Chinese monolingual children, Li *et al.* (2002) assessed phonological awareness and morphological awareness, and related these to reading ability in Chinese. While their findings showed that both phonological and morphological awareness were important, morphological awareness (measured, for example, by tests of radical awareness and lexical morpheme awareness) predicted more of the variance in Chinese reading performance. That is, morphological awareness was indicated to be the more important factor of the two in predicting Chinese reading.

Sentence processing skills

Research on the development of sentence processing skills in Chinese is limited to only a few studies. Chang (1986) examined early utterances of Chinese children. His findings show that children start to develop two-word utterances at about age two (Chang, 1986), and that they produce SV (subject + verb) two-word sentences earlier than OV (object + verb) sentences. Chang also examined the acquisition of the BA and BEI constructions. The BA construction, as described above, indicates that the noun phrase it marks is the object both thematically and syntactically. This construction was found to be easier for children to understand than the BEI construction, which marks a sentence structure similar to passive in English. Jeng (1991) showed that Chinese children were more likely than adults to use a word-order strategy in processing sentences when the syntax (word order) of the sentence contradicted the semantic information. Such findings suggest that syntactic properties drive the development of language processing skills and shape the strategies adopted in achieving sentence comprehension from a very early age.

Chang (1992) in other work found that even six-year-old Chinese children have substantial difficulty with many common classifiers. Classifiers are morphemes whose function is to mark lexical items as belonging to the same semantic class. Chinese requires the addition of appropriate classifiers when indicating number on nouns that represent tangible (countable) referents. For example, 個 /ge/ is commonly used to count concrete objects such as *a person* (一個人, /yi-ge-ren/, "a person"); 本 /ben/ is used to count books (一本書 /yi-ben-shu/, "a book"), and 隻 /zhi/ is commonly used to count animals (一隻狗 /yi-zhi-gou/, "a dog"). Chang's findings also showed that the rate of acquisition for classifiers depends on the type of classifier. For example, the most common Chinese classifier, the above-mentioned 個 /ge/, appears in the spontaneous speech of children at about two years of age and much earlier than other classifiers. Nevertheless, it is not clear what cognitive mechanisms underlie the differential acquisition for the different classifiers.

Learning to read in a second language

Transfer of phonological processing skills

As described above, Chinese phonological information is assigned holistically to a character whether that character is used independently as a single-component character, or as the phonetic radical in a compound character. Therefore phonological decoding in Chinese requires retrieving phonological information from the whole character, the phonetic radical, or both. In contrast, the basic unit of representation in English orthography is the phoneme. Readers of English need to obtain phonological codes through, first, intraword phonological segmentation and then through integration of the segmental phonological information. Thus, the fundamental differences in the basic units of representation in the logographic and alphabetic systems mandate qualitatively different phonological processing procedures. The critical questions are, first, whether processing skills developed to accommodate the first-language features transfer to second-language reading, and second, to what extent, and how, transferred skills contribute to the formation of second-language reading skills, particularly when the two languages are typologically different.

In one recent study, Wang *et al.* (2003) systematically investigated the effects of alphabetic and non-alphabetic first languages. They compared native Chinese and Korean college students (matched on English proficiency) who were learning to read English as a second language (ESL) to examine the learners' reliance on phonological and orthographic information in English word identification. First, in a semantic category judgment task, Wang *et al.* found that the Korean ESL learners made more false positive errors in judging the stimuli that were homophones to category exemplars than they did in judging spelling controls. However, there were no significant differences in responses across these two conditions for the Chinese ESL learners. On the other hand, Chinese ESL learners responded more accurately for stimuli that were less similar to category exemplars in spelling than for stimuli that were more similar.

The patterns of responses for the two groups suggest that the Chinese ESL learners relied less on phonological information and more on orthographic information when identifying English words than did their Korean counterparts. Further evidence supporting this argument was seen in a subsequent phoneme deletion task. In this task, Chinese subjects performed more poorly overall than their Korean counterparts and made more errors that were phonologically incorrect but orthographically acceptable. The authors suggested that the differences in the first language writing systems and transfer of first language reading skills may be responsible for these differences in performance for the two learner groups (see Wang *et al.*, 2004, for a detailed discussion).

Koda (1998) examined the effects of first-language processing experience on phonemic sensitivity, subsequent decoding skills, and reading comprehension among college-level ESL learners with contrasting first-language backgrounds: logographic Chinese and alphabetic Korean. Koda predicted that Korean ESL learners would perform better than Chinese ESL learners in both phonemic manipulation and decoding given Korean students' experience in intra-word phonological analysis in their first language. While the results showed little difference between the two groups in phonemic awareness, decoding, and reading comprehension, there were contrasting patterns found in the way phonemic awareness, decoding, and reading comprehension were related. For the Korean ESL learners, results on these three types of tasks were closely interconnected; however, no such direct relationships were found in the data for the Chinese ESL learners. Subsequent analyses showed that more than half of the reading comprehension variance among the Korean ESL learners was accounted for by phonemic awareness and decoding. In contrast, only 27 percent of the Chinese variance was explained by the same variables. These results suggest that first-language phonological processing experience may not necessarily be associated with quantitative differences in processing efficiency, but may lead to a strong preference for particular procedures for phonological processing in second-language reading. Thus, second-language visual input may be processed differently by second-language learners through the transfer of qualitatively different procedures. These findings also suggest that second-language processing competence is likely to emerge through different developmental paths among learners with typologically different first-language backgrounds.

Gottardo *et al.* (2001) studied Chinese-language children in Canada in grades one through eight and found that rhyme detection in Chinese was associated with English-reading skill and English phonological processing measures. Regression analyses on separate English and Chinese phonological processing variables indicated that each contributed unique variance to English reading. These findings were taken as showing that first language phonological processing skills can be applied to and influence second language reading performance, even when the first language is not alphabetic. However, it should be noted that the children in this study had been studying in English classrooms for varying periods of time; some had been born in Canada and had received all schooling in English, while others had been in Canada for shorter periods of time. A further study of these relationships between first and second language phonological processing should involve children with more limited exposure to English instruction.

Transfer of morphological processing skills

Cross-linguistic analyses of English and Chinese have indicated that the morphological structures of the two languages differ in several ways. English morphological formation involves an addition of affixes either before or after a base morpheme in a fairly systematic, linear, fashion. In contrast, Chinese character formation relies on a non-linear integration of character components whose primary function is to provide either phonological or semantic information for a whole character. The contrasting nature of Chinese and English morphological structures provides a window for examining reading skill transfer among second-language learners.

Koda (1999, 2000) examined the specific ways in which first-language processing experience influences second-language morphological awareness among second-language learners of English with Korean and Chinese first-language backgrounds. Since morphological processing in Korean and English are similar, it was predicted that Korean ESL learners would show overall better performance compared to the Chinese. That is, the Chinese ESL learners were expected to be less sensitive to the internal morphological structure of English words, and also less adept at morphological analysis. The data showed that, although the two groups were similar in processing structurally salient words, the Korean ESL learners were far superior to the Chinese learners in morphological analysis of structurally less salient words. These findings suggest that first-language processing experience influences the development of some, but not all, aspects of second-language morphological awareness. Of note is the fact that a salience effect was found in the data. This finding indicates that other factors, such as experience in processing the second language, also play an important role in shaping second-language processing competence, and that emerging second-language processing competence cannot be adequately described in terms of either first-language or second-language factors alone. Rather, it should be conceptualized as resulting from complex interactions of a learner's experiences in processing both the first and the second language data.

In research on spelling performance in English as a second language by Chinese (Cantonese) children, Wang and Geva (2003) examined the implications of the logographic nature of the Chinese writing system. Their results showed that even for children whose exposure to Chinese literacy was limited to heritage schools and thus far below that of peers educated in China, effects of learning to read in their first language were found. Specifically, a strong facilitation effect for processing whole-word information and poorer performance on pseudo-word spelling was observed for the Chinese ESL learners as compared to English first-language children. In addition, the difference between pseudo-word and real-word spelling performance was much greater for the Chinese children. These findings demonstrated that visual processing skill, which has been shown in other research to be important for literacy learning in Chinese, can be applied to second language learning of English, an alphabetic language. However, the authors also noted that the Chinese children had had only limited exposure to English at the time of assessment, and this also may have played a role in their performance.

Transfer of morphosyntactic skills

Variations between English and Chinese in the lexical processing skills required might be expected given the functional and structural differences of the two languages, particularly with regard to the basic word formation rule. In English, the combination of individual morphological components constructs the meaning of a morphologically complex word. In principle, therefore, inferring the meaning of an unknown word is possible through integrating the meanings of its morphological constituents. In contrast, in Chinese, the semantic radical provides an indication of a character's meaning, but does not completely provide the full meaning. The semantic radical information is generally limited to the semantic category (e.g. female, plant, tree) or a physical attribute of the referent of a character (e.g. something metallic, something made out of thread), and thus it is very unlikely that a reader will be able to determine a character's full meaning by relying only on the information provided by the semantic radical.

The fact that Chinese has a large number of multiple-character words makes determining the meaning of such words more complicated than just a simple summation of each character's meaning. This is especially true for multiple-character words that express abstract meanings. Quite often, a component character's meaning may not be fully reflected in the meaning of the word of which the character is a part. A competent reader of Chinese must integrate the semantic information derived from the radical within the character and from the character itself together with other sources of information, such as neighboring characters and sentential context, in order to determine the contribution of each character to the meaning of the full compound word. The metalinguistic competence of a Chinese reader is shaped by the properties of the Chinese writing system, and this meta-linguistic competence is likely to influence the way the Chinese reader will process reading in a second language.

Several studies (Koda, 2000; Mori & Nagy, 1999; Su, 2001) have been conducted to investigate how Chinese ESL learners utilize their first language morphological processing strategies in comprehending second language sentences. For example, Su (2001) examined the effect of the context on sentence processing, using the Competition Model framework. The data first demonstrated that Chinese monolinguals compared to English mono-linguals depend more heavily on contextual information in processing sentences. Su further investigated learners' use of contextual cues in processing sentences in their second languages, comparing Chinese learners of English, and English learners of Chinese. In the sentence processing tasks, Chinese learners of English relied on the sentential context to a greater extent than did the English learners of Chinese. This finding implies that Chinese learners transferred their first-language sentence comprehension skills to process-ing English as a second language. That is, the Chinese learners tended primarily to use word order information and contextual cues in processing English sentences.

Such language transfer phenomena also apply to other language learning tasks as well. Koda (2000) predicted that Chinese ESL learners compared to Korean ESL learners would be more efficient in integrating both word-internal (morphological) information and word-external (contextual) information, given the differences in first language experience for the two groups. The findings confirmed this predicted difference between Chinese and Korean ESL learners

Social/cultural factors affecting Chinese literacy development

Literacy instruction in schools

Strategies for teaching reading vary from one area to another in the Chinese education system. In the PRC, children learn Pinyin during the first ten weeks of the first grade (at six to seven years of age) before beginning to read and write Chinese characters (Shu & Anderson, 1997; Shu *et al.*, 2000). Pinyin is a Roman alphabetic system in which the letters correspond to phonemes. First, the teachers teach vowels (/a/, /o/, /e/) and consonants (/b/, /p/, /m/, /f/) separately, and then they teach how to combine consonants and vowels. Children are given ample practice in combining onsets and rimes to form meaningful syllables. The Pinyin are used in early reading instruction to assist children in learning new characters. Usually, the Pinyin appears above characters in a text. Children also learn the symbols for the four tones used in Mandarin, and these symbols are always indicated above the rime of the Pinyin. Children are taught to read single-component characters before they begin to learn multiple-component characters.

The instructional approach in Taiwan is similar to that of the PRC. Children in Taiwan learn a separate non-Roman phonetic script known as Zhu-Yin-Fu-Hao during the first ten weeks of the first grade, before any instruction in reading and writing of Chinese characters is introduced (see Hanley *et al.*, 1999, for a review).

In contrast to literacy instruction in the PRC and Taiwan, in Hong Kong, there is no separate phonetic system used to aid children in learning to read Chinese. Children are taught by a whole character approach and rote-learning strategies (Ho & Bryant, 1997a, 1997b). Typically, the teacher reads a new character aloud and explains the meaning, and then the children learn the character through copying and memorization.

Different instructional approaches for teaching reading in Chinese have been shown to differentially affect the readers' phonological processing skills. Chinese readers who are experienced with Pinyin are more successful in manipulating speech sounds than those who learned Chinese characters without any phonetic aids (e.g. Cheung *et al.*, 2001; Read *et al.*, 1986). Children in Taiwan show significant improvement in phonological aware-ness after being taught the Zhu-Yin-Fu-Hao phonetic script (e.g. Huang & Hanley, 1997). Similarly, children from the PRC who have learned Pinyin have been shown to have higher performance on tests of phonological awareness than Hong Kong children, who learn characters without a phonetic script system (Cheung *et al.*, 2001).

With regard to the internal structure of characters, Anderson *et al.* (2003) note that typically teachers do not teach children about the role of the phon-etic radical, and suggest that this may be due to the fact that in a large number of cases it is unreliable. However, the researchers' findings regarding the use of phonetic information in learning new characters by children in grades two and four leads them to suggest that there may be a benefit for average- and low-performing students if the partial information available in characters were to be directly pointed out to them.

Whole class instruction is dominant in China in contrast to the often more individualized instruction in North America. There are about 40 to 50 stu-dents in each class, seated at immobile desks that are arranged in long col-umns with the teacher's desk in front. This whole-class instructional approach does not provide teachers with much opportunity to accom-modate individual differences in learning to read. Teachers follow the text-books strictly, and the same textbooks are used nationwide; there has been only one version of the primary textbooks for many years. Thus, instructional approaches are consistent across the entire country, including in rural and urban, public and private schools.

Literacy support at home

Chinese have a long tradition of valuing education and literacy. Schooling at the elementary and junior high levels is mandatory in the PRC and parents place a very high value on their children's academic achievement. Environmental print exposure is abundant in China. The numerous bookstores and libraries are popular places for people to spend their leisure time, and children's books constitute a prominent section in bookstores and libraries.

As Shu *et al.* (2002) have noted, parents spend more than 20 percent of the family income on their children's education-related activities and materials, including books, magazines, and other extra-curricular materials. The study found that the home literacy environment played an important role in learning to read in Chinese. Considering three major parameters of the home literacy environment, parent-child literacy-related activities, children's literacy-related activities, and parents' education, all three were shown to contribute significantly to children's reading proficiency as early as fourth grade. Many Chinese parents engage their children in reading and writing exercises well before formal schooling begins. However, these literacy activities at home typically involve a heavy reliance on drill and memorization without much instruction on comprehension of the materials.

Home–school language mismatch

There are many dialects of Chinese, including Mandarin, Cantonese, Xiang, and Min, among others. However, all Chinese who are literate use the same writing system, regardless of their spoken dialect. This is the case even though most of the dialects are mutually unintelligible. In the PRC, most children learn to speak, read, and write Mandarin from the first grade. Learning to map newly learned spoken Mandarin elements onto characters is a challenge for those children who are non-native Mandarin dialect speakers. However, there are apparently no studies that focus on this issue for Chinese learners. Anderson *et al.* (2003) noted that children from Guangzhou, who learn Mandarin as a second language, were less able to use phonetic information to learn the pronunciation of characters than were first-language Mandarin speakers from Beijing. Clearly, further research is needed in this area.

Summary and conclusions

The Chinese language and writing system differ in many ways from other languages in the world. These cross-language and orthography contrasts have a significant impact on learning to read in English as a second language for native speakers of Chinese. In this chapter, we first presented linguistic analyses of the Chinese language including its phonology, orthography, morphology, syntax, and discourse. We summarized the metalinguistic

competences required in learning to read Chinese. We then reviewed literature on reading Chinese by adult skilled Chinese readers and by young
native Chinese children. Studies on how Chinese readers learn to read in
English as a second language were also reviewed. Last but not least, we
discussed social/cultural factors influencing Chinese literacy acquisition
including literacy instruction in schools, literacy support at home, and differences between the dialects used at home and the language used at school.
Taken together, we emphasized the cross language and orthography differences between Chinese and other languages. We argued that these differences are responsible for the distinct cognitive processes observed for native
Chinese learners in reading and learning to read in Chinese, as well as in
learning to read in English as a second language.

Note

We appreciate the contribution from Hisae Fujiwara in writing the literature review
of second language studies and Ran Zhao in writing the section on discourse.

References

Adams, M. J. (1990) *Beginning to read*. Cambridge, MA: MIT Press.

Anderson, R. C., Li, W., Ku, Y.-M., Shu, H. & Wu, N. (2003) Use of partial information in learning to read Chinese characters. *Journal of Experimental Psychology*,
95(1), 52–7.

Bates, E. & MacWhinney, B. (1989) Functionalism and the competition model. In
B. MacWhinney & E. Bates (eds.), *The crosslinguistic study of sentence processing* (pp. 3–73). Cambridge, UK: Cambridge University Press.

Britton, Bruce K. (1994) Understanding expository text: building mental structures
to induce insights. In M. A. Gernsbacher, (ed.), *Handbook of psycholinguistics*
(pp. 641–74). San Diego: Academic Press.

Chan, L. & Nunes, T. (1998) Children's understanding of the formal and functional
characteristics of written Chinese. *Applied Psycholinguistics*, 19(1), 115–31.

Chang, H. W. (1986) Young children's comprehension of the Chinese passive. In
H. Kao & R. Hoosain (eds.), *Linguistics, psychology, and the Chinese language*.
Hong Kong: University of Hong Kong Press.

Chang, H. W. (1992) The acquisition of Chinese syntax. In H. C. Chen & O. J.
L.Tzeng (eds.), *Language processing in Chinese*. North-Holland: Elsevier Science
Publishers.

Chao, Y. R. (1968) *A grammar of spoken Chinese*. Berkeley: University of California
Press.

Chen, H. C. & Shu, H. (2001) Lexical activation during the recognition of Chinese
characters: evidence against early phonological activation. *Psychonomic Bulletin
and Review*, 8(3), 511–18.

Chen, P. (1984) *Discourse analysis of third-person zero anaphora in Chinese*. Bloom-
ington, Indiana: Indiana University Linguistics Club.

Chen, Y.-P. (1993) Word recognition and reading in Chinese. Unpublished doctoral
dissertation, University of Oxford.

Chen, Y.-P. & Allport, A. (1995) Attention and lexical decomposition in Chinese word recognition: conjunctions of form and position guide selective attention. *Visual Cognition*, 2, 235–68.

Chen, H. C., Flores d'Arcais, G.B., & Cheung, S. L. (1995) Orthographic and phonological activation in recognizing Chinese characters. *Psychological Research/Psychologische Forschung*, 58(2), 144–53.

Cheung, H., Chen, H-C., Lai, C. Y., Wong, O. C., and Hills, M. (2001) The development of phonological awareness: effects of spoken language experience and orthography. *Cognition*, 81, 227–41.

Chua, F. K. (1999) Phonological recoding in Chinese logograph recognition. *Journal of Experimental Psychology: Learning, Memory, and Cognition*, 25, 876–91.

DeFrancis, J. (1989) *Visible speech: the diverse oneness of writing system*. Honolulu: Univeristy of Hawaii.

Fang, S.-P., Horng, R.-Y., & Tzeng, O. J. L. (1986) Consistency effects in the Chinese character and pseudo-character naming task. In H. S. R. Kao & R. Hoosain (eds.), *Linguistics, psychology, and the Chinese character*. Hong Kong: Center of Asian Studies, University of Hong Kong.

Feldman, L. B. & Siok, W. W. T. (1999a) Semantic radicals contribute to the visual identification of Chinese characters. *Journal of Memory and Language*, 40(4), 559–76.

Feldman, L. B. & Siok, W. W. T. (1999b) Semantic radicals in phonetic compounds: implications for visual character recognition in Chinese. In J. Wang, A. W. & H. C. Chen (eds.), *Reading Chinese script: a cognitive analysis* (pp. 19–35). Mahwah, NJ: Lawrence Erlbaum Associates Inc.

Gottardo, A., Yan, B., Siegel, L. S., & Wade-Woolley, L. (2001) Factors related to reading performance in children with Chinese as a first language: more evidence of cross-language transfer of phonological processing. *Journal of Educational Psychology*, 93(1), 530–42.

Hanley, J. R., Tzeng, O., & Huang, H.-S. (1999) Learning to read Chinese. In M. Harris & G. Hatano (eds.), *Learning to read and write: a cross-linguistic perspective*. Cambridge, UK: Cambridge University Press.

Ho, C. S.-H. & Bryant, P. (1997a) Development of phonological awareness of Chinese children in Hong Kong. *Journal of Psycholinguistic Research*, 26, 109–26.

Ho, C. S.-H. & Bryant, P. (1997b) Learning to read Chinese beyond the logographic phase. *Reading Research Quarterly*, 32, 276–89.

Ho, C. S.-H. & Bryant, P. (1997c) Phonological skills are important in learning to read Chinese. *Developmental Psychology*, 33, 946–51.

Ho, C. S.-H. & Ma, R. N. L (1999) Training in phonological strategies improves Chinese dyslexic children's character reading skills. *Journal of Research in Reading*, 22(2), 131–42.

Ho, C. S.-H., Law, T. P.-S., & Ng, P. M. (1998) The phonological deficit hypothesis in Chinese developmental dyslexia. *Reading and Writing: An Interdisciplinary Journal*, 10, 1–23.

Hoosain, R. (1991) *Psycholinguistic implications for linguistic relativity: a case study of Chinese*. Hillside, NJ: Erlbaum.

Hu, C.-F. & Catts, H. W. (1993) Phonological recoding as a universal process? Evidence from beginning readers of Chinese. *Reading and Writing: An Interdisciplinary Journal*, 5, 325–37.

Hu, C.-F. & Catts, H. W. (1998) The role of phonological processing in early reading ability: what we can learn from Chinese. *Scientific Studies of Reading*, 2(1), 55–79.

Huang, C.-T. J. (1984) On the distribution and reference of empty pronouns. *Linguistic Inquiry*, 15, 531–74.

Huang, H. & Hanley, R. (1994) Phonological awareness and visual skills in learning to read Chinese and English. *Cognition*, 54, 73–98.

Huang, H. & Hanley, R. (1997) A longitudinal study of phonological awareness, visual skills and Chinese reading acquisition among first-graders in Taiwan. *International Journal of Behavioral Development*, 20, 249–68.

Hung, D. L. & Tzeng, O. J. (1981) Orthographic variations and visual information processing. *Psychological Bulletin*, 90(3), 377–414.

Jeng, L. Y. (1991) Young children's comprehension of canonical Mandarin sentence. *Chinese Journal of Psychology* (in Chinese).

Kao, H. S. R., Leong, C. K., & Gao, D. G. (2002) *Cognitive neuroscience studies of the Chinese language*. Hong Kong: Hong Kong University Press.

Kilborn, K. & Ito, T. (1989) Sentence processing strategies in adult bilinguals. In B. MacWhinney & E. Bates (eds.), *The crosslinguistic study of sentence processing* (pp. 257–95). Cambridge, UK: Cambridge University Press.

Koda, K. (1989) Effects of L1 orthographic representation on L2 phonological coding strategies. *Journal of Psycholinguistic Research*, 18, 201–22.

Koda, K. (1990) The use of L1 reading strategies in L2 reading. *Studies in Second Language Acquisition*, 12, 393–410.

Koda, K. (1998) The role of phonemic awareness in second language reading. *Second Language Research*, 14(2), 194–216.

Koda, K. (1999) Development of L2 intraword orthographic sensitivity and decoding skills. *Modern Language Journal*, 83(1), 51–64.

Koda, K. (2000) Cross-linguistic variations in L2 morphological awareness. *Applied Psycholinguistics*, 21(3), 297–320.

Li, C. N. & Thompson, S. A. (1981) *Mandarin Chinese: a functional reference grammar*. California: University of California Press.

Li, C. N. & Thompson, S. A. (1984) Third person pronouns in zero-anaphora in Chinese discourse. In T. Givon (ed.), *Discourse and syntax* (pp. 311–35). New York: Academic Press.

Li, P., Bates, E., & MacWhinney, B. (1993) Processing a language without inflections: a reaction time study of sentence interpretation in Chinese. *Journal of Memory and Language*, 32(2), 169–92.

Li, P., Bates, E., Liu, H., & MacWhinney, B. (1992) Cues as functional constraints on sentence processing in Chinese. In H. C. Chen & O. J. L. E. Tzeng (eds.), *Language processing in Chinese*. Amsterdam: North-Holland.

Li, W., Anderson, R. C., Nagy, W., & Zhang, H. (2002) Facets of metalinguistic awareness that contribute to Chinese literacy. In W. Li, J. Gaffney, & J. Packard (eds.), *Chinese children's reading acquisition: theoretical and pedagogical issues*. Boston: Kluwer Academic, pp. 87–106.

MacWhinney B., Bates, E. & Kliegl, R. (1984) Cue validity and sentence interpretation in English, German, and Italian. *Journal of Verbal Learning & Verbal Behavior*, 23(2), 127–50.

Mattingly, I. G. (1992) Linguistic awareness and orthographic form. In R. Frost & L. Katz (eds.), *Orthography, phonology, morphology, and meaning* (pp. 11–26). Amsterdam: Elsevier Science Publishers.

McBride-Chang, C., & Ho, C. S.-H. (2000) Developmental issues in Chinese children's character acquisition. *Journal of Educational Psychology*, 92(1), 50–5.

Miao, X. C. (1981) Word order and semantic strategies in Chinese sentence comprehension. *International Journal of Psycholinguistics*, 8, 109–22.

Miao, X. C., Chen, G. P., & Ying, H. C. (1984) Reexamination of the roles of word order and lexical meaning in Chinese sentence comprehension. *Report of Psychological Science* (in Chinese), 6, 1–7.

Mori, Y. & Nagy, W. E. (1999) Integration of information from context and word elements in interpreting novel kanji compounds. *Reading Research Quarterly*, 34(1), 80–101.

Muljani, D., Koda, K., & Moates, D. (1998) Development of L2 word recognition. *Applied Psycholinguistics*, 19(1) 99–113.

Perfetti, C. A. (1985) *Reading ability*. New York: Oxford University Press.

Perfetti, C. A. & Zhang, S. (1991) Phonological processes in reading Chinese characters. *Journal of Experimental Psychology*, 17, 633–43.

Perfetti, C. A. & Zhang, S. (1995) Very early phonological activation in Chinese reading. *Journal of Experimental Psychology: Learning, Memory, and Cognition*, 21, 24–33.

Perfetti, C. A. & Tan, L. H. (1998) The time course of graphic, phonological, and semantic activation in Chinese character identification. *Journal of Experimental Psychology: Learning, Memory, and Cognition*, 24(1), 101–18.

Perfetti, C. A., Zhang, S., & Berent, I. (1992) Reading in English and Chinese: evidence for a "universal" phonological principle. In R. Frost & L. Katz (eds.), *Orthography, phonology, morphology, and meaning* (pp. 227–48). Amsterdam: North-Holland.

Perfetti, C., Liu, Y., & Tan, L.-H. (2002) How the mind meets the brain in reading: a comparative writing systems approach. In H. S. R. Kao, C. K. Leong, & D. G. Gao (eds.), *Cognitive neuroscience studies of the Chinese language*. Hong Kong: Hong Kong University Press.

Perfetti, C. A., Liu, Y., & Tan, L. H. (2005) The lexical constituency model: Some implications of research on Chinese for general theories of reading. *Psychological Review*, 112(1), 43–59.

Read, C., Zhang, Y.-F., Nie, H.-Y., & Dmg, B.-Q. (1986) The ability to manipulate speech sounds depends on knowing alphabetic writing. *Cognition*, 24, 31–44.

Seidenberg, M. S. (1985) The time course of phonological code activation in two writing systems. *Cognition*, 19, 1–30.

Scollon, R., Scollon, S. W., & Kirkpatrick, A. 2000 *Contrastive discourse in Chinese and English*. Beijing: Foreign Languages Teaching and Research Press.

Shu, H. & Anderson, R. C. (1997) Role of radical awareness in the character and word acquisition of Chinese children. *Reading Research Quarterly*, 32(1), 78–89.

Shu, H. & Anderson, R. C. (1999) Learning to read Chinese: the development of metalinguistic awareness. In J. Wang, A. W. Inhoff, & H. C. Chen (eds.), *Reading Chinese script: a cognitive analysis* (pp. 1–18). Mahwah, NJ: Lawrence Erlbaum Associates.

Shu, H., Anderson, R. C., & Wu, N. N. (2000) Phonetic awareness: knowledge of orthography–phonology relationships in the character acquisition of Chinese children. *Journal of Educational Psychology*, 92(1), 56–62.

Shu, H., Li, W-L., Anderson, R., Ku, Y-M., & Yue, X. (2002) The role of home-literacy environment in learning to read Chinese. In W. Li, J. S. Gaffney, & J. L.

Packard. (eds.), *Chinese children's reading acquisition: theoretical and peda-gogical issues*. Norwell, MA: Kluwer Academic Publishers.

Siok, W. T. & Fletcher, P. (2001) The role of phonological awareness and visual-orthographic skills in Chinese reading acquisition. *Developmental Psychology*, 37(6), 886–99.

Siu, P. K. (1986) Understanding Chinese prose: effects of number of ideas, metaphor, and advance organizer on comprehension. *Journal of Educational Psychology* 78(6): 417–23.

So, D. & Siegel, L. S. (1997) Learning to read Chinese: semantic, syntactic, phono-logical and working memory skills in normally achieving and poor Chinese readers. *Reading and Writing: An Interdisciplinary Journal*, 9, 1–21.

Su, I. R. (2001) Transfer of sentence processing strategies: a comparison of L2 learn-ers of Chinese and English. *Applied Psycholinguistics*, 22(1), 83–112.

Sun, C. & Givon, T. (1985) On the so-called SOV word order in Mandarin Chinese: a quantified text study and its implications. *Language*, 61, 329–51.

Tai, James H-Y. (1978) Anaphoric constraints in Mandarin Chinese narrative dis-course. In J. Hinds (ed.), *Anaphora in discourse*. Edmonton, Alberta, Canada: Linguistic Research Inc.

Tan, L.-H. & Perfetti, C. (1998) Phonological codes as early sources of constraint in Chinese word identification: a review of current discoveries and theoretical accounts. *Reading and Writing: An Interdisciplinary Journal*, 10, 105–200.

Tan, L.-H., Hoosain, R., & Soik, W. W. T. (1996) Activation of phonological codes before access to character meaning in written Chinese. *Journal of Experimental Psychology: Learning, Memory, and Cognition*, 22, 865–82.

Taylor, I., & Taylor, M. M. (1995) *Writing and literacy in Chinese, Korean, and Japanese*. Philadelphia: John Benjamins.

Tsao, F. (1977) A functional study of topic in Chinese: the first step toward discourse analysis. Doctoral dissertation, USC, Los Angeles, California.

Tzeng, O. J., Hung, D. L., & Wang, W. S. Y. (1977) Speech recoding in reading Chinese characters. *Journal of Experimental Psychology: Human Learning and Memory*, 3(6), 621–30.

van den Broek, P. (1994). Comprehension and memory of narrative texts: Inferences and coherence. In M. A. Gernsbacher, (ed.), *Handbook of psycholinguistics*, (pp. 539–88). San Diego: Academic Press.

Vellutino, F. R. & Scanlon D. M. (1991) The preeminence of phonologically based skills in learning to read. In: S. A. Brady & D. P. Shankweiler (eds.), *Phonological processes in literacy: a tribute to Isabelle Y. Liberman*, (pp. 237–52). Hillsdale, NJ, England: Lawrence Erlbaum Associates.

Wang, L. (1955) *Zhongguo yufa lilun (theories of Chinese grammar)*. Shanghai: Commercial Press.

Wang, M. & Geva, E. (2003) Spelling performance of Chinese children using English as a second language: lexical and visual-orthographic processes. *Applied Psycholinguistics*, 24, 1–25.

Wang, M., Koda, K., & Perfetti, C. A. (2003) Alphabetic and non-alphabetic L1 effects in English word identification: a comparison of Korean and Chinese English L2 learners. *Cognition*, 87, 129–49.

Wang, M., Koda, K., & Perfetti, C. A. (2004) Language and writing systems are both important in learning to read: a reply to Yamada. *Cognition*, 93, 133–37.

Yang, C.-L., Gordon, P. C., Hendrick, R., & Wu, J. T. (1999) Comprehension of referring expressions in Chinese. *Language and Cognitive Processes*, 14, 715–43.

Yang, C.-L., Gordon, P. C., Hendrick, R., & Hue, C. W. (2003) Constraining the comprehension of pronominal expressions in Chinese. *Cognition*, 86, 283–315.

Yang, C.-L., Gordon, P. C., Hendrick, R., Wu, J. T., & Chou, T. L. (2001) The processing of co-reference for reduced expressions in discourse integration. *Journal of Pycholinguistic Research*, 30, 21–35.

Zhang, H. & Hoosain, R. (2001) The influence of narrative text characteristics on thematic inference during reading. *Journal of Research in Reading* 24(2): 173–86.

Zhou, X. & Marslen-Wilson, W. (1996) Direct visual access is the only way to access the Chinese mental lexicon. In G. Cottrell (ed.), *Proceedings of 18th Annual Conference of the Cognitive Science Society* (pp. 714–19). Hillsdale, NJ: Lawrence Erlbaum Associates.

Zhou, X. & Marslen Wilson, W. (1999) The nature of sublexical processing in reading Chinese characters. *Journal of Experimental Psychology: Learning, Memory, and Cognition*, 25(4), 819–37.

Zhu, X. (1988) Analysis of the cuing function of the phonetic in modern Chinese. *Proceedings of the Symposium on Chinese Language and Character*. Beijing: Guang Ming Daily Press (in Chinese).

7 Facets of metalinguistic awareness related to reading development in Hebrew

Evidence from monolingual and bilingual children [1]

Esther Geva

Introduction

It has been argued that readers of different languages face different cognitive and metalinguistic demands when they read and write, and that these differences are motivated by typological differences in orthographic and language features (Akamatsu, 1999; Feldman, 1987; Frost, 2005; Geva & Siegel, 2000; Koda, 1999; Leong & Tamaoka, 1998; Oney *et al.*, 1997; Saiegh-Haddad & Geva, in press; Seymour *et al.*, 2003; Shimron, 1993; 2006; Taylor & Taylor, 1983; Wang & Koda, 2005). The "orthographic depth hypothesis" (Feldman, 1987; Katz & Frost, 1992) has been used as a framework for discussing cross-orthography similarities and differences in word recognition processes. Researchers have argued that pre-lexical phonology plays a more important role in lexical access in "shallow" or "transparent" orthographies such as Spanish or voweled Hebrew, in which there is a direct and consistent grapheme to phoneme correspondence, than in orthographies such as English, where the mapping of graphemes to phonemes is more opaque or "deep." In languages that are orthographically transparent, the lexical outcome of assembling a series of matched graphemes-phonemes into words is unequivocal. Developmental studies have shown that individuals rely also on other orthographic, visual, and linguistic information sources to achieve accurate and quick lexical access in word recognition (Breznitz, 2006). Reliance on these cognitive resources varies as a function of the simplicity of the phonological structure of a given language as well as the extent to which direct training in phoneme awareness has been provided (Ziegler & Goswami, 2005).

Other researchers have focused instead on "universal" processes. They examine common cognitive and neurological processes that might underlie the reading process and the development of reading skills and that prevail in spite of typological differences in the spoken language or the orthography. To date the focus of this research has been on pinpointing commonalities and differences in the role that cognitive-linguistic processes such as phonemic awareness, rapid serial naming, phonological memory, verbal working memory, and visual perception might play in word reading skills. Studies demonstrating the role of these cognitive-linguistic processes have been conducted with individuals learning to read in different languages, e.g. Cossu *et al.* (1988) for Italian; Durgunoglu & Oney (1999) for Turkish; Mann (1985), Siegel & Ryan (1989), Stanovich *et al.* (1984) for English; Hu & Catts (1998), Ho *et al.* (2000), and So & Siegel (1997) for Chinese; Näslund & Schneider (1996), Wimmer *et al.* (2000), Wimmer & Goswami (1994) for German; Breznitz & Share (2002), Shatil (1997), for Hebrew.

Evidence supporting the "universal" position comes from cross-linguistic comparisons within and across students. It also comes from a growing body of research literature demonstrating the relevance of various units of phonological and visual processes in reading in logographic languages (e.g. Perfetti & Zhang, 1995). Studies comparing good and poor readers (e.g. DaFontoura & Siegel, 1995; Everatt *et al.*, 2000; Ho *et al.*, 2000) also suggest that, regardless of the orthographies involved, bilinguals who have decoding and spelling problems in their L1 have difficulties in their L2 as well. At the same time, evidence from research on bilingual children (e.g. Geva & Siegel, 2000; Mumtaz & Humphreys, 2001; Wang & Geva, 2003) also indicates that the *type* of reading and spelling errors observed reflects typological influences. Taken together these two literatures suggest that it may be more prudent to consider the universal and script-dependent perspectives as complementary (Geva & Wang, 2001).

Based on the current state of knowledge, recently, Ziegler & Goswami (2005) have proposed the "psycholinguistic grain size theory" as an integrated theoretical framework for studying reading development in different languages. They suggest that over time, the relationship between reading ability and phoneme awareness is reciprocal, in that children begin to learn about phonemes through their experience with letters, but they also suggest that in order to grasp the alphabetic principle, a certain level of phonemic awareness may be necessary. They propose a progression from awareness of large units (such as words and syllables), to awareness of multi-phonemic, sub-syllabic, units such as onsets and rimes, and then finally to smaller phonemic units. Results of recent research with European languages supports the argument that awareness of supra-phonemic/sub-syllabic units is a precursor to later phonemic awareness (Anthony & Lonigan, 2004; Carroll *et al.*, 2003; Ziegler & Goswami, 2005).

It has been suggested that children have to learn to distinguish between similar words in their spoken language. When words have many "neighbors", i.e. other similar words that differ from it by a few phonemes, it forces the children to restructure their phonological representations and to attend to the finer distinctions among the words (Goswami, 2000; Metsala & Walley, 1998). But, awareness of small units is likely an outcome of experiences with the particular orthography and reading instruction (Burgess & Lonigan, 1998; Morais *et al.*, 1979; Tolchinsky & Teberosky, 1998; Ziegler & Goswami, 2005). That is, it is probably universally true that progress in knowledge of grapheme-phoneme mappings enhances further development and refinement of phonemic awareness. However, consistency of grapheme-phoneme relations in terms of pronunciation and spelling influences the process of learning to read in different languages.

The goal of this chapter is to review and consider facets of metalinguistic awareness related to reading acquisition in Hebrew as a first (L1) or second language (L2). To allow for coherence and focus, only developmental research pertaining to elementary school children is reviewed. Two aspects of metalinguistic awareness that have received attention in the research literature are discussed: phonological awareness and morphological awareness. For a better understanding of how facets of metalinguistic awareness are related to reading in Hebrew it is essential to describe features of the spoken and written language that affect reading performance in Hebrew. This description is provided in the second section of this chapter. The following section reviews pertinent research with regard to school children learning to read Hebrew as their L1 or home language. In the next section, the focus is on L2 learners and two bodies of research are reviewed: research on native speakers of English (English L1) students learning to read Hebrew as a second language, and research on native Hebrew (Hebrew L1) speakers learning to read English as a second language. The subsequent section discusses the role of metalinguistic awareness in understanding dyslexia in Hebrew readers, and conclusions and some thoughts about areas that require additional research are offered in the final section of the chapter.

Description of the Hebrew language and writing system

Characteristics of the Hebrew orthography

Hebrew is written and read from right to left. There are twenty-two consonants in Hebrew, which can be written in a cursive or print form. Five of the consonants are written differently when they appear at the very end of a word. In comparison to the Latin alphabet, the shape of printed Hebrew letters is more uniform and block-like. Most letters are formed with horizontal and vertical strokes and only a few letters include curves and diagonals. Hebrew letters are recognized more slowly than English letters, a finding that has been attributed to the relative uniformity of the letters (Shimron & Navon, 1981). The effects of this uniformity have been also documented in a study by Geva and Siegel (2000). Their study involved children in elementary grades one to five who were learning to read concurrently in English (their home language, or L1) and Hebrew (their L2). One category of decoding errors that did not occur when children's word recognition skills were assessed in English but that did occur with some frequency in Hebrew, especially in the lower grades, involved confusion among visually similar letters, (e.g. xet/tav; bet/kaf).

Some scholars (e.g. Gelb, 1963) have argued that early Semitic scripts, which were unvoweled (or "unpointed"), were syllabaries rather than alphabets. Currently, however, there is agreement among scholars of Hebrew that the unpointed (or unvoweled) Hebrew is a consonantal alphabet, where graphemes represent individual phonemes (Bentin & Frost, 1987; Frost & Bentin, 1992; Levin *et al.*, 1996; Navon & Shimron, 1994; Shimron, 2006).

Modern Hebrew has five vowel phonemes: /a/, /e/, /i/, /o/, and /u/. Hebrew vowels in the form of dots and dashes are placed below, above or to the left of letters. These vowels are quite close to the cardinal vowels in their phonetic realization (Berman, 1978). The voweled Hebrew orthography can be described as shallow in that there is a direct and rather consistent correspondence between graphemes and phonemes. Unlike English, the pronunciation of graphemes in Hebrew rarely varies as a function of specific letter strings, the nature of neighboring consonants or vowels, or their position in the word (Geva & Siegel, 2000). However, unlike the transparency of the grapheme-to-phoneme system, the phoneme-to-grapheme relationships in Hebrew are more variable. This is related to the fact that certain grapheme pairs that were phonetically distinct in ancient Hebrew (e.g. alef/ayin, xet/xaf, tet/taf; kaf/Qof) have been neutralized and now represent the same phoneme in the spoken language. As a result, many Hebrew words are homophones, a fact that is especially challenging for young spellers (Gillis & Ravid, 2000), for individuals with learning disabilities, and for learners of Hebrew as a second language (Geva & Wade-Woolley, 1998).

Two separate systems of voweling have evolved and are in use in Hebrew. As noted above, historically, the Hebrew orthographic system was consonantal in nature. There were either no vowels, or some vowel support was provided by the "mothers of reading" letters. These "matres lectionis" or "mothers of reading" (/iMoT HaʾKRiʾAh/ in Hebrew) represent the oldest voweling system. This system employs four of the consonantal letters alef, hei, vav, and yod. In other words, these letters serve two functions: they can signify vowels and they can signify consonants. For example, vav signifies the consonant /v/ (e.g. VeReD "rose") as well as the vowels /o/ and /u:/ (as in the words YoM "day" or Mu:m "defect"). The fact that the same grapheme can represent both a vowel and a consonant is a source of ambiguity, and the use of these graphemes is inconsistent and incomplete (Levin *et al.*, 1999; Shimron, 1993, 2006). In contemporary books, newspapers, and magazines two of these "mothers of reading" letters (yod; vav) appear inconsistently and their absence is not considered a spelling error. However, the other two (alef; hei), which appear word-finally, are obligatory even when they function as a vowel, and their absence is considered a spelling error.

The second system of vowelization that employs diacritical marks emerged gradually in the eighth to ninth centuries C.E. The diacritics system provides a complete and unambiguous representation of the vowels. On the whole, in its vowelized form, Hebrew orthography is rather consistent and transparent. Thanks to the almost universal correspondence between graphemes and phonemes, the development of skills associated with grapheme-phoneme correspondence rules, and the development of decoding skills, is straight-forward (Geva & Siegel, 2000; Share & Levin, 1999). For this reason, voweled Hebrew is used consistently in children's books and in texts for beginning Hebrew as L2 learners, as well as in poetry and sacred texts.

The semantic core of a Hebrew word (the root) is usually consonantal, and the vowels (and additional infixes, suffixes and prefixes) provide morpho-syntactic information such as person, number, and gender. However, the use of vowels in Hebrew is optional, and the prevailing practice is to "wean" readers from reliance on vowels. As they become skilled readers, learners are gradually exposed to texts without the diacritic vowels, and by the time they reach grades four or five, children read unvoweled texts. This practice alters the orthographic depth of the script to be read; it becomes deep, or opaque, and reading it requires heavy reliance on contextual and linguistic know-ledge (Berman, 1985; Geva *et al.*, 1997; Shimron, 1993, 2006; Shimron & Navon, 1982; Shimron & Sivan, 1994). In other words, reading voweled Hebrew requires command of phonological skills, whereas reading unvow-eled Hebrew requires command of morphological and syntactic skills (Bentin & Frost, 1995; Shimron, 1999). This is so because of the derivationally and morphologically dense nature of the language, and the prevalence of homographs in unvoweled printed words (see below).

Some characteristics of Hebrew phonology

One feature of the oral language that impacts the challenges to reading and in particular to spelling in Hebrew involves the need to overcome the neutralization of five phonological distinctions (alef vs. ayin, xet vs. xaf, tet vs. tav, kaf vs. qof, and samex vs. sin). In the past, these orthographic pairs were associated with distinct phonemes. However, in modern spoken Hebrew the phonemic distinction between these phoneme pairs has disap-peared, whereas the spelling continues to maintain the orthographic distinc-tions that once existed. This constitutes one of the key factors leading to the high number of homophones in Hebrew, and native speakers of Hebrew have to learn to overcome the challenges presented by the preponderance of homophonous spelling (Gillis & Ravid, 2000). Geva *et al.* (1993) have shown that this conclusion also applies to Hebrew L2 learners whose L1 is English, and they suggest that Hebrew may be more opaque for spelling than for decoding.

It is also important to consider phonotactic complexity. Hebrew allows only relatively simple syllable structures (primarily CV, VC, and CVC), whereas languages such as English allow for complex syllable structure (e.g. CCVC, CCCVC, CVCC, CCVCC, and CCVCCC). Consider for example the complex onsets in bride, scrupulous, and spring, the complex rimes in hand, tumble, and swift, or the existence of complex onsets and rimes in the same words as seen in words such as prompt, storm, or skunk. When Hebrew speakers encounter complex syllable structures in English they are likely to re-syllabify the complex syllable by adding a schwa that splits the complex rime (e.g. /fĭ'lem/ for film). Phonotactic complexity probably affects beginning Hebrew L2 readers, as it may partially determine the difficulty of segmenting phonemic units and of identifying aurally and metalinguistically the linguistic units represented by graphemes. Since syllabic units are more complex in English than in Hebrew, there may not be a complete match between performance on certain phonemic awareness tasks in Hebrew and English. It may be difficult for Hebrew L1 children who are learning English to keep these complex and less familiar structures in working memory, and to isolate the phonemes in a reliable manner in to order to read and spell words with such syllabic complexity. Thus, this is an example where a consideration of typological differences might modify specific predictions about Hebrew L2 learners based on the universal position.

Some characteristics of Hebrew morphology

The Hebrew language is considered morphologically rich. Hebrew word formation utilizes two types of word procedures: non-linear root plus pattern Semitic forms, and concatenated, linear structures (Berman, 1985; Bolozky, 1999). Content words consist of a "root," most typically comprised of three consonants; the root provides the semantic core of a word. The Hebrew lexicon is based on about 2,000 roots. Content words are produced by integrating a pattern ("mishkal") with the root. These patterns consist of infixes, prefixes, or suffixes into which the root is amalgamated. The combination of the root and the word patterns yields specific phonological and semantic information about the word. Different words can have in common a root or a word pattern (Berent & Shimron, 1997; Frost & Bentin, 1992). For example, nouns derived from the three-consonant root LMD include: LiMuD "study", LoMDa "educational software", MiT-LaMeD "apprentice", and LaMDaN "scholar". Some noun patterns represent semantic categories. For example, the pattern CaCaC, characteristic of names of professions, is evident in KaTaV "journalist", NaGaR "carpenter", and SaPaN "sailor".

Typically, verb forms operate on the same root-plus-pattern principle. Hebrew verbs are morphemically dense because tense, person, number, voice, and gender are indicated by inflecting roots (Berman, 1982). To illustrate, the following verb forms are derived from the root LMD : LiMeD "he taught", LaMaD "he studied", ALaMeD "I will teach", YeLaMeD "he will teach", and Te'LaMDi "you (feminine, singular) will teach".

Hebrew "words" are morphologically dense for another reason: many function words (e.g. to, from, in, and, the) and possessives (my, your, our) are function letters that are typically affixed to nouns. For example, the two-"word" sentence HaYeLaDiM BaKiTah is mapped onto a six-word sentence in English: "The children (are) in the classroom." In this example the function word /Ha/ "the" is affixed to the noun YeLaDiM "children", (masculine). The second word BaKiTah consists of three morphemes. In this case two function words: /Ha/ "the" and /Be/ "in", are fused into one syllable: /Ba/ "in the" which is affixed to KiTah "classroom". These examples illustrate the considerable morphosyntactic "unpacking" that needs to be carried out by Hebrew readers. It also illustrates the methodological challenges in conducting cross-linguistic comparisons (Geva *et al.*, 1997).

The combination of morphemic density and lack of vowels results in homographs that can be disambiguated on the basis of top-down sentential context. For example, in the absence of vowels it is not clear whether the word BXR stands for BaXuR "lad" or BaXoR "in the hole". In this example, the reader needs to decide whether the syllable associated with the grapheme B is part of the root BXR, or whether Ba "in the" is affixed to XR "hole". In a study of adult Hebrew as L2 learners, Wade-Woolley and Geva (1999) have shown that language proficiency facilitates this disambiguation process, and that adults for whom Hebrew is a second language are less efficient in reading such words than native speakers of Hebrew, probably because they have fewer linguistic resources to draw on.

Another source of complexity comes about when the phonemic neutralization process discussed above interacts with morphological and orthographic processing demands. For example, because there is no distinction in modern spoken Hebrew between the pronunciation of /xaf/ and /xet/, the words MaLaX "sailor", written with /xet/ and MaLaX "(he) reigned", written with /xaf/), are homophones. There is another complication here as well in that /xaf/ is one of the letters that is spelled differently when it appears in word-final position. In order to spell this word accurately, the speller of MaLaX "he reigned" would need to derive the intended root from the sentential context, apply the appropriate derivational pattern, and, in addition, consider the orthographic conventions concerning the representation of /xaf/ in word-final position. Shimron (2006) underscores the importance of top-down contextual processes in disambiguating such items. Gillis and Ravid (2000) suggest that the ability to analyze Hebrew words into their morphological components should help individuals to realize the differences in spelling. Native speakers of Hebrew rely on complex morphophonological cues in deciding how to spell such ambiguous words (Ravid, 2002).

Metalinguistic awareness and learning to read Hebrew as a first language

Phonological awareness and learning to read Hebrew

The notion of continuity in literacy and language development has been offered to describe and understand the developmental salience of specific linguistic and literacy components at different points along the developmental spectrum (Aram, 2005). For example, vocabulary at age three predicts subsequent phonological awareness (Metsala & Walley, 1998; Ziegler & Goswami, 2005). Phonological awareness at age four predicts phonological awareness at age five (Burgess, 1997). Numerous studies point to the important role that early language and pre-literacy skills, including vocabulary, phonological awareness, and letter knowledge, in kindergarten play in predicting decoding accuracy, reading efficiency, and reading comprehension in later years (e.g. Bowey, 1995; Chaney, 1998; Hart & Risley, 1999; Lonigan *et al.*, 2000; Näslund & Schneider, 1996; Scarborough, 2002; Storch & Whitehurst, 2001).

These findings have been replicated with Hebrew speakers. For example, longitudinal and concurrent research suggests that phonemic awareness significantly predicts subsequent reading skills of Hebrew L1 speakers. Kozminsky and Kozminsky (1993/94) conducted an intervention study with kindergarten children. Children were randomly assigned to the experimental or control class. The children in the experimental group received training focused on syllabic, sub-syllabic, and phonemic awareness, while those in the control class received a program that focused on visual-motor integration. The results provided strong evidence for the merits of early and systematic intervention. There were lasting gains in the experimental class and these significant gains were related to better reading comprehension both at the end of grade one and two years later, at the end of grade three.

Bentin and Leshem (1993) also report positive and significant correlations between phonemic awareness tasks and various reading indices for Israeli children learning to read in their home language, Hebrew. However, the results of Bentin and Leshem (1993) demonstrate the merits of considering as complementary the typological perspective and the universal or central processing perspective of reading development. Bentin and Leshem (1993) conducted a training study in which they examined the effect of phonemic awareness training in kindergarten on reading skills in grade one for a large sample of Israeli children learning to read Hebrew, their L1. Comparison of the results for students receiving the intervention with the results for students within a control group indicated that early intervention focused on phonemic awareness skills in kindergarten enhanced reading skills in grade one. The pattern of results pointed also to mutual facilitation between phonemic awareness and reading skills acquisition, a result that echoes similar results reported with regard to other orthographies. Reading acquisition was facilitated by prior training in phonemic awareness, and training on word segmentation skills correlated highly with subsequent word reading skills. In turn, learning to read was the main factor that accounted for further improvement in phonemic awareness.

However, the response patterns in the Bentin and Leshem (1993) study point to typological differences between English and Hebrew. In kindergarten, the most common response on the phoneme segmentation tasks was the production of sub-syllabic CV segments (36 percent). By comparison, the mean on the phoneme-based responses was 19 percent, and the mean of syllable-level responses was 12 percent. The correlation between phoneme-based responses and end-of-grade-1 reading was higher (r=.35) than the correlation between CV-based responses and end-of-grade-1 reading (r=.19). A year later, in grade one, children committed fewer errors than in kindergarten, but the drop on syllabic errors was more pronounced. Results of a cross-sectional study by Bentin *et al.* (1991) that examined phoneme segmentation also showed that the sub-syllabic CV unit plays a prominent role in Hebrew reading acquisition. The authors report that in kindergarten 25 percent of the errors constituted the sub-syllabic CV unit, and only 12 percent of the errors involved syllables. The preferred breakup of the syllable may not correspond with the onset/rime division believed to be characteristic of English (see Goswami & Bryant, 1990; Treiman, & Zukowski, 1996).

A recent cross-sectional study of preliterate (kindergarten) and literate (grade two) Hebrew speakers by Share and Blum (2005) supports the argument that multi-phonemic units are an intermediate stage before children are able to access phonemes. At the same time, however, the study also shows that the nature of syllable splitting may be different in Semitic languages such as Hebrew.

The authors hypothesized that Hebrew predisposes children to body-plus-coda (i.e. CV+C) rather than to onset-plus-rime (C+VC) units as is the case in English because, as discussed above, Hebrew prefers simple, open-syllables. In the study, an unstructured task required children to divide spoken monosyllabic CVC words into two. Also, one structured task required children to divide syllables into onset-rime units, and another task required them to divide syllables into body-coda units. Results pertaining to the literate, grade two, children confirmed a preference for the body-plus-coda division. However, preliterate kindergarten children had difficulty in dealing with phoneme-size units. The results demonstrated that, just as in English, there exists a sub-syllabic/supra-phonemic level of phonological awareness in Hebrew. However, the natural, sub-syllabic/supra-phonemic constituent is not the rime but the body of the syllable.

Two studies point to the relative salience of consonants (vs. vowels) in Hebrew. In one study of kindergarten children, Lapidot *et al.* (1995–6) found evidence for the salience of consonants (vs. vowels) in Hebrew. They report that children were able to identify and isolate consonants with more ease than they could vowels. Insensitivity to vowels was also revealed in errors such as those stating that eSHKoLiT "grapefruit" and SHuLXaN "table" begin with the same sound. Children also experienced greater difficulty in identifying a common terminal vowel (e.g. TMuN*ah* "picture") than a common terminal consonant (e.g. GeZe*R* "carrot"/SiR "pot". In a second study, Tolchinsky and Teberosky (1998) compared segmentation strategies in two groups of grade two children, Hebrew L1 children, and Spanish L1 children. The children in both groups were asked to divide words into "little parts." Most Hebrew speakers pronounced only consonants, but this strategy did not occur in the matched Spanish-speaking group.

In this regard it is also useful to note that the reported correlations between phonemic awareness measures and word reading measures, albeit positive and significant, were lower in these Hebrew-based studies (with correlations ranging from .31 to .42 with a median of .36) than parallel correlations reported in the English L1 literature (e.g. Stanovich *et al.*, 1984; Yopp, 1988). (See also Geva *et al.*, 1993, for similar results concerning Hebrew L2 children.)

In general then, these results suggest that while phonemic awareness is a significant predictor of subsequent acquisition of Hebrew reading skills, the strength of the relationship is somewhat weaker than in English, and the crucial linguistic units involved are not completely identical in English and Hebrew. The developmental trajectories might vary as a function of typological differences in the two orthographies. It is possible that because of the shallowness of voweled Hebrew, and the regularity of grapheme-phoneme correspondences, that decoding voweled Hebrew does not require high levels of phonological awareness. As will become evident below, it is possible that phoneme awareness is less critical in reading Hebrew than in reading English because other linguistic and orthographic information sources (and in particular, morphological information) enable reading and spelling in Hebrew.[2] At the same time it is possible that the prevalence of the simple (CV) open structure of Hebrew spoken syllables may prime Hebrew speakers to prefer the CV structure. Among children whose native language is Hebrew, individual differences in phonemic awareness are related to individual differences in learning to read Hebrew, but in comparison to English, there exist subtle differences in the nature of the linguistic units implicated. At the same time, it is important to bear in mind that Hebrew is a Semitic language and, as will become evident later, another possibly unique feature of phonological awareness in Hebrew relates to its affinity to Hebrew morphology.

Shatil (1997) conducted a longitudinal study of the cognitive and psycholinguistic factors associated with early reading achievement, in a representative large sample of Hebrew L1 children. At the end of kindergarten, a large battery of tasks that assessed domain-specific skills, including visual-orthographic processing, phonological awareness, phonological memory, and tasks that assessed early literacy, was administered. The domain-general set focused on general ability, metacognitive functioning, and oral language, and explained jointly 5 percent of the variance in word recognition skill assessed at the end of grade one. On the other hand, domain-specific factors explained jointly 33 percent of the variance in word recognition. The contribution of domain-specific variables to word recognition remained unchanged even when these variables were entered after controlling for all domain-general and higher-order language tasks. Reading comprehension in grade one was predicted longitudinally by domain-specific as well as domain-general skills. As for the longitudinal prediction of decoding skills in grade one, phonological awareness was a significant predictor, explaining

11 percent of the variance. In addition to phonological awareness, other factors significantly predicted decoding in grade one: visual-orthographic processing (11 percent), phonological memory (16 percent), and early literacy (19 percent). Meyler and Breznitz (1998) also reported that visual-spatial factors play a significant role in predicting early reading in Hebrew.[3] One of the findings in Shatil's study underscores further the suggestion that sub-syllabic CV units are significant in Hebrew reading acquisition. One of the early literacy predictor tasks that Shatil administered required children to learn three spoken CV labels for letter-like symbols, and then to read and write words which combined these newly acquired elements. Performance on this task significantly predicted reading a year later.

Morphological awareness and learning to read Hebrew, the L1

Morphological awareness and its relation to reading performance are topics that have been receiving increased attention in recent years. Morphological awareness involves the ability to reflect on word components and their functions. It is a complex construct that involves phonological, semantic, syntactic, and orthographic knowledge (Ravid & Malenky, 2001; Spencer, 1991). Emerging research has shown that morphological awareness is essential for word identification, spelling, and reading comprehension not only in alphabetic languages such as English and French (e.g. Carlisle, 1995, 2000; Carlisle & Fleming, 2003; Carlisle & Stone, 2005; Frank *et al.*, 2002; Plaza, 2003), but also in non-alphabetic languages such as Chinese (e.g. McBride-Chang *et al.*, 2003). Children's morphological knowledge continues to develop, and over time there is probably mutual facilitation between phonological awareness, morphological awareness, and reading (Carlisle & Nomanbhoy, 1993). Research has shown that as they reach late elementary years, school children's morphemic awareness and their ability to segment and manipulate morphemes within complex words continue to develop, and that morphemic awareness makes an independent contribution to reading over and above phonemic awareness and decoding skills (Fowler & Liberman, 1995; Singson *et al.*, 2000). Morphological awareness also plays an important role in understanding individual differences in reading comprehension (Carlisle, 2000; Carlisle & Fleming, 2003).

The English morphology can be characterized, on the whole, as concatenative (Marchand, 1969). That is, prefixes and suffixes are affixed to the original base word before or after the base in a linear fashion (e.g. help, helpful, helpless, helplessness, unhelpful, unhelpfulness). Hebrew morphology, on the other hand, is a mix of concatenative and non-concatenative principles (Bentin & Frost, 1995).

While inflectional morphology is concerned with the application of obligatory rules, derivational morphology is a richer and less constrained domain that correlates with vocabulary size. Command of inflectional morphology involves an integration of knowledge concerning conventions for forming words with semantic content and formal structure—in other words, literacy-related domains that continue to develop in school. Skills involving derivational morphology are mastered later than the skills involving inflectional morphology. Derivational morphology develops gradually throughout the school years, and is related to literacy skills (Anglin, 1993; Ravid, 2004; Tyler & Nagy, 1989).

As is evident from the review of Hebrew morphology offered in the previous section, Hebrew can be characterized as a synthetic language that is rich in morphological structures. Recent research evidence suggests that from a young age, children whose L1 is Hebrew are influenced by their language typology and use its characteristics, including information about the root as a core morphological entity, when they read and spell in Hebrew (e.g. Ben Dror *et al.*, 1995; Gillis & Ravid, 2000; Levin *et al.*, 2001; Ravid & Bar-On, 2005; Ravid & Malenky, 2001).

In their longitudinal study of young Hebrew spellers, Levin *et al.* (1999) found that, in addition to phonological information, young children utilize morphological information when they spell, and that morphological awareness skills in kindergarten predict success in writing a year later, in grade one. A study conducted by Ben-Dror *et al.* (1995) demonstrates the contribution of morphological awareness to reading. The study compared the semantic, phonological, and morphological skills of reading-disabled grade five children to the performance of a group of age-matched normal readers, and a younger group of normal readers who were matched on vocabulary. The children were asked to judge relatedness on various metalinguistic tasks. They had to judge phonemic identity and semantic relatedness, and in a morphological relatedness task they had to decide whether two words shared a common root. Reading-disabled children were particularly challenged on the morphological awareness task.

In a longitudinal study of young Hebrew L1 children, Aram (2005) found that performance in kindergarten on various aspects of emergent literacy skills and on phonological awareness tasks correlated positively and significantly with performance on a task that assessed morphological skills at the end of grade two. Morphological awareness continues to develop through the school years, and Ashkenazi and Ravid (1998) have shown that more sophisticated aspects of morphological awareness, such as the ability to provide explicit explanation of morphologically based riddles and jokes in Hebrew, is achieved only in adolescence.

The majority of studies that have compared performance on various tasks under voweled versus unvoweled conditions in Hebrew typically show that individuals benefit from the presence of vowels, because the phonological information provided by vowels in Hebrew is consistent. For example, in a cross-sectional study of elementary school children, Shimron (1999) has demonstrated that the presence of explicit vowel diacritics enhanced word recognition memory, word recall, and text comprehension in comparison to unvoweled conditions. At the same time, Shimron points out that the readers were not crippled when the vowel diacritics were omitted. The explanation he offers is that skilled Hebrew L1 readers can and do apply morphological skills, such as the extraction of the root that encodes the general semantic field. They also use information about tense, number, person, and syntactic and semantic aspects clues (e.g. active-passive) that are embedded in word templates. By applying morphological skills such as these, skilled Hebrew L1 readers are able to achieve lexical access even in the absence of vowels. The root and template-based information provides the skilled Hebrew readers with sufficient clues to enable them to obtain lexical and morphosyntactic information embedded in the printed words, even when the texts are unvoweled. Carlisle and Nomanbhoy (1993) have suggested in their research on literacy skills in English that there is mutual facilitation between phonological awareness, morphological awareness, writing, and reading, and that over time, these skills enhance each other. Clearly, this developmental process takes place among Hebrew learners as well.

The conclusion emerging from the review of recent research underscores the morphologically rich nature of the Hebrew language and the fact that, from a young age, native speakers of Hebrew are influenced by their language typology; they use its characteristics, and their growing awareness of morphological features, when acquiring word-level reading and spelling skills (Ben Dror *et al.*, 1995; Gillis & Ravid, 2000; Levin *et al.*, 1999, 2001).

Ravid (2001) has shown that elementary school children learn to spell function words correctly before they reach correct spelling of content words (Ravid, 2001), arguably because the challenges involved in extracting relevant morphological information are larger for content words. Ravid (2001) found that homophonic root letters in content words remained a source of spelling errors, and that these errors declined significantly only between grades four and six.

Hebrew spelling is related to morphological awareness skills, and Hebrew L1 children utilize morphological cues in figuring out how to spell homophonous letters in words (Ravid, 2005). Levin *et al.* (2001) offer an explanation for this continuity between performance on language and pre-literacy skills before the onset of formal reading instruction and Hebrew literacy skills in later years. They suggest that becoming aware of common spelling features of semantically related words contributes to an awareness of the morphemic connection between these words. Because of the synthetic nature of Hebrew, awareness of its code provides children with clues to its morphological infrastructure. By becoming sensitive to the infrastructure of morphological features such as morphemic connections at the root and word pattern levels, children gradually learn to appreciate the centrality of these features, and to derive the spellings of unknown words on the basis of known words (Levin *et al.*, 2001).

The distinction between inflectional morphemic awareness and derivational morphemic awareness is highly relevant for Hebrew readers and spellers. For example, already in the preschool years, Hebrew L1 children are able to identify and use appropriately obligatory morphological constructions such as the marking of plural suffixes: YeLeD "child" (male, singular); YeLaDiM "children" (male, plural). However, it takes longer to master rules concerning the optional use of morphological rules. For example, Cahana-Amitay & Ravid (2000) have shown that the analytic, simpler (and obligatory) form of the genitive "her palace," /Ha-ARMoN SHeLah/, emerges early, whereas the parallel bound form /ARMoN-ah/, whose use is optional, may emerge only in adulthood, and its emergence and use may be related to educational level.

Recent research provides evidence that being able to analyze Hebrew words into their morphological components is critical also for making semantic and syntactic sense, and for noting discourse coherence in reading and writing (Frost, 2005; Levin *et al.*, 2001; Schiff & Ravid, 2004). For example, in a longitudinal study, Levin *et al.* (2001) tracked children from kindergarten to grade one. They found that mastering derivational morphology is more challenging than mastering inflectional morphology, that morphological awareness was related to subsequent progress in representing vowels in writing, and that writing in kindergarten was related to development in derivational morphology over time.

In conclusion, English makes relatively little use of morphology and the process of English word formation involves, to a large extent, simple concatenation. By comparison, Hebrew is a highly synthetic language, and Hebrew word structures express a wide array of semantic and morphosyntactic ideas. Therefore, developing metalinguistic awareness of inflectional and derivational morphology in Hebrew is critical for learning to read and spell. From a young age, native speakers of Hebrew are influenced by the morphological features of their language, and use its characteristics when acquiring word level reading and spelling skills. However, this awareness does not develop in a vacuum; its development depends on other linguistic achievements, including phonological awareness, increase in vocabulary size, and learning to read and spell. In turn, morphological awareness can facilitate higher levels of reading and writing in Hebrew.

Metalinguistic awareness and bilingual learners

Research on children learning to read in a second language (L2) or in bilingual contexts has led to a refinement of theoretical conceptions of reading skills development. Two theoretical frameworks have been dominant. One framework referred to as the "universal" perspective (Geva & Siegel, 2000) searches for commonalities in underlying processes across language. This perspective has received support from studies demonstrating that individual differences on linguistic-cognitive processing component skills (measured in the L1 and/or L2) can be utilized to explain variance in performance on word-level reading and spelling skills in L2 and bilingual children as well (Geva & Genesee, 2006). For example, a growing body of research has established the relation between phonological awareness and word-level reading skills for: (a) English Language Learners (ELLs) coming from various linguistic backgrounds who are learning to read English, the societal language (e.g. Chiappe & Siegel, 1999; DaFontura & Siegel, 1995; Durgunoglu *et al.*, 1993; Geva *et al.*, 2000; Geva *et al.*, 2005; Gottardo *et al.*, 2006; Gottardo & Geva, 2006; Gottardo *et al.*, 2001; Lesaux & Siegel, 2003; Lindsey *et al.*, 2003; Quiroga *et al.*, 2002; Wade-Woolley & Siegel, 1997); (b) children whose home language is English who are learning to read English and French concurrently in French immersion programs (e.g. Comeau *et al.*, 1999; Lafrance & Gottardo, 2005; (c) children whose home language is English who are learning to read concurrently, within the school context, an additional orthography such as Arabic, Portuguese, Farsi, or Hebrew (e.g. DaFontura & Siegel, 1995; Geva & Siegel, 2000; Saiegh-Haddad & Geva, in press; Gholamain & Geva, 1999; Arab-Moghaddam & Sénéchal, 2001); and, (d) children living in various countries who are learning to read English in a foreign language context (e.g. Abu-Rabia, 1997; Dufva, & Voeten, 1999; Muter & Diethelm, 2001; Kahn-Horowitz *et al.*, 2005). Relatedly, individuals with deficits in cognitive and linguistic processing skills are expected to experience difficulties in acquiring basic reading skills, in spite of typological differences in features of the language and the script involved, and regardless of whether they are learning to read in their L1, their L2, or both (e.g. Brown & Hulme, 1992; DaFontura & Siegel, 1995; Doctor & Klein, 1992; Durgunoglu *et al.*, 1993; Geva & Siegel, 2000; Ho *et al.*, 2000; Katzir *et al.*, 2004; Quiroga *et al.*, 2002).

The second framework that has informed research on L2 learning, including studies of Hebrew learners, is the Contrastive Analysis Hypothesis (Lado, 1964) that was proposed to explain differences between a learner's L1 and L2 language development.[4] In various forms this framework continues to permeate research on L2 learning. More recently, numerous studies on literacy development and its antecedents have been conducted that examine the effects of typological differences between the L1 and L2 on the acquisition of specific aspects of literacy. The assumption of this "script dependent" perspective is that L1–L2 differences create difficulties for L2 learners that result in inappropriate transfer of L1 patterns to the L2 (Lado, 1964). Within the area of literacy development, the "orthographic depth hypothesis" framework has been proposed for studying how typological differences between writing systems can account for differences in how students learn to read in different languages, for errors they make as they acquire specific skills in the L2 (Genesee *et al.*, 2006), and for subtle differences in the role that metalinguistic skills might play in literacy acquisition in different languages, and how these might be related to the identification of reading disabilities in bilingual learners (Durgunoglu, 2002; Geva, 2000). One way of studying the nature of difficulties and errors that occur in the course of L2 reading development is to compare the two language systems. Corresponding phonological, morphological, and syntactic structures in L1 and L2 may be studied in order to figure out whether difficulties and errors in the course of L2 reading acquisition are primarily a result of "interference" at one or more of these levels (Durgunoglu, 2002). This framework can be conceived of as a yardstick for evaluating the degree to which phonological analysis of the structures of spoken words needs to be supplemented by morphological, orthographic, and lexical knowledge in order to read or spell correctly (Durgunoglu *et al.*, 2001).

Studies of normally developing children suggest that, in contrast with shallow orthographies such as German and Dutch, phonological awareness continues to be predictive of word-level reading and spelling skills in normally developing children in middle school when they need to read in a deep orthography such as English. In German and Dutch, it is naming speed rather than phonemic awareness that is a better predictor of word-level reading (de Jong & van der Leij, 1999; Wimmer *et al.*, 2000; Wolf *et al.*, 1994).

Indeed, research involving bilingual learners has shown that typological and orthographic differences between the oral and written forms of L1 and L2 are important mitigating factors in cross-language transfer (e.g. Geva & Siegel, 2000; Geva *et al.*, 1993; Geva & Wang, 2001; Gholamain & Geva, 1999; Mumtaz & Humphreys, 2001; Wade-Woolley & Geva, 2000), and cognitive and linguistic processes that are associated with reading acquisition may show different patterns of relationships in different L1–L2 language combinations (Geva & Wade-Woolley, 2004).

Given this brief overview, two sets of recent studies are briefly discussed here. One set of studies pertains to children whose home language is not Hebrew but who are acquiring Hebrew, the societal language, in a Hebrew immersion context. The second set pertains to studies of children living in English-speaking environments who were acquiring Hebrew language and literacy skills at school only.

Acquiring Hebrew, the societal language: the case of Ethiopian children

A study of kindergarten children (Shany *et al.*, 2006) provides evidence for the significant role played by phonemic awareness in the emergence of word-reading skills in young pre-school children whose parents immigrated to Israel from Ethiopia. The study compared the performance of Ethiopian-Israeli senior kindergarten children (ages 5–6) whose home language was Amharic with performance of children whose parents did not come from Ethiopia. Children in both language groups came from low SES—low home literacy backgrounds, and attended schools where Hebrew, the societal language, is the sole language of instruction. Even though the home language of this target group was Amharic, they actually spoke or understood very little Amharic, and had no literacy skills in Amharic. Two points are noteworthy in the present context: (a) performance of the Ethiopian-Israeli children on two tasks involving phonological awareness (an elision task that required children to delete syllables in Hebrew words and indicate the outcome, and a task that focused on elision of phonemes in Hebrew words) was poorer than that of children in the non-Ethiopian group, and (b) phonemic awareness in kindergarten correlated positively and significantly with performance on a word-reading task in kindergarten (r=.45).

In a cross-sectional study, Geva and Shany (2006) compared the performance of Israeli children from Ethiopian and non-Ethiopian backgrounds in grades one and two on a large battery of cognitive, linguistic and literacy tasks. Again, both groups came from various low SES neighborhoods, and attended the same schools. With the introduction of literacy skills in grade one, group differences on code-related components disappeared. Even though Ethiopian-Israeli children performed more poorly on phonemic awareness in the kindergarten study, performance of the two groups on the phoneme and syllable segmentation-elision tasks in grade one did not differ. The groups did not differ either on (voweled) word recognition or pseudo-word decoding tasks. In other words, they did not differ on the modular, core-related basic components of reading. However, as part of an alarming trend towards an increasing gap in language skills, in both grade levels the performance of the Ethiopian-Israeli children was significantly lower on two morphemic tasks, one that required children to complete sentences and another that required them to apply their knowledge of rules governing adjectival inflections in Hebrew. Their spelling scores were also lower than those of children in the non-Ethiopian comparison group.

As for the anticipated correlations between metalinguistic awareness and performance on word reading and spelling skills, results pointed to different patterns in the two groups. In the non-Ethiopian group, phonemic awareness correlated positively and significantly with word reading (r=.52) and spelling (r=.49). Interestingly, syllable awareness did not correlate with word reading, though it correlated highly with spelling (r=.71), a result echoing the salience of CV in Hebrew. In contrast, in the Ethiopian-Israeli group, the correlations between phoneme awareness and word reading and spelling were not significant. However, as was the case in the non-Ethiopian group, syllable awareness correlated significantly with spelling (r=.44). In other words, in both groups syllable awareness was related to spelling skills.

In this same study, Geva and Shany (2006) found that the gap in Hebrew morphemic awareness between the two groups increased from grade one to grade two. Morphemic awareness played a significant, although not identical, role in Hebrew word reading and spelling in the two groups. In the non-Ethiopian group, morphemic awareness correlated significantly with both word reading (r=.43) and spelling (r=.36). In the Ethiopian group, morphemic awareness did not correlate with word reading, but it correlated positively and significantly with spelling (r=.44).

These results indicate that general aspects of metalinguistic awareness other than phonemic awareness are related to word and spelling skills in Hebrew. They also point to the importance of considering socio-cultural factors such as poverty and lack of opportunities to develop language and literacy skills. The command of the home language (Amharic) was extremely low, and the children had very little exposure at home and at school to books and writing (either in the home language or in Hebrew). Concomitantly, their Hebrew language skills (e.g. vocabulary, grammar, morphology) were not at par with their Hebrew-speaking counterparts. Yet, even though the Ethiopian-Israeli children were found to lag behind the comparison group (and national norms) in terms of their age-appropriate morphemic awareness, individual differences in morphemic awareness were related to early literacy skills such as spelling and reading fluency. The results suggest that phonological awareness and morphological awareness develop gradually in the Ethiopian-Israeli group although they lag behind those noted for Hebrew as L1 children. But these two aspects of metalinguistic awareness do not develop in tandem. Phonological awareness, which is less complex, develops at a reasonable rate, and is related to basic decoding and spelling skills. By grade one the Ethiopian children have caught up with their Hebrew as L1 peers on the phonological awareness skills. However, morphological awareness is more complex, and it takes much longer to master in children who are acquiring Hebrew language and literacy skills within a L2 context. Morphological awareness presumably affects, and in turn is affected by, vocabulary development and more advanced literacy skills. More research is needed to find out whether these observations reflect the specific socio-cultural and L2 context of this series of studies, or whether these observations are true of other groups of Hebrew L2 learners. It is necessary to unpack the contributions of poor home literacy, typological distance between Hebrew and the home language, curricular features and approaches to instruction, and the interaction of these factors, to the development of language and literacy skills in children learning Hebrew as a second language.

Acquiring Hebrew as a foreign language at school only

In a different socio-cultural and educational context, Geva and her colleagues conducted a series of studies on children living in Canada. The home language of these children was English, and these middle-class children were studying in bilingual, English-Hebrew, private schools. In one cross-sectional study involving children in grades one to five, Geva and Siegel (2000) examined parallel English and Hebrew word recognition, pseudo-word reading, and cognitive skills. Results indicated that parallel measures in English and Hebrew correlated positively and significantly with each other. Of relevance in the present context was the demonstration of the effects of differences in orthographic depth between the two orthographies. In particular, children were able to decode words with more accuracy in (voweled) Hebrew than in English, their L1, even though their Hebrew language proficiency was low. By grade five accuracy rates on word reading and word decoding continued to be higher for Hebrew than for English, although the gap between the two languages became smaller.

In a longitudinal study of English L1-Hebrew L2 bilingual children, Geva *et al.* (1993) also reported that grade one and grade two children achieved higher accuracy in Hebrew word reading than in English word reading. The correlation between phonemic awareness and Hebrew word reading was positive and significant but weaker (r=.32) than the corresponding correlation between the parallel English tasks (r=.62). Phonemic awareness correlated significantly with spelling skills in each language. This result is similar to what has been reported for Hebrew L1 learners, and it suggests that the relationship between phonological awareness and decoding and spelling skills is not as strong in Hebrew as it is in English.

Phonological awareness, novel phonemes and learning to read: Hebrew L2 learners

In the last decade numerous studies have examined the extent to which phonological awareness plays a facilitating role in learning to read in a second language. Some studies have also examined the effect of typological differences on literacy acquisition, and whether features of the L1 and L2 might influence the processing of the L2. With regard to phonological awareness one possible scenario is that phonological awareness is a universal metalinguistic ability that underlies phonemic analysis in a learner's L1 and L2, regardless of typological similarities and differences in the elements that comprise the phonological repertoire of the L1 and L2.

At the same time, research evidence suggests that new phonemes that do not exist in the child's L1 present a specific challenge to L2 spelling. However, developmental research with English L2 learners and Hebrew L2 learners has shown that over time, with exposure and literacy acquisition, L2 children acquire these new phonemes and the frequency of L1-specific errors in spelling gradually diminishes (e.g. Geva *et al.*, 1993; Wang and Geva 2003). Wade-Woolley & Geva (2000) examined the possibility that phonological awareness in the L2 could depend on the extent to which the L1 and L2 share most phonemes or syllable structures. L2 learners may experience difficulties with specific novel linguistic features introduced in the L2 such as imprecise phonological representations of novel phonemes. This has been studied with respect to the phoneme /ts/ for Hebrew L2 young children (Geva *et al.*, 1993; Wade-Woolley & Geva, 2000), the phoneme /th/ for Chinese L1 children acquiring English in an immersion context (Wang & Geva, 2003), and for novel syllable structures such as CVC or CCVC introduced in the L2 (Caravolas & Bruck, 1993).

A study involving grade two children who were native English speakers, and who were learning Hebrew at school in a bilingual day-school, was conducted to examine this issue further (Wade-Woolley & Geva, 2000). The authors examined the more nuanced hypothesis that L2 learners who are less skilled readers may be more challenged in acquiring new phonemes or phonemic contrasts that exist in the L2 but not in their L1. The study sought to determine the relative difficulty of unfamiliar orthography and unfamiliar (L2-specific) phonological elements for young L2 readers. An experimental, cross-modal, auditory-written, multiple-choice, pseudo-word recognition task was developed. In the task, children listened to pseudo-words, and for each, circled the written word they thought they had heard. In addition to the correct answer, the written options included both phonological and visual distracters. The phonological aspect of the task was designed to tap sensitivity to the phonemic contrast (/ts/ versus /s/) that occurs productively in Hebrew but is phonotactically constrained in English.

As predicted, children experienced more difficulty discriminating the /ts/ versus /s/ contrast in onsets than in rimes. Word-level reading skills in both Hebrew and English correlated significantly with performance on this measure. Phonological awareness in the native language (English) was related to the ability to read words and understand oral language in the L2 (Hebrew). The hypothesis that there would be an interaction of reading level and language transfer was not supported: both skilled and less skilled Hebrew L2 readers had more difficulty discriminating the /ts/—/s/ phonemic contrasts in syllable positions that were novel to them (i.e. in syllable onsets). This study provides additional evidence for the complementarity of the universal and language specific frameworks outlined earlier. Phonological awareness is required for reading to develop in English, the L1, or Hebrew, the L2. However, phonological elements characteristic of the L2 present additional specific challenges to L2 learners.

Metalinguistic awareness: Hebrew L1/English L2 and English
L1 and Hebrew L2 learners

Kahn-Horwitz *et al.* (2005) examined whether factors predicting Hebrew L1 reading acquisition would also predict acquisition of reading in English acquired as a foreign language in Israel. Children were tested in Hebrew, the L1, at the beginning of grade four, and in English, the L2, at the end of grade four, following the first full year of instruction in English. Of particular relevance in the present context is the finding that Hebrew morphological and phonological awareness, orthographic ability, and Hebrew word-reading efficiency (accuracy and speed) predicted letter-sound and letter-name knowledge in English, as well as pseudo-word decoding and reading comprehension in English. The authors argue that these results provide support for the argument about a common, underlying, core of metalinguistic and linguistic skills that influence first and subsequent language reading acquisition.

The available developmental research on the acquisition of Hebrew L2 reading skills suggests that phonological awareness plays a role also when Hebrew is being acquired as a second language, and this observation appears to hold whether Hebrew skills develop in a foreign language context or when Hebrew is the societal language. Furthermore, in general the available studies on L2 learners provide additional support for the universal position in that phonological awareness in children's L1 (English) as well as in the L2 (Hebrew) correlate with word recognition and spelling skills in Hebrew L2 (Geva *et al.*, 1993; Geva & Siegel, 2000). The reverse also appears to hold, namely, that Hebrew L1 metalinguistic skills predict reading performance in English, the L2 (Kahn-Horwitz *et al.*, 2005). While a general level of phonological awareness is required for reading to develop in the L1 or the L2, phonological elements characteristic of the L2 present additional challenges to L2 learners who need to master those new linguistic structures. There is also some evidence that morphological awareness is slower to develop in Hebrew L2 learners, and that this development may depend on a myriad of school and home factors, though this area has not been sufficiently studied to date.

There has been almost no systematic research on the development of basic morphological skills and morphological awareness in children acquiring Hebrew within bilingual or L2 contexts. It is reasonable to hypothesize that a certain (as yet unspecified) level of language proficiency would be necessary for L2 learners to be able to analyze Hebrew words into their morphological components with sufficient accuracy and fluency that allows them to derive word meanings when they engage in reading or writing tasks. In fact, as suggested by Carlisle with regard to children learning to read in their L1, it is reasonable to hypothesize that, over time, the relationships between language proficiency, vocabulary, word reading and spelling skills, and morphological skills are mutually enhancing. It is reasonable to expect that Hebrew L2 learners would be less sensitive to derivational morphology, and less able to apply morphological knowledge to perceive word families, and to derive word meaning. They may have more difficulty in comprehending and producing words on the basis of systematic application of derivational morphology. Moreover, it is reasonable to hypothesize that the cognitive-linguistic demands associated with reading and comprehending unvoweled Hebrew texts may be exacerbated by the demands of the highly inflected and morphologically dense nature of the Hebrew language (Wade-Woolley & Geva, 1999).

Clearly, a myriad of questions pertaining to the development of meta-linguistic awareness in learners of Hebrew as a second language, and the role of metalinguistic awareness in the development of proficiency in reading and writing skills, remain unanswered. These include questions on topics such as (a) patterns of morphemic awareness development in Hebrew L2 children; (b) the extent to which this development affects and is affected by development on various aspects of literacy, growth in vocabulary, and phonemic awareness in the L1 and L2; (c) the relationship between morphemic awareness and L1 and L2 linguistic proficiency; (d) the relationships between the emergence of phonemic, morphemic, and syntactic awareness, inter alia; and (e) the nature of metalinguistic awareness that can transfer from children's L1 to Hebrew, the L2. The impact of contextual factors such as home literacy, SES, and the effects of instruction should not be ignored either.

Metalinguistic awareness and dyslexia in Hebrew readers

Research has shown that the two aspects of metalinguistic awareness that have been the focus of this chapter, phonological awareness and morphological awareness, distinguish normally developing Hebrew readers from dyslexic Hebrew readers.[5] The research suggests that deficits in phonological awareness are related to reading failure in Hebrew, though the shallowness of Hebrew orthography is an important mitigating factor. Difficulties with morphological skills are especially detrimental, however, to Hebrew readers (Share, 2003).

Research on English has shown that access to phonemes is a significant predictor of later reading and that early training in phonemic awareness enhances later reading ability. As has been shown amply with regard to English L1 dyslexic children, the research on Hebrew L1 children has shown that elementary school dyslexic children have deficits on various aspects of phonological awareness tasks. Lapidot *et al.*, (1995–96) examined the extent to which phonological awareness assessed in kindergarten predicted difficulties in grade one. Out of a sample of 100 children, eighteen children experienced poor phonological awareness in kindergarten. One year later, in grade one, nine of these children were identified as having reading difficulties, while none of the children who scored within the normal range on the phonological awareness task in kindergarten were identified with reading difficulties in grade one.

In another study, Ben-Dror *et al.* (1995) reported that Hebrew L1 reading-disabled children were inferior to the two comparison groups in their ability to identify first phonemes in words that were presented orally and in decoding pseudo-words. The authors concluded that children with developmental reading-disabilities have deficits in the metalinguistic skills necessary for conscious application of linguistic rules to word reading. Breznitz (1997) also found that dyslexic children in grade three had difficulties on various phonological awareness tasks. In addition, they were slower on various reading tasks.[6]

Having poor morphological awareness may be especially problematic for reading disabled individuals, since understanding words in Hebrew depends on efficient access to the constituent morphemes (i.e. roots, templates, and affixes) (Ben-Dror *et al.*, 1995). Ben-Dror *et al.* (1995) compared the phonological, morphological, and semantic skills of grade five Hebrew-speaking dyslexics with those of an age-matched group and a younger, vocabulary-matched group. The most pronounced gap between the groups was on a morphological awareness task, where children had to decide whether two words shared a common root. On the phonological and semantic awareness tasks, the performance of the reading disabled readers was significantly inferior only with regard to the age-matched group. In other words, differences on morphological awareness reflected reading ability in each of the groups.

A study by Cohen *et al.* (1996) provides additional information about the impact of morphological awareness deficits in Hebrew L1 school children on literacy tasks involving story writing and story telling. In that study, dyslexic and matched non-dyslexic children in grades three to six, were asked to tell and write stories in response to pictures. The stories were analyzed in terms of aspects such as morphological richness, syntactic and narrative complexity, and text length. On each of these indices, dyslexic children performed more poorly than non-dyslexic children, although the differences between the groups was especially pronounced in the more demanding writing task. In general then, it is clear that dyslexic children with Hebrew as their first language have poor morphological skills and poor morphological awareness, and that these difficulties are related to the difficulties they experience on various literacy tasks.

In the same vein, Katzir *et al.* (2004) report on a cross-national study that compared underlying processes in a group of grade three and grade four monolingual Hebrew dyslexic children living in Israel with a monolingual English dyslexic group living in the U.S. A battery of reading, phonological, orthographic, and cognitive tasks was administered to the children in the two matched groups. The study revealed that dyslexic individuals reading in different orthographies shared some characteristics but also demonstrated unique characteristics associated with the interface of their difficulties and the nature of the orthography they were struggling with. Hebrew- and English-speaking readers with dyslexia were similar on verbal IQ, performance IQ, and speed of processing of non-linguistic stimuli (Symbol Search and Coding). Of theoretical and clinical significance is also the finding that children in both groups experienced difficulties in pseudo-word decoding. These results point to a universal phonological core deficit for readers with dyslexia. The results of Kahn-Horwitz *et al.* (2005) lead to similar conclusions with regard to Hebrew L1 speakers learning to read English in a foreign language context.

Yet, even though the cognitive profiles were similar in the two groups, results of the Katzir *et al.* study (2004) also point to findings that do not apply equally to both groups. The Hebrew dyslexic children achieved higher scores on word and connected-text reading rate compared to the English dyslexics. The Hebrew dyslexic children also performed significantly better on the orthographic measures, and on reading comprehension than did their English-speaking counterparts. These results suggest that Hebrew L1 dyslexics are less challenged when they read vowelized Hebrew than are their

English-speaking counterparts in reading English. The vowelized and "shallow" Hebrew orthography presents fewer challenges to the dyslexic Hebrew reader, as it does in the case of normally achieving readers of Hebrew (Geva and Siegel, 2000; Geva *et al.*, 1997).

To conclude, dyslexic children whose L1 is Hebrew, just like their English-speaking counterparts, experience phonological and morphemic awareness deficits, and these deficits (in conjunction with other underlying visual and processing speed processes) impede their performance on pseudo-word reading skills, and on higher-level literacy skills. However, from the perspective of metalinguistic awareness the profiles of English and Hebrew dyslexics are not identical, since certain aspects are more sensitive to typological differences in the spoken and written language. Thus, even though the regular vowelized Hebrew orthography is somewhat less challenging for the impaired Hebrew reader than for the impaired reader of English, having poor morphological awareness may be rather detrimental for Hebrew-reading dyslexics, especially if they have to tackle unvoweled texts. This issue has not been studied yet in a systematic way either in a cross-linguistic or a bilingual context. It is also not known whether providing systematic intervention for Hebrew L2 dyslexics with phonemic awareness and/or morphemic awareness would yield positive results and enhance reading skills in their L1 and L2.

Conclusions

Universal and language specific frameworks

In Hebrew as in English, metalinguistic skills begin to emerge before the systematic introduction of literacy skills. This chapter focused on phonological and morphological awareness, their development, and their roles in acquiring literacy skills in Hebrew. These skills enhance subsequent literacy development, and in turn, as a result of learning to read and write, they develop further. From a universal perspective, it is possible to conclude that in English and Hebrew the orthographic system encodes linguistic concepts at the phonemic, sub-syllabic, syllabic, morphemic, lexical, and sentential level, and these concepts affect and are affected by growth in literacy skills. At the same time, the instantiation of these concepts is not identical across English and Hebrew, because Hebrew and English differ in their orthography, phonology, syllable structure, and morphology. Children have to learn to represent and integrate these levels in their oral language as well as when they engage in reading and writing activities. Gradually, with development and increased literacy skills, children become increasingly sophisticated in understanding and utilizing information about how these linguistic concepts are mapped onto the particular orthography they are learning. Moreover, because of these typological differences in the spoken language, different component parts of the linguistic and writing system may be activated to varying degrees in English and Hebrew.

L2 issues

It could be argued that when children acquire language and literacy skills in an L2 context they should be able to take advantage of the abstract linguistic concepts that they have figured out in their L1, and utilize them where relevant in the L2. Indeed cross-language correlations between phonemic awareness in English and Hebrew suggest that phonological awareness is a language-general skill that needs to be acquired only once (Durgunoglu, 2002).

However, caution should be exercised in interpreting inter-lingual correlations as "transfer." For example, it is clear that Hebrew morphology and English morphology are very different from each other. Therefore, if morphemic awareness in Hebrew correlates with morphemic awareness in English it would be difficult to explain this co-relation as transfer of skills, unless one is able to demonstrate what skills have been "transferred." The transfer framework is useful but not sufficient for understanding L2 literacy development, and it is not the only source of influence (Genesee *et al.*, 2006). Other cognitive underlying abilities (e.g. working memory, processing speed) that underlie performance on specific literacy skills in the L1 and L2 may explain this co-relation (Geva & Ryan, 1993).

In terms of assessment of L2 learners, certain error types can be understood in terms of typological differences between English and Hebrew (and interpreted as "negative transfer"). Other processes, such as phonemic awareness, are less complex and more modular, and can therefore be assessed reliably in English and in Hebrew. Difficulties with phonemic awareness tasks are indicative of reading disabilities regardless of the language under scrutiny, and are less sensitive to variation in language proficiency. However, well-developed oral language and literacy skills may be necessary to evaluate morphemic awareness, and difficulties in developing appropriate Hebrew morphological skills may be one of the hallmarks of reading disabled individuals, regardless of their L1 or L2 status. Clearly, normally developing children utilize their understanding of the Hebrew morphology as they develop their spelling and reading skills. Because the Hebrew morphology is more complex it may take longer to master, and in the absence of vowels dyslexic readers and L2 learners may be especially challenged by under-developed skills in this domain.

Notes

1   This chapter was prepared while the author was on a sabbatical leave from the University of Toronto.

2   Ben-Dror *et al.*, (1995) explored this observation in a study that involved adults who were either native Hebrew-speakers or native English-speakers. Hebrew speakers were more likely (84 percent versus 65 percent) to delete (correctly) the initial phoneme in CVC words in which the medial vowel was represented by a "mother of reading" (e.g. KiR (=wall), than in CVC words in which the medial

vowel was represented by a vowel letter (e.g. GaN, =kindergarten). The authors maintain that "The basic sub-word phonological unit induced by exposure to Hebrew letters may take the form of a CV phonological unit" (Ben-Dror *et al.*, 1995, p.181).

3 Shatil argues that the more important role played by visual-spatial ability in explaining individual differences in word reading skills in young children learning to read Hebrew can be attributable to multiple factors such as lack of orthographic redundancy in Hebrew script, the fact that readers need constantly to segment multi-morphemic strings into constituent morphemes, and the visual complexity involved in attending to the diacritic vowel symbols. The requirement to distinguish among visually similar letters could be a contributing factor, as well. A review of research on the contributions of visual-spatial processes to reading in Hebrew is beyond the scope of this chapter.

4 A detailed discussion of the contrastive analysis hypothesis and its critiques is beyond the scope of this chapter.

5 The role of other cognitive processes associated with reading disability of bilingual or L2 learners is not discussed here. For a recent review of pertinent research see Durgunoglu, 2002; Genesee & Geva, 2006; Garcia & McKoon, 2006; and Lesaux & Geva, 2006.

6 For a comprehensive discussion of issues concerning rate of processing of auditory-phonological, and visual-orthographic information and its impact on reading performance see Breznitz (2006).

References

Abu-Rabia, S. (1997) Verbal and working-memory skills of bilingual Hebrew–English speaking children. *International Journal of Psycholinguistics*, 13(1), 25–40.

Akamatsu, N. (1999) The effects of first language orthographic features on word recognition processing in English as a second language. *Reading and Writing: An Interdisciplinary Journal*, 11(4), 381–403.

Anglin, J. M. (1993) Vocabulary development: a morphological analysis. *Monographs of the Society for Research in Child Development*, 58, Serial #238.

Anthony, J. & Lonigan, C. (2004) The nature of phonological awareness: converging evidence from four studies of preschool and early grade school children. *Journal of Educational Psychology*, 96(1), 43–55.

Arab-Moghaddam, N. & Sénéchal, M. (2001) Orthographic and phonological processing skills in reading and spelling in Persian/English bilinguals. *International Journal of Behavioral Development*, 25, 140–7.

Aram, D. (2005) Continuity in children's literacy achievements: a longitudinal perspective from kindergarten to school. *First Language*, 25: 259–89.

Ashkenazi, O. & Ravid, D. (1998) Children's understanding of linguistic humor: an aspect of metalinguistic awareness. *Current Psychology of Cognition*, 17, 367–87.

Ben-Dror, I., Bentin, S., & Frost, R. (1995) Semantic, phonologic and morphologic skills in reading disabled and normal children: evidence from perception and production of spoken Hebrew. *Reading Research Quarterly*, 30, 876–93.

Bentin, S. & Frost, R. (1987) Processing lexical ambiguity and visual word recognition in a deep orthography. *Memory & Cognition*, 15, 13–23.

Bentin, S. & Frost, R. (1995) Morphological factors in visual word identification in Hebrew. In L. B. Feldman (ed.), *Morphological aspects of language processing* (pp. 271–92).

Bentin, S. & Leshem, H. (1993) On the interaction of phonologic awareness and reading acquisition: it's a two-way street. *Psychological Science*, 2, 271–74.

Bentin, S., Hammer, R., & Cahan, S. (1991) The effects of aging and first year schooling on the development of phonological awareness. *Psychological Science*, 2, 271–74.

Berent, I. & Shimron, J. (1997) The representation of Hebrew words: evidence from the contour principle. *Cognition*, 64, 39–72.

Berman, R. (1978) *Modern Hebrew Structure*. University Publishing Projects: Tel Aviv.

Berman, R. (1982) Verb pattern alternation: the interface of morphology, syntax, and semantics in Hebrew child language. *Journal of Child Language*, 9: 169–91.

Berman, R. (1985) The acquisition of Hebrew. In D. Slobin (ed.), *The cross-linguistic study of language acquisition*, Vol. I: *The data* (pp. 255–371). Hillsdale, NJ: Erlbaum.

Bolozky, S. (1999) *Measuring productivity in word formation: the case of Israeli Hebrew*. Boston: Brill.

Bowey, J. A. (1995) Socioeconomic status differences in preschool phonological sensitivity and first-grade reading achievement. *Journal of Educational Psychology*, 87, 476–87.

Breznitz, Z. (1987) Enhancing the reading of dyslexic children by reading acceleration and auditory masking, *Journal of Educational Psychology*, 89(1), 103–13.

Breznitz, Z. (2006) *Fluency in reading: synchronization of processes*. New York: Lawrence Erlbaum Associates.

Breznitz, Z. & Share, D. (2002) Introduction on timing and phonology. *Reading and Writing: An Interdisciplinary Journal*, 15: 1–3.

Brown, G. D. A. & Hulme, C. (1992) Cognitive psychology and second language processing: the role of short-term memory. In R. J. Harris (ed.), *Cognitive processing in bilinguals* (pp. 105–21). Amsterdam: Elsevier.

Burgess, S. (1997) The role of shared reading in the development of phonological awareness: a longitudinal study of upper class children. *Early Child Development and Care*, 127–8, 191–8.

Burgess, S. R. & Lonigan, C. J. (1998) Bidirectional relations of phonological sensitivity and prereading abilities: evidence from a preschool sample. *Journal of Experimental Child Psychology*, 70, 117–41.

Cahana-Amitay, D. & Ravid, D. (2000) Optional bound morphology in the development of text production. In S. C. Howell, S. A. Fish & T. Keith-Lucas (eds.) Proceedings of the 24th Annual Boston University Conference on Language Development, Vol. I. Somerville, MA: Cascadilla Press, 176–84.

Caravolas, M. & Bruck, M. (1993) The effect of oral and written language input on children's phonological awareness: a cross-linguistic study. *Journal of Experimental Child Psychology*, 55, 1–30.

Carlisle, J. F. (1995) Morphological awareness and early reading achievement. In L. B. Feldman (ed.). *Morphological aspects of language processing* (pp. 189–209). Hillsdale NJ: Lawrence Erlbaum Associates.

Carlisle, J. F. (2000) Awareness of the structure and meaning of morphologically complex words: impact on reading. *Reading and Writing: An Interdisciplinary Journal*, 12, 169–90.

Carlisle, J. F. & Nomanbhoy, D. M. (1993) Phonological and morphological awareness in first graders. *Applied Psycholinguistics*, 14, 177–95.

Carlisle, J. F. & Fleming, J. J. (2003) Lexical processing of morphologically complex words in the elementary years. *Scientific Studies of Reading*, 7, 239–53.

Carlisle, J. F. & Stone, C. (2005) Exploring the role of morphemes in word reading. *Reading Research Quarterly*, 40, 428–49.

Carroll, J., Snowling, M., Hulme, C., & Stevenson, J. (2003) The development of phonological awareness in pre-school children. *Developmental Psychology*, 39(5), 913–23.

Chaney, C. (1998) Preschool language and metalinguistic skills are links to reading success. *Applied Psycholinguistics*, 19, 433–46.

Chiappe, P. & Siegel, L. S. (1999) Phonological awareness and reading acquisition in English- and Punjabi-speaking Canadian children. *Journal of Educational Psychology*, 9, 20–8.

Cohen, A., Schiff, R., & Gillis-Carlebach, M. (1996) Complexity of morphological, syntactic, and narrative characteristics: a comparison of children with reading difficulties and children who can read. *Megamot*, 37, 273–91 (in Hebrew).

Comeau, L., Cormier, P., Grandmaison, E., & Lacroix, D. (1999) A longitudinal study of phonological processing skills in children learning to read in a second language. *Journal of Educational Psychology*, 91, 29–43.

Cormier, P. & Landry, S. (2000) The role of phonological and syntactic awareness in the use of plural morphemes among children in French immersion. *Scientific Studies in Reading*, 4, 267–93.

Cossu, G., Shankwieler, D., Liberman, I. Y., Katz, L., & Tola, G. (1988) Awareness of phonological segments and reading disability in Italian children. *Applied Psycholinguistics*, 9, 1–16.

DaFontoura, H. A. & Siegel, L. S. (1995) Reading, syntactic, and working memory skills of bilingual, Portuguese–English Canadian children. *Reading and Writing: An Interdisciplinary Journal*, 7, 139–53.

de Jong, P. F. & van der Leij, A. (1999) Specific contributions of phonological abilities to early reading acquisition: results from a Dutch latent variable longitudinal study. *Journal of Educational Psychology*, 91, 450–76.

Doctor, E. A. & Klein, D. (1992) Phonological processing in bilingual word recognition (pp. 237–52). In R. J. Harris (ed.), *Cognitive processing in bilinguals*. Amsterdam: Elsevier.

Dufva, M. & Voeten, M. J. M. (1999) Native language literacy and phonological memory as prerequisites for learning English as a foreign language. *Applied Psycholinguistics*, 20(3), 329–48.

Durgunoglu, A. (2002) Cross-linguistic transfer in literacy development and implications for language learners. *Annals of Dyslexia*, 52, 189–204.

Durgunoglu, A. Y. & Oney, B. (1999) A cross-linguistic comparison of phonological awareness and word recognition. *Reading and Writing*, 11, 281–99.

Durgunoglu, A. Y., Nagy, W. E., & Hancin-Bhatt, B. J. (1993) Cross-language transfer of phonological awareness. *Journal of Educational Psychology*, 85, 453–65.

Durgunoglu, A. Y., Snow, C., & Geva, E. (2001) Theoretical issues in literacy development of ELL students. *International Dyslexia Association Commemorative Booklet*, 21–6.

Everatt, J., Smythe, I., Adam, E., & Ocampo, D. (2000) Dyslexia screening measures and bilingualism. *Dyslexia*, 6, 42–56.

Feldman, L. B. (1987) Phonological and morphological analysis by skilled readers of

Serbo-Croatian (pp. 197–210). In A. Allport, D. G. MacKay, W. Prinz, & G. Scheerer (eds.), *Language perception and production*. London: Academic.

Fowler, A. E. & Liberman, I. Y. (1995) The role of phonology and orthography in morphological awareness. In L. B. Feldman (ed.) *Morphological aspects of language processing* (pp. 157–88). Hillsdale, NJ: Erlbaum.

Frank, J., Vigliocco, G., & Nicol, J. (2002) Subject-verb agreement errors in French and English: the role of syntactic hierarchy. *Language and Cognitive Processes*, 17, 371–404

Frost, R. (2005) Orthographic systems and skilled word recognition processes in reading (pp. 272–95). In C. Hulme & M. Snowling (eds.), *The science of reading: a handbook*. Oxford: Blackwell.

Frost, R. & Bentin, S. (1992) Processing phonological and semantic ambiguity: evidence from semantic priming at different SOAs. *Journal of Experimental Psychology: Learning, Memory, and Cognition*, 18, 58–68.

García, G. E. & McKoon, G. (2006) Language and literacy assessment of language-minority students. In D. August & T. Shanahan (eds.), *Developing literacy in second-language learners: a report of the National Literacy Panel on Language-Minority Children and Youth*. Mahwah, NJ: Lawrence Erlbaum Associates.

Gelb, I. J. (1963) *A study of writing*, 2nd edn. Chicago: University of Chicago Press.

Genesee, F. & Geva, E. (2006) Cross-linguistic relationships in working memory, phonological processes, and oral language. In D. August & T. Shanahan (eds.), *Developing literacy in second-language learners: a report of the National Literacy Panel on Language-Minority Children and Youth*. Mahwah, NJ: Lawrence Erlbaum Associates.

Genesee, F., Geva, E., Dressler, D., and Kamil, M. (2006) Synthesis: cross-linguistic relationships. In D. August & T. Shanahan (eds.), *Developing literacy in second-language learners: a report of the National Literacy Panel on Language-Minority Children and Youth*. Mahwah, NJ: Lawrence Erlbaum Associates.

Geva, E. (2000) Issues in the assessment of reading disabilities in L2 children: beliefs and research evidence. *Dyslexia* 6, 13–28.

Geva, E. & Ryan, E. B. (1993) Linguistic and cognitive correlates of academic skills in first and second language. *Language Learning*, 43, 5–42.

Geva, E. & Wade-Woolley, L. (1998) Component processes in becoming English–Hebrew biliterate (pp. 85–110). In A. Durgunoglu, & L. Verhoeven (eds.), *Acquisition of literacy in a multilingual context: a cross-cultural perspective*. Hillsdale, NJ: Lawrence Erlbaum Associates.

Geva, E. & Siegel, L. S. (2000) Orthographic and cognitive factors in the concurrent development of basic reading skills in two languages. *Reading and Writing: An Interdisciplinary Journal*, 12, 1–31.

Geva, E. & Wang, M. (2001) The role of orthography in the literacy acquisition of young L2 learners. *Annual Review of Applied Linguistics*, 21, 182–204.

Geva, E. & Wade-Woolley, W. (2004) Issues in the assessment of reading disability in second language children (pp. 195–206). In I. Smythe, J. Everatt, & R. Salter (eds.), *International book of dyslexia: a cross language comparison and practice guide*. Chichester, UK: John Wiley.

Geva, E. & Genesee, F. (2006) First-language oral proficiency and second-language literacy. In D. August & T. Shanahan (eds.), *Developing literacy in second-language learners: a report of the National Literacy Panel on Language-Minority Children and Youth*. Mahwah, NJ: Lawrence Erlbaum Associates.

Geva, E. & Shany, M. (2007 under review) Do vulnerable bilingual-bicultural children close the gap on cognitive, linguistic, and literacy skills? A cross-grade comparison.

Geva, E., Wade-Woolley, L., & Shany, M. (1993) The concurrent development of spelling and decoding in two different orthographies. *Journal of Reading Behavior*, 25, 383–406.

Geva, E., & Wade-Woolley, L., & Shany, M. (1997) The development of reading efficiency in first and second language. *Scientific Studies of Reading*, 1, 119–44.

Geva, E., Yaghoub Zadeh, Z., & Schuster, B. (2000) Understanding individual differences in word recognition skills of ESL children. *Annals of Dyslexia*, 50, 123–54.

Gholamain, M. & Geva, E. (1999) Orthographic and cognitive factors in the concurrent development of basic reading skills in English and Persian. *Language Learning*, 49, 183–217.

Gillis, S. & Ravid, D. (2000) Effects of phonology and morphology in children's orthographic systems: a cross-linguistic study of Hebrew and Dutch (pp. 203–10). In E. Clark (ed.), *The Proceedings of the 30th Annual Child Language Research Forum*. Stanford: Center for the Study of Language and Information.

Goswami, U. (2000) Phonological representations, reading development and dyslexia: towards a cross-linguistic theoretical framework. *Dyslexia*, 6, 133–51.

Goswami, U. & Bryant, P. (1990) *Phonological skills and learning to read*. London, UK: Lawrence Erlbaum Associates.

Gottardo, A., Chiappe, P., Yan, B., Siegel, L., & Gu, Y. (2006) Relationships between first and second language phonological processing skills and reading in Chinese English speakers living in English speaking contexts. *Educational Psychology*, 26, 367–93.

Gottardo, A., Yan, B., Siegel, L. S., & Wade-Woolley, L. (2001) Factors related to English reading performance in children with Chinese as a first language: more evidence of cross-language transfer of phonological processing. *Journal of Educational Psychology*, 93, 530–42.

Hart, B. & Risley, T. R. (1999) *The social world of children learning to talk*. Baltimore: Brookes Publishing Co.

Ho, C. S., Law, T. P., and Ng, P. D. (2000) The phonological deficit hypothesis in Chinese developmental dyslexia. *Reading and Writing*, 13, 57–79.

Hu, Chieh-Fang & Catts, H. W. (1998) The role of phonological processing in early reading ability: what we can learn from Chinese. *Scientific Studies of Reading*, 2, 55–7.

Kahn-Horwitz, J., Shimron, J., & Sparks, R. L. (2005) Predicting foreign language reading achievement in elementary school students. *Reading and Writing*, 18, 237–558.

Katz, L. & Frost, R. (1992) The reading process is different for different orthographies: the orthographic depth hypothesis (pp. 67–84). In R. Frost & L. Katz (eds.), *Orthography, phonology, morphology, and meaning*. Amsterdam: Elsevier.

Katzir, T., Shaul, S., Breznitz, Z. & Wolf, M. (2004) The universal and the unique in dyslexia: a cross-linguistic investigation of reading and reading fluency in Hebrew and English-speaking children with reading disorders. *Reading and Writing*, 17, 739–68.

Koda, K. (1999) Developing L2 intra-word orthographic sensitivity and decoding skills. *The Modern Language Journal*, 83, 51–64.

Kozminsky, L. & Kozminsky, E. (1993/94) In Hebrew: Hahashpa'a shel ha'imun be'mudaut phonologit be'gil ha'gan al ha'hatslacha be'rechishat ha'kri'ah be'vet ha'sefer. [The effects of phonological awareness training in kindergarten on reading acquisition in school]. Chelkat HaLashon, 15–16, 7–28.

Lado, R. (1964) *Language reading: a scientific approach*. New York: McGraw Hill.

Lafrance, A. & Gottardo, A. (2005) A longitudinal study of phonological processing skills and reading in bilingual children, *Applied Psycholinguistics*, 26, 559–78.

Lapidot, M., Tubul, G., & Wohl, A. (1995–6) Mivchan eranut fonologit kekli nibuj be'rechishat ha'kri'a. [A rest of phonological awareness as a predictor of reading acquisition]. *Chelkat Lashon*, 19–20, 169–88.

Leong, C. K. & Tamaoka, K. (eds.) (1998) *Cognitive processing of the Chinese and the Japanese languages*. Dordrecht: Kluwer Academic Publishers.

Lesaux, N. & Siegel, L. S. (2003) The development of reading in children who speak English as a Second Language (ESL). *Developmental Psychology*, 39, 1005–19.

Lesaux, N. & Geva, E. (2006) Synthesis: development of literacy in language-minority students. In D. August & T. Shanahan (eds.), *Developing literacy in second-language learners: a report of the National Literacy Panel on Language-Minority Children and Youth*. Mahwah, NJ: Lawrence Erlbaum Associates.

Levin, I., Korat, O., & Amsterdamer, P. (1996) Emergent writing among kinder-gartners: cross-linguistic commonalities and Hebrew-specific issues (pp. 398–419). In G. Rijlaarsdam, H. van der Bergh, and M. Couzijn (eds.), *Current trends in writing research: theories, models and methodology*. Amsterdam: Amsterdam University Press.

Levin I., Ravid, D., & Rapaport, S. (1999) Developing morphological awareness and learning to write: a two-way street (pp. 77–104). In T. Nunes (ed.), *Learning to read: an integrated view from research and practice*. Amsterdam: Kluwer.

Levin, I., Ravid, D., & Rapaport, S. (2001) Morphology and spelling among Hebrew-speaking children: from kindergarten to first grade. *Journal of Child Language*, 28, 741–72.

Lindsey, K. A., Manis, F. R., & Bailey, C. E. (2003) Prediction of first-grade reading in Spanish-speaking English-language learners. *Journal of Educational Psychology*, 95, 482–94.

Lonigan, C. J., Burgess, S. R., & Anthony, J. L. (2000) Development of emergent literacy and early reading skills in preschool children: evidence from a latent-variable longitudinal study. *Developmental Psychology*, 36, 596–613.

McBride-Chang, C., Shu, H., Zhou, A., Wat, C.-P., & Wagner, R. K. (2003) Morphological awareness uniquely predicts young children's Chinese character recognition. *Journal of Educational Psychology*, 95, 743–51.

Mann, V. A. (1985) Why some children encounter reading problems: the contribution of difficulties with language processing and phonological sophistication to early reading disability (pp. 133–54). In J. K. Torgesen & B. Y. L. Wong (eds.), *Psychological and educational perspectives on learning disabilities*. New York: Academic Press.

Marchand, H. (ed.). (1969) *The categories and types of present-day English word-formation*. Munich: C.H. Becksche, Verlagsbuchhandlung.

Metsala, J. & Walley, A. (1998) Spoken vocabulary growth and segmental restructuring of lexical representations: precursors to phonemic awareness and early reading ability. In J. Metsala & L. Ehri (eds.), *Word recognition in beginning reading*. Mahwah, NJ: Lawrence Erlbaum Associates.

Meyler, A. & Breznitz, Z. (1998) Developmental aspects of visual and verbal short-term memory and the acquisition of decoding skill. *Reading and Writing: An Interdisciplinary Journal.* 10, 519–40.

Morais, J., Cary, L., Alegria, J., & Bertelson, P. (1979) Does awareness of speech as a sequence of phones arise spontaneously? *Cognition*, 7, 323–31.

Mumtaz, S. & Humphreys, G. W. (2001) The effects of bilingualism on learning to read English: evidence from the contrast between Urdu–English bilingual and English monolingual children. *Journal of Research in Reading*, 24(2), 113–34.

Muter, V. & Diethelm, K. (2001) The contribution of phonological skills and letter knowledge to early reading development in a multilingual population. *Language Learning*, 51(2), 187–219.

Näslund, J. C. & Schneider, W. (1996) Kindergarten letter knowledge, phonological skills and memory processes: relative effects on early literacy. *Journal of Experimental Child Psychology*, 62, 30–59.

Navon, D. & Shimron, Y. (1994) Reading Hebrew: how necessary is the graphemic representation of vowels? In L. Henderson (ed.), *Orthographies and reading: perspectives from cognitive psychology, neuropsychology, and linguistics.* London: Lawrence Erlbaum Associates.

Oney, B., Peter, M., & Katz, L. (1997) Phonological processing in printed word recognition: effects of age and writing system. *Scientific Studies of Reading*, 1, 65–83.

Perfetti, C. A. & Zhang, S. (1995) Very early phonological activation in Chinese reading. *Journal of Experimental Psychology: Learning, Memory, and Cognition*, 21, 24–33.

Plaza, M. (2003) The role of naming speed, phonological processing and morpho-logical/syntactic skill in the reading and spelling performance of second-grade children. *Current Psychology Letters*, 10, Vol. 1, 2003, Special Issue on Language Disorders and Reading Acquisition. http://cpl.revues.org/document88.html

Quiroga, T., Lemos-Britton, Z., Mostafapour, E., Abbott, R.D., & Berninger, V. W. (2002) Phonological awareness and beginning reading in Spanish-speaking ESL first graders: research into practice. *Journal of School Psychology*, 40, 85–111.

Ravid, D. (2001) Learning to spell in Hebrew: phonological and morphological factors. *Reading and Writing*, 14, 459–85.

Ravid, D. (2002) A developmental perspective on root perception in Hebrew and Palestinian Arabic. In Y. Shimron (ed.) *The processing and acquisition of root-based morphology.* Amsterdam: Benjamins.

Ravid, D. (2004) Later lexical development in Hebrew: derivational morphology revisited. In R.A. Berman (ed.), *Language development across childhood and adolescence: psycholinguistic and cross-linguistic perspectives* (pp. 53–82). Philadelphia: Benjamins.

Ravid, D. (2005) Hebrew orthography and literacy (pp. 339–63). In R. M. Joshi & P. G. Aaron (eds.), *Handbook of orthography and literacy.* Mahwah, NJ: Lawrence Erlbaum Associates.

Ravid, D. & Malenky, D. (2001) Awareness of linear and non-linear morphology in Hebrew: a developmental study. *First Language*, 21, 25–56.

Ravid, D. & Bar-On, A. (2005) Manipulating written Hebrew roots across development: the interface of semantic, phonological and orthographic factors. *Reading and Writing*, 18, 231–56.

Saiegh-Haddad, E. & Geva, E. (in press) Morphological awareness, phonological awareness, and reading in English-Arabic bilingual children. *Reading and Writing: An Interdisciplinary Journal.*

Scarborough, H. S. (2002) Connecting early language and literacy to later reading (dis)abilities: evidence, theory and practice (pp. 97–110). In S. B. Neuman & D. K. Dickinson (eds.), *Handbook of early literacy development.* New York: Guilford.

Schiff, R. & Ravid, D. (2004) Vowel representation in written Hebrew: phonological, orthographic and morphological contexts. *Reading and Writing,* 17, 245–65.

Seymour, P. H., Aro, M., & Erskine, J. M. (2003) Foundation literacy acquisition in European orthographies. *British Journal of Psychology,* 94, 143–74.

Shany, M., Geva, E., & Melech, L. (under review) Emergent literacy in Ethiopian kindergarten children in Israel: socio-cultural, contextual, cognitive, and linguistic factors.

Share, D. (2003) Dyslexia in Hebrew (pp. 208–34). In N. Goulandris (ed.), *Dyslexia in different languages.* London: Whurr Publishers Ltd.

Share, D. & Levin, I. (1999) Learning to read and write in Hebrew (pp. 89–111). In M. Harris and G. Hatano (eds.), *Learning to read and write: a cross-linguistic perspective.* Cambridge: Cambridge University Press.

Share, D. & Blum, P. (2005) Syllable splitting in literate and pre-literate Hebrew speakers: onsets and rimes or bodies and codas? *Journal of Experimental Child Psychology,* 92 (2), 182–202.

Shatil, E. (1997) Predicting reading ability: evidence for cognitive modularity. Unpublished doctoral dissertation. University of Haifa.

Shimron, J. (1993) The role of vowels in reading: a review of studies in English and Hebrew. *Psychological Bulletin,* 114, 52–67.

Shimron, J. (1999) The role of vowels signs in Hebrew: beyond word recognition. *Reading and Writing: An Interdisciplinary Journal,* 11, 301–19.

Shimron, J. (2006) *Reading Hebrew: the language and the psychology of reading it.* New York: Lawrence Erlbaum Associates.

Shimron, J. & Navon, D. (1981) The distribution of information within letters. *Perception & Psychophysics,* 30, 483–91.

Shimron, J. & Navon, D. (1982) The dependency on graphemes and their translation to phonemes in reading: a developmental perspective. *Reading Research Quarterly,* 17, 210–28.

Shimron, J., & Sivan, T. (1994) Reading proficiency and orthography: evidence from Hebrew and English. *Language Learning,* 44, 5–27.

Siegel, L. S. & Ryan, E. B. (1989) Development of grammatical sensitivity, phonological, and short-term memory skills in normally achieving and learning disabled children. *Developmental Psychology,* 24, 28–37.

Singson, M., Mohany, D., & Mann, V. (2000) The relation between reading ability and morphological skills: evidence from derivational suffixes. *Reading and Writing: An Interdisciplinary Journal,* 12, 219–52.

So, D. & Siegel, L. S. (1997) Learning to read Chinese: semantic, syntactic, phonological and short-term memory skills in normally achieving and poor Chinese readers. *Reading and Writing: An Interdisciplinary Journal,* 9, 1–21.

Spencer, A. (1991) *Morphological theory.* Basil Blackwell, Oxford.

Stanovich, K. E., Cunningham, A. E., & Feeman, D. J. (1984a) Intelligence, cognitive skills, and early reading progress. *Reading Research Quarterly,* 19, 278–303.

Stanovich, K. E., Cunningham, A. E., & Cramer, B. B. (1984b) Assessing phonological awareness in kindergarten children: issues of task comparability. *Journal of Experimental Child Psychology*, 38, 175–90.

Storch, S. A. & Whitehurst, G. J. (2001) The role of family and home in the literacy development of children from low-income backgrounds. In P. R. Britto & J. Brooks-Gunn (eds.), *The role of family literacy environments in promoting young children's emerging literacy skills: new directions for child and adolescent development* (pp. 53–71). San Francisco, CA: Jossey Bass/Pfeiffer.

Taylor, I. & Taylor, M. M. (1983) *The psychology of reading*. New York: Academic.

Tolchinsky, L. & Teberosky, A. (1998) The development of word segmentation and writing in two scripts. *Cognitive Development*, 13, 1–25.

Treiman, R. & Zukowski, A. (1996) Children's sensitivity to syllables, onsets, rimes, and phonemes. *Journal of Experimental Child Psychology*, 6, 193–215.

Tyler, A. & Nagy, W. (1989) The acquisition of English derivational morphology. *Journal of Memory and Language*, 28, 649–67.

Wade-Woolley, L. & Siegel, L. S. (1997) The spelling performance of ESL and native speakers of English as a function of reading skill. *Reading and Writing: An Interdisciplinary Journal*, 9, 387–406.

Wade-Woolley, L. & Geva, E. (1999) Processing inflected morphology in second language word recognition: Russian-speakers and English-speakers read Hebrew. *Reading and Writing: An Interdisciplinary Perspective*, 11, 321–43.

Wade-Woolley, L. & Geva, E. (2000) Processing novel phonemic contrasts in the acquisition of L2 word reading, *Scientific Studies of Reading*, 4, 267–93.

Wang, M. & Geva, E. (2003) Spelling acquisition of novel English phonemes in Chinese children. *Reading and Writing: An Interdisciplinary Journal*, 16, 325–48.

Wang, M. & Koda, K. (2005) Commonalities and differences in word identification skills among English second language learners. *Language Learning*, 55, 73–100.

Wimmer, H. & Goswami, U. (1994) The influence of orthographic consistency on reading development: word recognition in English and German children. *Cognition*, 51, 91–103.

Wimmer, H., Mayringer, H., & Landerl, K. (2000) The double deficit hypothesis and difficulties in learning to read a regular orthography. *Journal of Educational Psychology*, 92, 668–80.

Wolf, M., Tuffs, U., Pfeil, C., Lotz, R. & Biddle, K. (1994). Towards a more universal understanding of the developmental dyslexias: the contribution of orthographic factors. In V.W. Berninger (ed.) *The varieties of orthographic knowledge: Theoretical and developmental issues*, (pp. 137–71). New York: Kluwer Academic.

Yopp, H. K. (1988) The validity and reliability of phonemic awareness tests. *Research Reading Quarterly*, 23, 159–77.

Ziegler, J.C. & Goswami, U. (2005) Reading acquisition, developmental dyslexia and skilled reading across languages: a psycholinguistic grain size theory. *Psychological Bulletin*, 131, 3–29.

8   Learning to read in Khmer

Annette M. Zehler and Saloni Sapru

Cambodian, or Modern Standard Khmer, is understood and used through-out Cambodia. Variants of Khmer that are considered to be mutually under-standable are used by many speakers in communities outside Cambodia, including speakers in Thailand and in southern Vietnam. Although Khmer is an alphabetic language, there are characteristics of the writing system that depart from a strict alphabetic system and that have led some to characterize it as a syllabic system.

Description of the Khmer language and writing system

Characteristics of the Khmer orthography

The Khmer language uses an alphabetic, phonologically based writing system. Khmer is written in two different styles of script, slanted script and round script. The slanted script is a fine-line script used for most text. There is also a straight line or vertical form of this script that is often used for chapter headings or subtitles, and which in some cases may even be used for a whole text, replacing the slanted script form entirely (Huffman, 1970a). The round script is a more ornamental and archaic form, typically a shadowed or double-lined version of its slanted form. It is used for titles of books, major headings, newspaper headlines, religious texts, proper names, and inscriptions on monuments and buildings (Huffman, 1970a; Ouk *et al.*, 1988).

Khmer is similar to English in that it is written from left to right and down the page, but it differs in that it is written as continuous script, that is, without spaces between individual words. Although boundaries between words are not marked, spaces and other marks are used to indicate the end of a clause or boundaries between sentences (Ouk *et al.*, 1988).

There are 33 consonant symbols in Khmer (to represent 18 consonant phonemes), and also separate subscript forms that are used when a conson-ant is the second of two consonants that occur together. This subscript form most typically is a somewhat modified, smaller version of the consonant; however, in some cases it is a form that does not resemble the original consonant in any way. The 33 consonant symbols include two sets or "series" of letters for representing the Khmer consonants, meaning that there are generally two consonant symbols for every consonant sound. Each series is associated with a different inherent vowel. In addition, the series of an initial consonant symbol determines the value of the vowel that follows it. Khmer also includes unwritten consonants in some environments (e.g. a medial consonant becomes a doubled consonant and results in an added syllable).

Vowels are represented by 21 vowel symbols. The vowel symbols are comprised of one or more elements that are written before, above, below, after, or surrounding, the consonant symbol. Each vowel symbol has at least two possible values, with the specific reading dependent upon the series of the consonant with which the vowel is associated. The final value of a vowel depends not only upon the consonant with which it is linked, but also upon the specific syllable environment (e.g. stress pattern, the final consonant in the syllable) in which it occurs. Huffman (1970a) identifies 39 such "configurations" in which vowels are regularly represented which take these environments into account. Finally, Khmer includes unwritten vowels in certain environments, and 14 independent vowel symbols, used in a limited number of words, that incorporate both an initial consonant and a vowel. (Some of these symbols, however, are used in quite common words).

Thus, as the above demonstrates, a syllable in Khmer is not read simply as a sequence in which there is a one-to-one relationship between individual symbols and sounds (Huffman, 1970a). Khmer orthography differs from a purely alphabetic system in that the reading of a syllable is based on the specific consonant and vowel pair, and the specific environment in which these occur. It is this complex relationship in the representation of consonants and vowels that has led Khmer to be described by some as a syllabic system (Huffman, 1970a; Ouk *et al.*, 1988). Despite the apparent complexity, however, the rules for combining consonant and vowel sounds are very consistent, and overall the Khmer system is considered to be much more regular than the English system.

The Khmer orthography also includes a system of diacritics. Some create a first series consonant out of a second series consonant (when a separate first series form does not exist), and vice versa. Other diacritics change the value of the vowel or consonant (e.g. to shorten a vowel or change the vowel sound), or insert a sound (e.g. to insert a vowel or a vowel plus consonant) (Huffman, 1970a). There are several Khmer punctuation marks and these are used together with several common Western punctuation marks (such as question mark, colon). In Khmer, space is one form of punctuation; a space is used to indicate clauses within a sentence, or to mark sentences within a cohesive group of sentences. It is also used between separate words in lists, and before and after numbers and proper names, among other uses. Other punctuation includes a specific mark to indicate the beginning of literary and religious texts, and three different stop symbols to mark the end of a paragraph/topic, the end of a chapter or text, and the absolute end of a text, typically of a religious or poetic text. There is also a separate symbol (/leik too/, "the figure 2") that indicates repetition of the preceding word (or phrase). This is most commonly used in writing two-syllable compound words in which both syllables are the same (Huffman, 1970a).

Characteristics of Khmer phonology

Khmer has a very rich phonological system. Huffman (1970a) lists 18 consonants, including one used only in loanwords. Thirteen of the consonants can occur in syllable-final position (Phap, 1980; Wright, 1998), while the remaining consonants are limited to syllable-initial positions. Approximately 85 different consonant clusters are possible in Khmer (Huffman, 1970a; Wright, 1998). There are many more initial consonant clusters possible in Khmer than in most languages (Ouk *et al.*, 1988), and many of these are clusters that do not occur in English (e.g. kb, db, ml, lm (Phap, 1988)). However, no consonant clusters occur at the end of Khmer syllables (Huffman, 1970a).

There are 13 vowel phonemes in Khmer, including 10 short vowels, and three short diphthongs (i.e. two vowels together) (Huffman, 1970a). These occur as both short and long vowels/diphthongs for a total of approximately thirty-one separate vowel sounds (Huffman, 1970a; Wright, 1998).

Original Khmer words are either monosyllabic, consisting of a single syllable, or are disyllabic, consisting of a semi-syllable (unstressed with a reduced vowel) followed by a single syllable (with stress), or of two stressed syllables (most typically for compound words). A single syllable in Khmer consists of a consonant or consonant cluster followed by a vowel or diphthong, sometimes with a single final consonant. Possible syllable structures are: CVC, CCVC, and (rarely) CCCVC for syllables with short vowels or diphthongs; and CVV, CVVC, CCVV, CCVVC, and (rarely) CCCVVC for syllables with a long vowel or long diphthong. There is a high percentage of disyllabic words in Khmer, and most words in colloquial speech are one or two syllables only. In formal speech and written texts, however, there are many polysyllabic words, mainly of a literate character, which have been borrowed from Sanskrit, Pali, or French sources (Huffman, 1970a) or, more recently, from English. In contrast to several other languages in South East Asia, Khmer is not a tonal language. Khmer uses stress and intonation, with the stress most frequently falling on the final syllable of a word.

Characteristics of Khmer morphology

Khmer is an "isolating" language; that is, there are no changes on nouns or verbs to mark case or other grammatical relationships that are signaled by inflections in non-isolating languages such as English. Instead, Khmer can rely on word order alone to convey such information. For example, possession in Khmer is indicated by word order, with the possessor following immediately after the object possessed (e.g. Som Nang's book = book Som Nang).

Number on nouns and tense on verbs are interpreted either from context alone (e.g. /kmawday/ refers to either, "pencil" or "pencils;" /tɨñ/, refers to "buy" or "bought," depending on the context), or by the addition of modifiers that make clear the specific number, or that indicate a past or future time (e.g. /kmawday pii/, "pencil(s) two;" /tɨñ msəlmən/, "buy(bought) yesterday") (Center for Applied Linguistics, 1978; Huffman, 1970b; Ouk *et al.*, 1988; Wright, 1998). Gender distinctions are indicated by use of words that have inherent referential gender, such as words for "son," or "daughter;" or by use of the additional word "male," or "female" when a gender-neutral word is used (e.g. /pqoun-proh/ "brother," consists of two words, /pqoun/, "younger relative of the same generation" and /proh/, "male"). Similarly, pronouns in Khmer do not inflect for differences in case or gender as in English. Nevertheless, the system of personal pronouns is quite complex since a different pronoun is used for "I" or "you" when speaking with persons unknown to the speaker versus with intimate friends, or with persons lower in social status, royalty, or clergy (Center for Applied Linguistics, 1978; Wright, 1999). For example, Huffman and Proum (1978, cited in Wright, 1999) identify 13 different categories for the second person pronoun "you," with variations for gender, politeness, age, relationship, and social status.

Khmer morphology includes derivation of disyllabic words from monosyllabic bases through use of prefixes and infixes to derive, for example, causative verbs from simple verbs (e.g. "put to sleep" from "sleep"), reciprocal verbs from simple verbs (e.g. "love one another" from "love"), and nouns from verbs (e.g. "birth" from "be born") (Huffman, 1970a; Chhim, 1994). However, as Huffman (1970b) notes, for the most part these affixes are not productive in the modern language, and are "crystallized" in the words in which they occur.

Khmer syntactic structure

Khmer uses Subject-Verb-Object (SVO) word order (Wright, 1998; Ouk *et al.*, 1988); however when the subject is clear from the context, then it can be omitted. In addition to an SVO structure, a topic-comment structure is also acceptable and common (Phap, 1980), as in : /kliə nuh, kñom prae mɨñ baan tee/, "That sentence, I can't translate" (Huffman, 1970b). Unlike English, modifiers typically follow the noun modified (e.g. "shirt white"). Khmer has two forms of the verb "to be" which are often used in different contexts; however, a sentence can be grammatical without the verb "to be" (e.g. "this mother I" for "This is my mother;" "I happy" for "I am happy" (Phap, 1980)).

Negative sentences are formed by the negative /mɨñ/ placed before the verb (e.g. "I no happy") or the use of the "discontinuous negative" /mɨñ. . .tee/ (e.g. /kñom <u>mɨñ</u> trəw-kaa kafei <u>tee</u>/, "I don't need any coffee"). Questions do not involve any change in the order of the subject and verb. They are formed in three ways, all with use of a rising intonation: use of a sentence-final question word; use of the final question particle /rɨ-tee/ (shortened to /tee/ in colloquial speech) for yes-no questions; and intonation only, without the use of a particle or question word, in contexts where the question follows up on a question already introduced into the conversation (Huffman, 1970b).

Relative pronouns exist in Khmer (e.g. /dael/, "who," "which," "that," Huffman, 1970b). However, these are not required, and word order alone can convey the relative clause (Phap, 1980). Word order alone can be used for subordinate conjunction as well. For example, the subordinate conjunction /dɑl/, "when," can be used as in English to introduce a subordinate clause, but it is not required in cases in which the subordinate clause precedes the main clause and is prior in time or is a logical requirement for the main clause (e.g. "[When] you get out of school, what work do [you] plan to do?" (Huffman, 1970b).

Khmer discourse structure

As for other languages, there are important differences observed between the spoken and written forms of Khmer. In the case of Khmer, however, these differences may be more pronounced in that, for example, written Khmer uses many archaic and polysyllabic words, while within everyday conversation, monosyllabic and disyllabic words predominate and polysyllabic words are few.

Written text in Khmer does not follow the linear, Western, model of discourse (Phap, 1980), and repetition of individual words or phrases is used frequently to provide emphasis. Repetition is marked by the use of the /leik too/ ("the figure 2") symbol. (This is the same symbol used to represent a repeated syllable in compound words, as noted above). The /leik too/ symbol is often used for repetition of adjectives as a means of providing emphasis (Huffman, 1970a).

Metalinguistic and other requisite competencies in learning to read Khmer

A broad search of the research literature (in English) did not reveal any research that specifically examined acquisition of reading in Khmer and the competencies involved. However, by analyzing the language, it is possible to propose competencies that are likely to underlie ability to read in Khmer.

Oral language competence

In listening to and speaking Khmer, the learner will become attuned to patterns such as the syllable-initial consonant clusters, restrictions on syllable-final consonants, and sequences of stressed and semi-stressed syllables that assist in segmenting the language into syllables and words. Use of the language also familiarizes a learner with the combinations of consonants and vowels and their occurrence within certain syllable environments. In addition, experience as a speaker and listener provides an understanding of the use of word order and topic-comment structures to convey meaning, the use of replication to insert emphasis or to make reference back to a prior sentence or clause, and the importance of using the context to accurately interpret the intended referent (e.g. to distinguish whether a male or female individual is indicated when gender-neutral words are used) or the intended tense of a verb (e.g. to interpret the time frame in the absence of a word that specifies the time reference).

Orthographic knowledge

Reading in Khmer requires recognition of the two sets of consonant symbols (representing the two series) and the separate subscript forms that are used when a consonant follows immediately after another consonant with no intervening vowel. In learning the vowel symbols, the reader must understand that each vowel symbol occurs in a fixed position in relation to the consonant (either above, below, left or right of, or surrounding, the consonant). In addition, there are different combination patterns ("configurations" identified by Huffman, 1970a) associated with certain syllable environments. Key to competence in the orthography also is knowledge of the diacritics and the functions of these in relation to consonants and vowels (e.g. to change a consonant from a first series to a second series consonant). The reader must also be familiar with the two main script types and their variations.

Grapho-phonological awareness

Developing an awareness of the relationship between sounds and their written representations requires processing of more than an individual symbol. Readers of Khmer must interpret additional markers and syllable-level characteristics in order to accurately link a sound and symbol. They must recognize the two separate forms (first and second series forms) that exist for many of the consonants, and also understand that the same vowel symbol is associated with two different sounds, and that its value is determined by the specific syllable context. In addition, the reader of Khmer must become skilled in understanding the use of diacritics, e.g. to signal insertion of a sound, or to signal a change in the value of a symbol (e.g. use of diacritics to change the series of a consonant, with implications for the reading of the vowel associated with it).

Grapho-morphological awareness

Most Khmer words are either a single-syllable, a semi-syllable followed by a single syllable, or a combination of single-syllable words. Since the script does not mark breaks between words, the reader must rely on an understanding of possible syllable structures and of allowable distributions of sounds within syllables in order to determine word boundaries. For example, a reader of Khmer who recognizes that consonant clusters can occur only at the beginning and not at the end of a syllable will be better able to identify syllable and word boundaries. This same skill will help the reader of Khmer to isolate a preceding syllable in order to match the /leik too/, the symbol for repetition, with the appropriate word or phrase.

Sentence-processing skills

Khmer sentences generally use SVO word order to identify the relationships among elements in a sentence. However, the sentence context also is important to understanding sentences. Since Khmer is an isolating language, the reader must rely on the context to interpret number, gender or verb tense when modifiers are not present to clarify these. Both clause order and context are important in understanding a subordinate clause and its relationship to the main clause when no subordinate conjunction is present. Context is necessary in interpreting those sentences that use topic-comment structure, which is also allowed in Khmer. Skilled readers in Khmer must interpret the appropriate function of the /leik too/ symbol within a sentence. For example, if it is used to repeat an adjective, then it signals emphasis/intensity on the meaning of that adjective.

Differences and similarities in learning to read in Khmer and English

A Khmer reader learning English as a second language will be able to benefit from some similarities in the writing systems. For example, both Khmer and English are phonologically based, requiring the reader to link individual symbols and sounds. However, Khmer is not based on a simple linear sequence of consonants and vowels as is English; the orthography is more complex. Each Khmer vowel is located in a specified position in relation to a consonant (above, below, before, after, or surrounding, the consonant). Its value is determined by the consonant with which it is associated and by the syllable environment. Thus Khmer is considered to be a syllabic system, in contrast to the alphabetic system of English, since it relies on the configuration of the vowel and consonant together to determine the reading of the symbols used. Khmer symbols are more complex as well. Khmer uses two separate sets of consonant symbols (first series and second series); consonants also have subscript forms that are used when one consonant follows immediately after another without an intervening vowel. While many subscripts are similar to the full consonant, some are very different in appearance and must be learned separately. Thus the system of consonants and vowels is more complex in Khmer than in English. However, despite this complexity, once the Khmer orthography has been mastered, it is generally predictable and consistent. In contrast, English is not as predictable and can be quite difficult for a beginning reader (e.g. the different readings of "ough" in "rough," "through," and "bough").

Although Khmer and English both utilize SVO word order, Khmer also allows for a topic-comment structure, and allows the subject to be dropped when it is easily understood from the context. Similarly, word order and context are used to interpret subordinate clauses in Khmer where English would require a conjunction. English marks word boundaries while Khmer requires the reader to identify word boundaries from within continuous script. The languages differ in the type of task required of the reader in other ways as well. While English includes morphological systems to indicate tense, number, and other modifications of meaning on nouns and verbs, Khmer, an "isolating" language, does not, and the reader must use the context alone to determine these in the absence of other sentence elements that specify the intended meaning (e.g. use of "yesterday" to indicate past time). Text coherence in Khmer is built through use of direct repetition of a preceding word or phrase through use of the /leik too/ symbol. However, English avoids direct repetition and uses various means of anaphoric-reference. Thus information integration in Khmer and English requires several different processes of the reader.

Research on literacy learning and processing involving Khmer speakers

No studies were identified (in English) that have examined the processes involved in learning to read in Khmer, and only a few studies have examined the development of literacy by Khmer speakers. For example, Barratt-Pugh and Rohl (2001) observed the biliteracy development of students enrolled in a four-year Khmer and English bilingual program in Australia. The study included observation of students' development of writing in both Khmer and English, and interviews with the students regarding the differences between the two languages (e.g. one child's comment that the placement of vowels in positions around the consonant in the Khmer writing system was "too tricky"). The authors describe the patterns of errors in writing in both languages, and note that some of these reflect the influence of one language on the other (e.g. lack of subject-verb agreement for number in English; placement of the adjective before the noun rather than after in Khmer). The authors suggest that some students employed a "visual strategy" in early stages of learning to spell Khmer words that appeared to lead to errors in spelling English words. However, they do not provide further description or examples of the observed strategy or specific errors. In other research, the findings reported on literacy and Khmer speakers are more general. For example, researchers have noted an apparent advantage in learning literacy in English for Cambodian adult ESL learners with some literacy in Khmer (Malicky & Derwing, 1993), and for grade K–12 students (Wright, 1998).

Socio-cultural factors affecting literacy development for Khmer speakers

The examination of the relationship between first language literacy in Khmer and literacy learning in a second language introduces additional, somewhat separate concerns to the analyses presented in this volume, in that many Khmer speakers of different ages/grade levels come to learning a second language with only limited literacy skills in their first language. This has been true for many Khmer speakers who have entered public schools in the United States over the last few decades, particularly those from rural areas (Smith-Hefner, 1995; Wright, 1998, 1999).

Large numbers of Cambodian children began to enter the United States in the 1980s. They entered as refugees who had experienced a long period of political upheaval and disruption; and most had been out of school for several years (Chhim, 1994). Of the more recent immigrants, particularly those from rural and remote areas, many have brought with them the legacy of a disrupted education system, in the form of limited educational and literacy experience individually and within their communities in Cambodia. For these students, the study of the relationship between literacy in a first language and literacy learning in a second language must take into account the learners' limited literacy skills in their first language, and limited exposure to literacy in their home and community.

Education in Cambodia

The Khmer Rouge regime (1975 to 1979) inflicted monumental damage on the overall Cambodian education system. The political conflicts and civil wars during and after the fall of the Khmer Rouge had a crippling effect on the process and quality of education. Teachers, students, professionals, and intellectuals were killed or managed to escape into exile; and there was no schooling for over four years (Dy & Ninomiya, 2003).

There have been concerted efforts to repair the damage sustained during the years of war, but there remain serious problems in the system, particularly in rural areas. These problems include: an insufficient number of schools; incomplete or inconsistent availability of instruction (e.g. 50 percent of schools in rural areas do not offer the full range of classes); high levels of dropout for children in remote areas; very large class sizes; and high repetition rates (e.g. almost 40 percent in grade one) (Dy & Ninomiya, 2003). Such problems suggest that particularly in rural areas many children do not achieve more than very basic literacy skills.

Education and literacy for Cambodian students in the United States

Given the history and problems in their home educational system, many of the Cambodian children who enrolled in schools in the United States over the past few decades entered with very limited schooling and literacy learning experience. Also, among the smaller numbers arriving in recent years, particularly for those families arriving from rural and remote areas of Cambodia, the parents themselves have experienced limited schooling and have low levels of literacy (Hopkins, 1996).

With increased time in the United States, many Cambodian children transition to using English, attain only limited skills in Khmer, and become less interested in traditional activities (Lopez, 2000; Zimmer, 2000). Generational differences in language use and conflict often develop in the homes as children use primarily English while parents and grandparents continue to use Khmer, and ability to communicate with one another decreases (Zimmer, 2000). One important consequence of these changes is that the traditional oral activities in Khmer that involved children in complex language use and extended discourse are being discontinued. Combined, the implication of these changes is that Cambodian-American children have lost opportunities for exposure to complex language and for practice in higher-order thinking skills in Khmer (Ouk *et al.*, 1988) while not yet having achieved sufficient proficiency in English (Wright, 1998).

In some large Cambodian communities, such as in Long Beach, California on the West coast and in Philadelphia, Pennsylvania, and Lowell, Massachusetts on the East coast, economic and social infrastructures have developed that contribute to the awareness and development of Khmer literacy. For example, there are shops selling Khmer language newspapers, videos, and music in the Cambodian community at Long Beach, CA (Needham, 2001). However, many families in such communities have few books or textual materials in Khmer or English (Hornberger, cited in Wright 1998; Hardman, 1998).

Even so, researchers and educators have noted a growing concern among the Khmer communities regarding the loss of the Khmer language and the linkage it offers to Cambodian culture and traditions. In response, programs have been set up in some communities to offer Khmer language and literacy instruction in conjunction with traditional cultural activities and experiences. Such programs typically meet once to a few times a week.

One such program is the Khmer Emerging Education Program (KEEP), an after-school, tuition-free program established in 1992 in Fresno, California. The program's aim is to bring Cambodian students back to their cultural roots, encourage them towards education, and create better communication channels between parents and children using both language and cultural programs. KEEP offers rigorous Khmer language instruction and, by the end of their fourth year in the program, students can speak, read, write, and translate Khmer text into English or translate English into Khmer. However, the KEEP program places a stronger focus on language and literacy than do many other after-school Khmer language and culture programs. More typically, Khmer literacy in these other programs is limited to basic decoding skills and reading of simple texts.

In some communities, there are temple schools based on the traditional model of education and Khmer literacy instruction. Generally, these schools utilize memorization of texts and group recitation as core learning activities (Needham, 2001; Sak-Humphry, personal communication, 2003). Within the public school systems, some (e.g. Long Beach Unified School District) have offered bilingual Khmer programs in the past (Wright, 1998). These programs are no longer provided by the schools, although Khmer may be offered as a foreign or heritage language in high school.

Conclusion

There has been very little research conducted on the acquisition of literacy in Khmer or on literacy learning in a second language by Khmer-language students. In general, however, observers have noted advantages in literacy learning in English as a second language for students with literacy skills in Khmer, their first language. For many Cambodians, a number of social and cultural factors have shaped their first language experience and the level of literacy skills attained in Khmer. This language and literacy history is likely to affect their learning of literacy in a second language. Further research should examine implications of limited literacy skills development in the first language, even for learners with several years of schooling; the role of oral language experience, in terms of levels of complexity and types of discourse experienced; and the impact of community-based literacy instruction on students' literacy learning in a second language.

References

Barratt-Pugh, C. & Rohl, M. (2001) Learning in two languages: a bilingual program in Western Australia. *Reading Teacher*, 54(7) 664–76.

Center for Applied Linguistics (1975) Indochinese Refugee Education Guides. Testing the reading ability of Cambodians (General Information Series No. 7). National Indochinese Clearinghouse, Arlington, VA: Author. (EDRS No. ED 116490).

Center for Applied Linguistics (1978) Indochinese Refugee Education Guides. Teaching English to Cambodian students. (General Information Series N. 18). National Indochinese Clearinghouse, Arlington, VA: Author. (EDRS No. ED 165467).

Chhim, S-H. (1994) Introduction to Cambodian culture. In Southeast Asia Community Resource Center (ed.), *Introduction to Indochinese Cultures.* Folsom, CA: Southeast Asia Community Resource Center, Cordova Unified School District.

Dy, S. S. & Ninomiya, A. (2003, December 18) Basic education in Cambodia: the impact of UNESCO on policies in the 1990s. Education Policy Analysis Archives, 11(48). Retrieved February 15, 2006 from http://epaa.asu.edu/epaa/v11n48/.

Elder, C. & Davies, A. (1998) Performance on ESL examinations: is there a language distance effect? *Language and Education,* 12(1) 1–17.

Hancock, C. R., DeLorenzo, W. E., & Ben-Barka, A. (1985) Teaching pre- and semi-literate Laotian and Cambodian adolescents to read. Helpful hints. Maryland State Department of Education. (EDRS No. ED360879).

Hardman, J. C. (1994) Language and literacy development in a Cambodian community in Philadelphia. Doctoral dissertation, University of Pennsylvania.

Hardman, J. C. (1998) Literacy and bilingualism in a Cambodian community in the U.S.A (pp. 51–81). In A. Y. Durgunoglu & L. Verhoeven (eds.), *Literacy development in a multilingual context: cross-cultural perspectives.* Mahwah, NJ: Lawrence Erlbaum Associates.

Hardman, J. C. (1999) A community of learners: Cambodians in an adult ESL classroom. *Language Teaching Research,* 3(2), 145–66.

Hardman, J. & Puchner, L. D. (1996) Family literacy in a cultural context. Southeast Asian immigrants in the US. NCAL Connections. National Center on Adult Literacy, University of Pennsylvania, (Internet).

Hopkins, M. C. (1996) *Braving a new world: Cambodian (Khmer) refugees in an American city.* Westport, CT: Bergin & Garvey.

Hornberger, N. H. & Hardman, J. (1991) Literacy as cultural practice and cognitive skill: biliteracy in a Cambodian adult ESL class and a Puerto Rican GED program. (EDRS No. ED331317).

Hornberger, N. H. & Skilton-Sylvester, E. (2000) Revisiting the continua of biliteracy: international and critical perspectives. *Language and Education,* 14(2) 96–122.

Huffman, F. E. (1970a) *Cambodian system of writing and beginning reader with drills and glossary.* New Haven: Yale University Press.

Huffman, F. E. (1970b) *Modern spoken Cambodian.* New Haven: Yale University Press.

Malicky, G. V. & Derwing, T. (1993) Literacy learning of adults in a bilingual ESL classroom. *The Alberta Journal of Educational Research,* 39(4) 393–406.

Lopez, M. G. (2000) The language situation of the Hmong, Khmer, and Laotian communities in the United States. In S. L. McKay & S. C. Wong (eds.), *New immigrants in the United States. Readings for second language educators.* Cambridge, UK, Cambridge University Press.

Needham, S. (2001) "How can you be Cambodian if you don't speak Khmer?" Language, literacy and education in a Cambodian "Rhetoric of distinction." In M. C. Hopkins & N. Wellmeier (eds.), *Negotiating transnationalism.* Selected Papers on Refugees and Immigrants, Vol. IX, 123–41.

Ouk, M., Huffman, F. E., & Lewis, J. (1988) *Handbook for teaching Khmer-speaking students*. Rancho Cordova, CA, Cordova Unified School District. (EDRS No. ED325581).

Phap, D. T. (1980) A contrastive approach for teaching English as a second language to Indochinese students. San Antonio, TX, Intercultural Development Research Association. (EDRS No. ED205018).

Seda, I. & Abramson, S. (1990) English writing development of young, linguistically different learners. *Early Childhood Research Quarterly*, 5, 379–91

Smith-Hefner, N. J. (1995) Language and identity in the education of Boston-area Khmer. In D. T. Nakanishi, T. Y. Nishida (eds.) *The Asian American educational experience: a source book for teachers and students* (pp. 198–211). Florence, KY, U.S.A.:Taylor & Francis/Routledge.

Wright, W. (1998) The education of Cambodian-American students in the Long Beach Unified School District: a language and educational policy analysis. Master's dissertation. California State University, Long Beach.

Wright, W. (1999) Linguistic perspective on the education of Cambodian-American students. In C. C. Park & M. Chi (eds.), *Asian-American education: prospects and challenges*. Westport, Connecticut: Greenwood Publishing Co.

Zimmer, J. (2000) Language barriers: for the new generation of Cambodian Americans, the Khmer language both unites and divides. *Asian Week*, Vol. 21, No.40, June 1.

9 Literacy experience in Korean

Implications for learning to read in a second language

Eunyoung Christine Park

Korean is written primarily through the use of Hangul, the Korean alphabetic script. There is also some very limited use of Hancha, Chinese characters, in combination with the Hangul (Taylor & Olson, 1995), although these are used only in South Korea and are not used at all in North Korea. Even in South Korea, the use of Hancha is very limited. Typically the characters appear only in texts targeted towards educated adults, such as newspapers and scholarly books (Cho *et al.*, 2000), and in these texts the Hancha are used only where they serve to differentiate the meanings of identically pronounced and spelled Hangul words. Consequently, South Korean students are not required to learn Hancha. Hangul is the only script taught in elementary schools, and instruction in Hancha is offered only on an elective basis at the middle and high school levels. Therefore, this chapter focuses on examination of Hangul in identifying the metalinguistic competencies that are directly related to literacy learning in Korean.

Descriptions of the Korean language and writing system

Characteristics of the Korean orthography

The Korean script, Hangul, is a non-Roman alphabetic script in which each symbol represents a single consonant or vowel. In contrast to the linear horizontal sequences used in English orthography, Hangul symbols are packaged into syllable blocks, according to relatively simple formation rules. Roughly 12,800 syllable blocks are possible given the total number of consonant and vowel symbols and their possible combinations; however, only approximately 2,000 syllable blocks are in common use (Taylor & Taylor, 1995). There are twenty-four basic Hangul symbols, including those for fourteen consonants (representing nineteen phonemes) and ten vowels. In addition, there are five twin consonants, twelve consonant clusters and eleven diphthongs.

When the Korean writing system was invented, consonant symbols were designed to depict the shapes of the speech articulators. For example, the symbol, representing /k/, ㄱ is the shape of the root of the tongue obstructing the throat. The vowel symbols were constructed to symbolize the natural pattern of the three powers of the Neo-Confucian universe: Heaven, Earth, and Man. Heaven is represented by a short stroke, originally a round dot; the symbol is used for the deep round vowel phonemes, such as ㅏ /a/ and ㅗ /o/). Earth is represented by a long horizontal stroke, used for the middle flat vowel phonemes, such as ㅜ /u/ and ㅠ /yu/), and Man by a long vertical stroke, used for the shallow upright phonemes, such as ㅣ /i/ and ㅟ /wi/ (e.g. Lee & Ramsey, 2000; Taylor & Taylor, 1995). All vowel symbols are comprised of one or more of these three types of strokes (Cho *et al.*, 2000).

The Hangul symbols are packed into syllable blocks, filling initial, medial, and final positions, defined top to bottom, and each positional slot is filled strictly in this order. There are three primary syllable structures: CV (consonant-vowel), CVC, and CVCC. Thus, the initial position in a syllable block is always filled by a consonant. When there is no initial consonant (simple consonant or twin consonant letters), the symbol "o," indicating a null sound, is used as a placeholder to fill the initial position (Taylor & Taylor, 1995).

The vowel position within a syllable block can be filled by either a vowel or diphthong (combination of a semi-vowel and a vowel, e.g. ㅛ /yo/). The specific placement of the vowel (or diphthong) as the second symbol within the syllable block differs depending upon whether it is represented by a horizontal or a vertical stroke. Those represented by horizontal strokes (ㅗ, ㅛ, ㅜ representing /o/, /yo/, /u/, respectively) are placed under the initial consonant symbol (고 /ko/, 교 /kyo/, 구 /ku/). Those with vertical strokes (ㅏ, ㅑ, representing as /a/, /ya/, respectively) appear on the right side of the initial consonant (가 /ka/, 갸 /kya/). Finally, all syllable-final consonants and consonant clusters, whether horizontal or vertical in formation, are placed under the preceding CV (Taylor & Taylor, 1995).

While grapheme-to-phoneme correspondences are highly consistent and reliable at the individual symbol level, syllable blocks do not always correspond with spoken syllable boundaries. This is because Hangul spelling conventions, or syllable block formations, tend to conform to the word's morphological composition, rather than to its phonetic constituents. For example, the word 깊은 (kiphun) is spelled with two syllable blocks, 깊 (kiph) (representing the morpheme "deep") and 은 (un) (representing the morpheme "to be"), even though the word is pronounced as /ki-phin/ (Sohn, 1999).

Characteristics of Korean phonology

Korean speech sounds consist of nineteen consonant phonemes and ten vowel phonemes. Korean has two semivowels, /w/ and /y/, and these combine with vowels to form eleven diphthongs, or complex vowels, such as /wu/, /wo/, and /wy/. When diphthongs occur, only one of the vowels can be the peak of a syllable (Lee & Ramsey, 2000).

Out of the nineteen consonant phonemes, only seven, /p/, /t/, /k/, /s/, /m/, /n/ and /l/, can occur in the syllable-final position in spoken Korean. The remaining twelve consonants can only be used as the initial consonant in a syllable. In addition, there are restrictions on consonant clusters (e.g. two or more consonants, such as /spr/ or /kl/). A syllable in modern spoken Korean cannot begin with a consonant cluster nor can it end with one. Note that the Hangul orthography allows for consonant clusters in the final position within a syllable block, because it is morphophonemic, representing both phonemes and morphemes. However, the pronunciation of a syllable never includes the final consonant cluster as such. Instead, when a consonant cluster occurs in syllable-final position, as in 닭, /talk/, "chicken," there are two rule-based alternatives for pronouncing the coda (syllable-final) consonants. When a syllable that ends in a consonant cluster is followed by a syllable that begins with a consonant or a pause, one of the consonants in the cluster is dropped. For example, 닭 is pronounced /tak/, instead of /talk/. However, when a syllable-final consonant cluster is followed by another syllable that begins with a vowel, then the last consonant of the cluster spills over the syllable boundary and is pronounced as the initial consonant of the following syllable (Lee & Ramsey, 2000).

Characteristics of Korean morphology

Korean, like English and many other languages, includes both free and bound morphemes.[1] In Korean, all nouns and adverbs are free morphemes, and can be used as freestanding words. Bound morphemes in Korean include inflectional and derivational affixes. Inflectional affixes provide information about the grammatical role of the word, while the primary function of derivational affixes is to generate new words. All inflectional affixes in Korean are suffixes that are attached to nouns, verbs, and adjectives; numerals, determiners, and adverbs do not permit inflectional suffix attachments (Sohn, 1999).

Noun inflections play a minor role in Korean morphology, given that Korean does not morphologically mark gender or plurality, and uses particles to signal noun case. However, inflections on verbs and adjectives are complex both in their structure and usage (Sohn, 1999). Unlike English, all verb- and adjective-stems in Korean are bound morphemes and cannot stand alone; they must be combined with inflectional suffixes. At minimum, a fully formed predicate must include a specific final inflectional suffix, or "ender." Other suffixes may be placed between the ender and the predicate stem. For example, the verb phrase 먹었다 /mek-ess-ta/, "ate" consists of three morphemes: the stem, 먹 /mek/, "to eat;" the past-tense morpheme, 었 /-ess/; and the ender, 다 /-ta/.

Predicate-ending suffixes can be divided into a number of subclasses. Lee and Ramsey (2000) have distinguished between the pre-final endings (e.g. the past-tense marker, 었 /-ess/, as in the above example) and final endings (the declarative ender, 다 /-ta/, in the·above example). They have noted that although pre-final endings are relatively few in number with straightforward functions, final endings have a number of subclasses. Final endings can be grouped either into sentence-final or non-sentence-final, embedded clause, endings. There are more than two dozen sentence-final endings, which indicate four distinct sentence types, declarative, interrogative, imperative, and propositive, and within each of these, six levels of politeness. There are four embedded clause types that take clause-ending suffixes: nominal, conjunctive, complement, and relative (Sohn, 1999). Nominal endings convert the inflected verb or adjective into a noun, while conjunctive endings are used to link clauses, and do not affect the original forms of the verbs or adjectives that are linked by these endings. Complement endings include the infinitive suffix and adverbializers, while relative endings connect a relative clause to a noun in the main clause (Sohn, 1999).

Korean derivational affixes include both prefixes and suffixes and are lexically restricted, meaning that a certain affix can be attached only to a specific set of words. There are about 270 prefixes in Korean (Sohn, 1999), and these are used to modify or limit a word's meaning without changing its grammatical category. For example, the negative can be expressed by attaching one of the following prefixes: 안 /an-/, 불 /pul-/, 비/pi-/, 부 /pu-/, 무 /mu-/, 몰 /mol-/, and 미 /mi-/ (comparable to English affixes im-, in-, dis-, un-, non-, de-, ir-, -less respectively) (Sohn, 1999).

In contrast with the more limited system of derivational prefixes, there is a rich and complex system of derivational suffixes in Korean. Nouns can be derived from verbs through the use of lexically restricted suffixes such as 이 /-i/, 개 /-kay/, 기 /-ki/, 음 /-(u)m/, and 보 /-po/. For example, 이 /-i/ attaches to the stem form of the verb 벌 /pel/, "to earn," to derive 벌이 /pel-i/, "earning"; 개 /-kay/, attaches to 싸 /ssa/, "to wrap," to derive 싸개 /ssa-kay/, "wrapper". Nouns can be derived also from adjectives and, as is the case for verbs, the adjective-stem and derivational suffix combinations are lexically restricted. There are also many other derivational possibilities in Korean using separate sets of derivational suffixes. It is possible, for example, to derive adjectives from other adjectives, nouns, and verbs; adverbs can be derived from other adverbs, nouns, adjectives, and determiners; and, there are derivations that form verbs from other verbs, nouns, and adjectives (Sohn, 1999).

In Korean morphology, compound nouns are large in number and diverse in structure. This reflects heavy lexical borrowing from Chinese, because most of the Chinese lexicon is compounds. In fact, Sino-Korean words constitute more than half (approximately 60 percent) of the contemporary Korean lexicon (Sohn, 1999). There are three basic formational rules for Korean compounding: (a) subcompounding (modifier+noun; e.g. 곱슬머리 / kopsul-meli/, "curly-hair"), (b) co-compounding (apposition; e.g. 눈물 / nwun-mul/, "eye-water" → "tear"), and (c) argument-predication (e.g. 목걸이 /mok-kel-i/, "neck-hang-thing" → "necklace").

Korean also includes compound verbs. A nominal can be placed in front of a verb to create a compound transitive or intransitive verb. For example, /kongpwu-hata/, "study-do", is "to study;" /son-pota/, "hand-see" is "to repair;" /tung-chita/, "back-hit" is "to blackmail;" /naymsay-nata/, "smell-occur" is "to smell;" /cheypho-toyta/, "arrest-become" is "to be arrested." The order of stems in these compounds reflects the subject-object-verb (SOV) word order of Korean (Sohn, 1994).

Korean syntactic structure

Korean is categorized as a subject-object-verb (SOV) language. Consistent with this categorization, subordinate clauses and relative clauses are generated at the left of the head nouns and precede the noun they modify. There is relative freedom of word order in Korean because well developed postpositional case markers or particles mark the grammatical roles of each noun phrase in a sentence.

Korean uses both canonical SOV word order and postpositional case markers to indicate the grammatical roles of sentence components. The postpositional case markers include particles such as /-ka/ (nominative or subject), /-ul/ (accusative or direct object), and /-eykey/ (dative or indirect object). Korean frequently allows use of other, non-canonical, word orders when the grammatical function of noun phrases is marked by the case particles. In fact, it is common, particularly in face-to-face conversations, for Korean sentences to deviate from the SOV word order. Lee and Ramsey (2000) explain that such flexibility in word order is an important stylistic device in that it allows a speaker to emphasize certain information by moving it closer to the predicate.

Alternatively, the case-marking particles are frequently omitted when the grammatical function of a noun phrase can be predicted from the word order or can be interpreted by other linguistic or non-linguistic cues. Also, sentential elements can be omitted when these are predictable from the discourse context. For example, Korean does not require any dummy elements to indicate grammatical function only, as is the case in the use of "it" or "there" in English (Sohn, 1999).

While there is relatively free word order in sentences given the well-developed system of case particles, word order related to modification is highly constrained. There is no variation in word order for combinations such as adnominal-noun (예쁜 꽃: /yey-ppun/ + /kkoch/, "pretty flower"); adverb-adjective (아직 젊은: /acik/ + /celmen/, "still young"); genitive case-noun (꽃의 줄기: /kkoch/uy/ + /culki/, "the flower's stem"), among others (Lee & Ramsey, 2000).

Morphology interacts with syntax in Korean, as is the case for most languages. For example, indications of degree or quantity are generated by attaching suffixes to stem morphemes: 만 /-man/, "only;" 까지 /-kkaci/, "as much as;" and 마저 /mace/, "even." Plurality is expressed by combining numerals and appropriate counters for modified nouns (e.g. a specific counter is used for thin, flat, objects, such as paper, sliced bread, shirts, and sweaters). Plural noun phrase construction involves concatenating either "noun + numeral + counter," as in 의 종이 + 세 + 장, "paper three sheets," or "numeral + counter + genitive + noun," as in 세 + 장 + 의 + 종이, "three sheets of paper" (Sohn, 1999).

Passive and causative verb phrases can be constructed by inserting inflectional suffixes, such as 이 /-i/, at the designated positions between the verb and the ender. For example, the active voice form of the verb "to see" is 보다 /po-ta/ and its passive form "to be seen" is 보이다 /po-i-ta/. Negative constructions are formed in two ways. For declaratives, interrogatives, and exclamations, the negative is formed by placing a negative adverb, 안 /an(i)/ or 못 /mos/, immediately before the predicate phrase. For propositives and imperatives, the negative is formed by use of the negative auxiliary verb 말 /mal-/ (Lee & Ramsey, 2000).

In running text, there is space before all types of noun phrases, including compounds, derived and inflected nouns, as well as pronouns. There is no space, however, between the morphological elements within a multi-morphemic word, or between case-marking particles and the nouns they mark. For all other word classes, there is a space before each free word (Sohn, 1999).

Korean discourse structure

A coherent discourse incorporates three levels of theme: local theme, previous theme, and global theme. The local theme reports what is going on at a given moment; the previous theme provides sequential continuity to the local theme; and the global theme is the theme of the entire discourse.

Morphosyntactic structure in Korean allows speakers to distinguish local and global discourse themes (Lee, 1999). Thus, discourse can be made thematically coherent through the use of the particle /ka/ (subject marker), which generally introduces new information into a discourse, and through use of the particle /nun/ (topic marker), which generally marks previously introduced information in a discourse, and thus establishes the global theme of a discourse (Kim, 1994, 1998).

Metalinguistic and other requisite competencies in learning to read Korean

Orthographic knowledge

As in other alphabetic languages, Korean written symbols correspond to sound units. Therefore, during early literacy acquisition, children must understand that print represents speech, and that speech can be segmented into smaller sound units. In learning to read Hangul, Korean children need to learn the individual symbols (vowels and consonants), their names (phonemic representations), and the rules for combining these symbols to form syllable blocks (e.g. when the vowel is represented by a horizontal stroke, it must be placed under the initial consonant symbol, and when it is represented by a vertical stroke, it must appear at the right side of the initial consonant symbol). Korean children typically acquire basic spelling skills in a short period of time (Taylor & Taylor, 1995), most likely due to the highly transparent sound-symbol correspondences in Korean orthography and the relatively simple syllable formation rules. However, the morphophonemic representation in Korean Hangul requires that children also recognize that Korean spelling reflects the morphological composition of words, rather than the phonetic pattern, and that the constituent syllables must be restructured accordingly.

Grapho-phonological awareness

Phonological awareness refers to children's emerging understanding of the phonological boundaries in speech, fostering their ability to manipulate segmental phonological information. Grapho-phonological awareness, on the other hand, pertains to an understanding of the relationship between orthography and phonology. Given the dual-level (phoneme and syllable) representation in Korean orthography, phonological manipulation in Korean requires both the recognition of syllables in speech, based on vowel-consonant combinations, and the ability to decompose syllables into their phonemic constituents. It has been reported that Korean children develop sensitivity to phonemes and syllables fairly early in their language development, and both phoneme and syllable manipulation skills uniquely predict Hangul word reading ability (Cho & McBride-Chang, 2005). Once the basic syllable formation rules are learned, Korean children need to know the specific spelling rules that apply to consonant clusters at the end of a syllable (i.e. when to drop the pronunciation of one consonant in the cluster and when to pronounce one consonant in the cluster as the initial consonant of the following syllable).

Grapho-morphological awareness

There are several basic metalinguistic competencies underlying grapheme-to-morpheme mappings in Korean. First, since most grammatical information is coded in the form of inflectional suffixes attached to predicates, children must understand what specific information can be added to verbs and adjectives through the use of the suffixes, and how the attachment procedures are syntactically and semantically constrained. Children also need to know that some designated affixes alter grammatical categories of words, while others limit the semantic information of words. Further, since Korean derivational affixes are lexically restricted, children must also know that some stem-affix combinations are permitted, while others are not; that is, they must develop sensitivity to the distributional constraints on stem-affix concatenations.

In using compound lexical items, children need to develop sensitivities to the linear structure of compound words, which contain a series of two or more semantic constituents. They must know that such morphologically complex Korean words can contain lexical items that may be used as independently meaningful and functional lexical items. And they must further understand that when such lexical items are used in a compound word they occur without spaces separating them and the individual lexical items contribute to the overall meaning of the compound word. Further, children must learn that there is more than one way of combining lexical items (e.g. sub-compounding and argument-predicate) to form compound words, and also that the semantic relation between the constituent items in a compound word differs from one structural type to another.

Sentence-processing skills

Korean utilizes dual case-signaling systems: case-marking particles and word order. Children must learn to use both in integrating word information across a sentence to uncover the underlying meaning. Also, since Korean uses a head-final structure, in which the central element or head of a phrase appears in the phrase-final position, children must learn to hold information segments in order to fully integrate them with the head of a phrase, clause, or sentence. Thus, children must recognize that the complete meaning of a sentence remains ambiguous until the end, where all of the information can be integrated and the meaning of the sentence fully understood.

Understanding sentences within a discourse, children need to know that accurate comprehension of text requires them to utilize clues at both the sentence and paragraph level. Also, since some particles, clauses, and phrases can be omitted from a sentence, Korean children need to learn how to integrate information from both local and global contexts. They must also develop sensitivity to how specific particles are used to signal the different types of themes (e.g. local or global themes) in a discourse.

Differences and similarities in learning to read in Korean and English

Although the Korean and English writing systems are both alphabetic, sharing the same general mapping principle, each orthography has distinct structural properties. Contrasting with the linear sequence of letters in English, Hangul symbols are packaged in syllable blocks. Therefore, in addition to learning individual symbols, Korean children must recognize that the individual Hangul symbols cannot be used independently and they must learn how to combine the symbols within syllable blocks. Thus, while English decoding involves linear horizontal processing of intraword elements, in contrast, Korean word reading requires the packaging and unpackaging of syllable blocks through an analysis of symbols aligned both horizontally and vertically.

The decoding of the individual Hangul symbols within the syllable blocks is straightforward and easily learned, given the very regular symbol-to-sound correspondence. Since many syllable blocks map onto morphemes rather than onto the spoken syllables, extracted sounds of a syllable block may not correspond with the spoken syllable boundaries. This can create problems in decoding and spelling multi-syllabic Hangul words. However, semantic access during Hangul word recognition may be facilitated because morphological information is visually preserved in the syllable blocks.

The morphological structures of English and Korean also reflect similarities and differences. Although both languages utilize inflectional and derivational affixes, Korean has a more extensive and more complex system of verb and adjective affixes. Korean predicates (verbs and adjectives) permit the sequential attachment of multiple suffixes, each providing different grammatical information (e.g. information on the sentence type, mode, politeness, tense). In addition, the concatenation of suffixes is constrained by strict ordering, and so children must learn both the specific function assigned to each suffix and the relevant attachment rules. For this reason, efficiency in segmenting predicate words into their stems and individual suffixes facilitates information extraction and integration for Korean word and sentence processing to a greater extent than for English. Similarly, at the sentence level, Korean differs from English in terms of the strong role of case-marking particles. Korean children must learn the functions of the different particles; however, they must also learn how to incorporate contextual clues to infer the meanings of sentences when particles and sometimes even words are omitted.

Research on literacy learning and processing involving Korean speakers

Learning to read Korean as a first language

The analyses of Korean linguistic structure and metalinguistic awareness indicate that the main factors contributing to reading development in Korean are the following: grapho-phonological awareness that recognizes the relationship between graphic symbols and speech sounds; grapho-morphological awareness that recognizes the manner in which elements of words are represented with graphic symbols; and syntactic awareness that recognizes word order and the linguistic devices used to signal syntactic and pragmatic functions of the constituent elements in sentences.

Much of the research on literacy learning and processing involved in reading Korean has examined phonological awareness. In one such study, Kang and Simpson (1996) used phonological and semantic priming procedures to investigate the extent to which beginning readers of Korean, ages eight to twelve, rely on phonological information in word recognition. In the phonological priming condition (Perfetti & Bell, 1991; Perfetti *et al.*, 1988), pseudo-homophones (i.e. non-words with the same pronunciation as real words) of the target words were used to prime children phonologically without activating any semantic information of those words. In the semantic priming condition (Lee & Lee, 1970), words that were meaningfully associated with the target words were used as primes to activate their semantic information without biasing the children phonologically.

Kang and Simpson (1996) noted that the patterns of the participants' latencies in naming the target words within the two priming conditions indicated a developmental difference. The phonological priming affected performance for both groups, but significantly more strongly for the younger children than for the older children. However, when semantic primes were used, only the older Korean children showed a priming effect on performance; no effect was found for the younger children. The authors concluded that younger Korean children rely more exclusively on phonological information than do older children. Thus the findings of this study suggest that age of the learner may be a factor in explaining uses of different information sources in the development of word recognition skills in Korean.

Using a large battery of tasks, Cho and McBride-Chang (2005) explored correlates of Korean Hangul acquisition among kindergarteners and second-grade children. They found that syllable and phoneme manipulation skills both were significantly related to Korean word reading ability. Thus, the dual-level representation in Korean Hangul requires children to be sensitive to the linguistic and orthographic units both at the syllable and phoneme levels.

In a cross-national study involving 100 second-grade children in Beijing, Hong Kong, Korea, and the United States (McBride-Chang, 2005), the relative contributions of phonological and morphological awareness to word recognition were compared. The researchers found that phonological and morphological awareness were related to one another, as well as to oral vocabulary knowledge in all three languages. The two facets of awareness, however, were differentially associated with word reading performance across languages. While phonological awareness was more closely linked to word reading in English and Korean than in Chinese, morphological awareness was a stronger predictor of word recognition in Chinese and Korean than in English. The researchers concluded that although phonological and morphological awareness are equally important in language development across cultures, their relative importance for reading development varies in accordance with each language's dominant linguistic and orthographic properties.

Song and Won (1998) carried out a study of phonological processing involving third-grade Korean children, including twelve children with normal reading skills and twelve children with reading disabilities. The children completed tasks designed to assess working memory, short-term memory, phonological processing, and syntactic processing. The findings showed that the children with reading disabilities had phonological processing deficits and smaller memory spans. No significant difference was found in syntactic processing for the two groups.

The important role of symbol-sound mappings in Korean reading has been also explored by examining adult Korean readers' Hangul word processing (Park, 1996, 1997; Park & Vaid, 1995; Nam *et al.*, 1997; Simpson & Kang, 2004). Cho and Chen (1999) found that adult readers of Korean exhibited strong phonological activation while carrying out tasks that required semantic processing of Hangul. In their study, forty Korean university students participated in tasks that included visually similar pseudohomophones, visually similar non-homophones, and their corresponding controls. The findings showed both phonological and visual similarity effects. However, the phonological similarity effect was significantly stronger than the visual similarity effect, suggesting that it is primarily through phonology that the meanings of Hangul words are obtained.

In other research comparing the processing of Hangul and Hancha (Chinese characters) words, several studies have found that adult native speakers of Korean use primarily phonological information in reading Hangul words. For example, Lee and Chard (2000) compared the processing of Hangul and Hancha word recognition in two pseudohomophone lexical decision experiments conducted with Korean adults (ages 25–36). In processing Hancha words, the participants' performance on the pseudohomophones was similar to their performance on the non-homophonic non-words, indicating the use of non-phonological information. However, in Hangul word recognition, participants processed Hangul pseudohomophones faster than non-homophonic non-words, indicating their strong reliance on phonological information.

Other experimental studies comparing Hangul and Hancha word recognition have yielded similar findings, indicating greater involvement of phonological processing in reading Hangul words than in reading Hancha words (Kang & Simpson, 2001; Kim, 1999; Simpson & Kang, 1994; Taylor & Park, 1995; Yoon *et al.*, 2002).

At the phrase or sentence levels, empirical evidence indicates that local grammatical cues are immediately integrated into the emerging interpretation of a sentence. For example, Kim (1998) conducted two experiments to determine whether syntactic parsing is affected by manipulation of case-marking particles in processing Korean sentences. Using a self-paced word-by-word reading task with relative clause and coordinated sentences, Kim compared the processing of sentences containing the nominative marker /ka/ with structurally matched sentences containing the topic marker /nun/. The topic marker changed overall patterns of word-by-word reading times for the sentences in both experiments. The results showed that local grammatical cues such as a topic maker affect overall Korean sentence processing efficiency.

In terms of the development of processing skills at a sentence level, there is evidence that Korean children develop grammatical sensitivity for SOV sentence structure early in development. A study by Cho *et al.* (2002) examined word order preference in forty Korean native-speaking children (four to seven years of age). The children were asked to respond to requests made using twenty sentence items that used different word orders. The results indicated that the children strongly preferred subject-object word order compared to the reverse order. This is not a surprising finding considering that the SOV order is the most frequent word order used within the input Korean children hear, and it indicates the strength of word order as a cue used for Korean sentence processing. However, Cho *et al.* also found that the Korean children preferred direct object-indirect object order even though the reverse (indirect object-direct object) order is more dominant in Korean sentences. The researchers concluded that the nature of the pragmatic situations conveyed by specific sentence structures is an important factor in Korean children's development of syntactic sensitivity. That is, the frequency of structures in the input alone is not sufficient for explaining the development of sentence processing skills in Korean.

A limited number of studies have also examined processing at the discourse level. In a study on subject assignment in Korean discourse, Kim (2002) examined native speakers' use of different subject markers to manage the thematic structure of a discourse. She used a picture-based story-telling methodology in which subjects were asked to produce a spontaneous narrative given a picture with a title. Forty university students in Korea were randomly assigned to one of two title conditions. The results indicated that the participants were sensitive to all three themes—local, global, and previous—and that, of the three, the local theme was most important in guiding subject assignment in Korean. In terms of marker choices, the topic particle /nun/ was predominantly used to refer to the global theme, while both /nun/ and the nominative marker /ka/ were used to refer to the local theme. There was a negative relationship between a previous theme and the use of the markers, a finding consistent with the fact that in Korean continuous subjects are typically not marked overtly, or not even mentioned.

In other research, Pak (1997) examined the cultural and schooling differences in production and comprehension of discourse for Korean and American children in grades one and four. First, the children were asked to create a story from a picture book. Next, they were read a story from a picture book, and then were asked to retell the story. Last, they were asked twelve open-ended questions to examine their comprehension of the story. The data were transcribed in the native languages of the children (Korean and English). The story-telling (production) data were analyzed in terms of three measures: ambiguity of reference, evaluative comments, and amount of information. Story comprehension was measured by the recall of the story and the responses to the comprehension questions. By analyzing the data for the degree of linguistic formality and function, Pak reported that the oral narratives produced by the Korean children were more context-dependent, more evaluative, and less informational than the narratives produced by the American children. The Korean children recalled peripheral information from the story better than did their American counterparts. However, there was no difference between the two groups (Korean vs. American children) in the accuracy of responses. This seems to indicate that cultural difference influences the manner in which children communicate through discourse.

Learning to read in a second language

The studies on literacy learning discussed thus far show that native Korean speakers develop the metalinguistic awareness unique to the Korean language and writing system through their first-language (L1) literacy experience. For second-language (L2) readers, those readers who already possess literacy skills in their L1 have the potential for transferring the L1 skills to enhance the development of their literacy in the L2. The transfer of literacy skills from the L1 to the L2 first entails the process of being sensitized to specific features of the L1. Such linguistic and functional conditioning then shapes the learner's cognitive strategies for processing a language, affecting the learner's perception and comprehension of L2 input. Thus, when L1 and L2 share similar processing requirements, it is likely that the L2 reader may have available sensitivities to specific language features gained from processing the L1 and will apply these sensitivities to building L2 processing skills. In fact, much research has shown that L2 readers transfer literacy skills acquired and developed in their L1 to their L2 reading tasks (Carlisle *et al.*, 1999; Hancin-Bhatt & Nagy, 1994).

Even among linguistically unrelated languages (i.e. those using Roman vs. non-Roman script), research studies (Koda, 1998, 2000; Muljani *et al.*, 1998) have consistently yielded empirical evidence that L2 adult readers transfer phonological awareness developed in their L1, given functional similarities associated with processing linguistic units of L1 and L2. Moreover, L2 reading researchers have come closer to understanding the specific ways in which the transfer seems to occur. Several of these studies have involved examination of L2 processing by native speakers of Korean. Due to the dearth of empirical research on L2 reading involving native Korean speakers, the following reviews include studies conducted both with adults and children.

Koda (1998) examined the effect of L1-processing experience on L2 phonemic awareness and decoding among proficiency-matched Korean (alphabetic) and Chinese (non-alphabetic) ESL students. The findings did not yield significant quantitative differences but did reveal significant qualitative variations between the two groups in both phonemic awareness and decoding during reading. These findings seem to indicate that L2 print experience may override L1 orthographic influences on L2 phonemic awareness, but the pattern of qualitative differences between the two groups suggests that previous L1 processing experience affects phonological processing procedures used in L2 reading.

Since Korean and English share similarities in phonological processing (in that in both languages each written symbol corresponds to a specific sound), there are implications of these findings for young Korean L1 learners of English as an L2. In other words, the development of decoding skills in Korean is essential to, and positively influences, the development of literacy skills in L2 English.

In general, more studies have been devoted to phonological processes than to morphological processes in connection with the development of literacy skills in English. Perhaps this trend has much to do with the fact that phonological processes are much more closely related to the learning-to-read stage and have implications for later reading to learn for school-aged children. Reading researchers have consistently identified deficiency in decoding skills as a key factor in level of success in reading in English, and substantial effort has been devoted to understanding the development of phonological awareness in L1 and its effect on L2 reading.

However, the potential role of morphological awareness in facilitating reading-to-learn has recently been studied for L2 English reading. Morphological awareness can have a facilitative effect on word identification in reading, since children can extract constituent morphemes by parsing unfamiliar words, and these in turn provide the basis of lexical inference in English (Carlisle, 2000; Nagy & Scott, 2000). For L2 readers, the transfer of L1 morphological awareness can facilitate the formation of L2 morphological awareness, and this awareness can then positively influence L2 reading comprehension. More specifically, transferred L1 morphological awareness expedites the process of acquiring the morphological awareness in L2 that is closely related to L2 literacy skills such as lexical inference.

In research with adults on morphological processing, Koda (2000) studied intraword structural sensitivity for two English as a Second Language (ESL) groups, Korean L1 and Chinese L1 university students. She hypothesized that processing skills in English as a second language would differ for these two groups based upon the differences in their first language morphological processing experience. Korean requires linear, componential processes, while Chinese logographic characters require non-linear, holistic processing. The findings seemed to suggest that L1 morphological processing experience influences the development of L2 morphological awareness in specific and predictable ways, in that the Korean L1 students employed different types of morphological processing skills from those of their Chinese counterparts. Koda concluded that the similarity in processing for Korean and English enabled the Korean learners of English as a second language, as compared to the Chinese learners, to develop and utilize more efficient English L2 morphological processing skills.

The results of research with young Korean L1 learners of English are consistent with those found for adults. In a recent study, Park (2004) examined the relationship between L1 and L2 morphological awareness among third, fourth, and fifth grade Korean L1 learners of English. Korean and English are assumed to require similar morphological processes since both involve linear affixation of morphological constituents. Given this similarity, Park hypothesized that the development of morphological processing skills in Korean should affect morphological processing skills in English and thus, at least partially, these processing skills should also affect lexical inference in English. In her study, Park found significantly high correlations for the segmental aspect of morphological awareness in Korean and English. An additional interesting finding in Park's study was that both Korean morphological awareness and English morphological awareness were strongly related to formal instruction, measured as number of years of schooling in which Korean or English was used as the language of instruction. However, morphological awareness was not related to listening comprehension in English. Park interpreted these findings as suggesting that exposure to formal (or academic) linguistic input is important in promoting the development of morphological awareness.

Thus, given similarity in Korean and English morphological formation processes, e.g. affixation of an element to a base morpheme, morphological processing skills in Korean are likely to influence the development of English L2 morphological awareness. The L2 English morphological awareness will in turn enhance the development of English literacy skills such as lexical inference. In addition, research indicates that the transfer of L2 morphological awareness is not simple one-to-one copying from one language to another, but rather, it involves complex restructuring.

In processing English sentences in reading, L2 learners encounter many different kinds of problems. One of the major difficulties is vocabulary. In several studies examining L2 English reading components, English vocabulary has been identified as a major factor for learners of L2 English reading across different age groups and L1 backgrounds (Carrell, 1988; De Bot *et al.*, 1997; Garcia, 1991; Hulstijn, 1993; Jimenez *et al.*, 1997). Kim (1995) identified English vocabulary as a key problem for Korean L1 high-school readers of English.

Thus, highly developed literacy skills such as lexical inference skills can be crucial in determining success in reading comprehension. It is at this juncture, then, that the transfer of word-level processing skills from L1 becomes very relevant to L2 readers, since their level of reading comprehension in the L2 can be greatly influenced by their L1 experience in morphological processing. If the two language systems involve similar lexical processing requirements, then the L2 readers should be able to take advantage of their

L1 morphological processing experience in developing L2 lexical inference skills in comprehending sentences.

However, successful lexical inference in reading requires more than the ability to integrate morphological information. It also requires the ability to integrate contextual information in order to construct the accurate meaning of unknown lexical items in a text (Mori & Nagy, 1999). Over-reliance on only one type of processing usually means that the other knowledge source is not being activated, and this will often result in an ineffective lexical inferencing procedure. Thus, it is important to examine how the transferred morphological awareness from L1 Korean is combined with contextual clues to successfully infer word meanings in English sentences.

In the above-mentioned study, Park (2004) also examined three-way relationships among L1 morphological awareness, L2 morphological awareness, and L2 lexical inference skills for Korean L1 children (grades three to five) learning English. Although there were strong relationships between L1 and L2 morphological awareness, as well as between L2 morphological awareness and L2 lexical inference, no significant relationship existed between L1 morphological awareness and L2 lexical inference. These results seem to suggest that L1 morphological awareness may provide support for L2 lexical inference only through L2 morphological awareness. Further qualitative analyses indicated that without an adequate level of L1 morphological awareness, the Korean L1 children did not appear to benefit from L2 language proficiency, in that they were less able to utilize contextual clues to infer the meaning of unfamiliar words in a sentence. Thus, for Korean learners of English, the results indicate that it is important to first develop a solid level of morphological awareness in Korean to successfully develop English reading sub-skills such as the use of lexical inference in context.

Socio/cultural factors affecting learning to read in Korean

In the development of literacy skills in any language, serious attention needs to be paid not only to linguistic and cognitive factors but also to instructional environments in which children are taught to read and write the language. Korean parents have high expectations for their children's educational attainment, and there is a strong emphasis on literacy, beginning in early childhood.

The majority of Korean parents consider reading and writing crucial readiness skills that children should acquire before entering elementary school (Lee *et al.*, 2000). Consequently, close to 90 percent of preschoolers learn basic Korean literacy skills such as letter and syllable knowledge and syllable formation rules from their parents at home (Choe, 1986), and so they have these skills when they enter elementary school. Most Korean children can read and write some consonant-vowel blocks at about age five (Lee *et al.*, 2000). Many Korean parents rely on private educational institutions to provide additional instruction to their children, and the parents' involvement is recognized as a very considerable factor in early childhood education (Lee *et al.*, 2000). Parents' contribution to their children's literacy development is significant enough that it has been identified as a major factor in increasing literacy rates in Korea (Lee, 2002), which have reached almost 100 percent in recent times (Taylor & Taylor, 1995).

In elementary school, literacy skills are taught through use of the Korean syllable chart. This chart is a matrix with the fourteen basic consonants as columns and the ten basic vowels as rows. The order taught in school is the following: simple consonant letters, twin consonants, consonant clusters, then vowels and diphthongs. Children begin by reading the chart aloud after the teacher, and then are taught to read and find the consonant-vowel blocks that make up real Korean words. Syllables are introduced to Korean children as a major unit of sound repetition. After this, children practice filling in blanks in the chart, and more complex syllable blocks are introduced in accompanying textbooks. Korean children are taught to treat syllabic blocks as the major unit when reading and spelling because syllables are perceptually and semantically more salient than phonemes (Taylor & Taylor, 1995). At these early stages of literacy acquisition, the children practice packaging letters in syllable block forms.

As Korean students progress through grades, most educational emphasis is placed on college entrance exams. It is very difficult to be admitted to college in Korea, and yet the extremely high social value placed on education motivates Korean students to study hard and to become academically successful (Taylor & Taylor, 1995).

Summary and conclusions

In learning to read Korean, children use linguistic knowledge specific to the Korean language and writing system, and develop metalinguistic awareness through this literacy experience. Although linguistic knowledge such as knowing the graphic symbols used in Korean may not affect second language literacy learning directly, the metalinguistic awareness children develop from their experience with Korean literacy seems to have an important impact on literacy development in a second language.

By identifying the different facets of metalinguistic awareness developed from Korean as a first language and understanding how this awareness can promote learning to read in a second language, it is hoped that children with L1 literacy experience can be assisted in applying the valuable L1 literacy skills they possess to the task of learning to read in a second language. In order to make this potential benefit from first-language literacy experience educationally sound, further research needs to be done to examine the nature and the extent of metalinguistic awareness developed in Korean and how it affects literacy learning in additional languages. More specifically, previous research on the role of metalinguistic awareness in children's L2 literacy development has been mostly focused on phonological awareness and its contribution to learning-to-read skills, that is, targeting kindergarten through second-grade learners. Research results indicate that it takes about four to seven years for English learners to attain academic proficiency in English (Hakuta *et al.*, 2000). Thus it is important also to focus on morphological awareness, which may have important implications for reading to learn, and may have a role in helping children learning English and other target languages in grades three and above.

Note

1 A free morpheme occurs on its own (e.g. the word "book"); a bound morpheme always occurs attached to another morpheme (e.g. the plural "s" in "books").

References

Carlisle, J. F. (2000) Awareness of the structure and meaning of morphologically complex words: impact on reading. *Reading & Writing*, 12(3–4), 169–90.

Carlisle, J. F., Beeman, M., Davis, L. H., & Spharim, G. (1999) Relationship of metalinguistic capabilities and reading achievement for children who are becoming bilingual. *Applied Psycholinguistics*, 20(4), 459–78.

Carrell, P. L. (1988) Some causes of text-boundedness and schema interference in EL reading. In P. Carrell, J. Devine, & D. Eskey (eds.), *Interactive approaches to second language reading* (pp. 101–13). Cambridge: Cambridge University Press.

Cho, J. & Chen, H. (1999) Orthographic and phonological activation in the semantic processing of Korean Hanja and Hangul. *Language & Cognitive Processes. Special Issue: Processing East Asian Languages*, 14, 481–502.

Cho, J. & McBride-Chang, C. (2005) Correlates of Korean Hangul acquisition among kindergarteners and second graders. *Scientific Studies of Reading*, 9(1), 3–16.

Cho, S., Lee, M., & O'Grady, W (2002) Word order preferences for direct and indirect objects in children learning Korean. *Journal of Child Language*, 29(4), 897–908.

Cho, Y., Lee, H. S., Schulz, C., Sohn, H., & Sohn, S. (2000) *Integrated Korean: Beginning 1*. Honolulu: University of Hawaii Press.

Cho, S., Lee, M., O'Grady, W., Song, M., Suzuki, T., & Yoshinaga, N. (2002) Word order preferences for direct and indirect objects in children learning Korean. *Journal of Child Language*, 29, 897–909.

Choe, H. S. (1986) Letter education in the early reading state. In *Seminar for Reforming Educational Process of National Language and Chinese Study*, Seoul, 157–77.

De Bot, K., Paribakht, T., & Wesche, M. (1997) Toward a lexical processing model for the study of second language vocabulary acquisition. Evidence from ESL reading. *Studies in Second Language Acquisition*, 19(3), 309–29.

Garcia, G. E. (1991) Factors influencing the English reading test performance of Spanish-speaking Hispanic children. *Reading Research Quarterly*, 26(4), 371–92.

Hakuta, K., Goto Butler, Y., & Witt, D. (2000) How long does it take English learners to attain proficiency? *University of California Linguistic Minority Research Institute Policy Report* 2000–1.

Hacin-Bhatt, B. & Nagy, W. E. (1994) Lexical transfer and second language morphological development. *Applied Psycholinguistics*, 15, 289–310.

Hulstijn, J. (1993) When do foreign-language readers look up the meaning of unfamiliar words? The influence of task and learner variables. *Modern Language Journal*, 77(2), 139–47.

Jimenez, R. T., Garcia, G. E., & Pearson, P. D. (1996) The reading strategies of bilingual Latina/o students who are successful English readers: opportunities and obstacles. *Reading Research Quarterly*, 31(1), 90–112.

Kang, H. & Simpson, G. (1996) Development of semantic and phonological priming a shallow orthography. *Developmental Psychology*, 32 (5), 860–6.

Kang, H. & Simpson, G. (2001) Local strategic control of information in visual word recognition. *Memory & Cognition*, 29, 648–55.

Kim, J. (1999) Investigating phonological processing in visual word recognition: the use of Korean Hangul (alphabetic) and Hanja (logographic) scripts. Unpublished Ph.D. dissertation, University of New South Wales, Australia.

Kim, J. & Davis, C. (2004) Characteristics of poor readers of Korean Hangul: auditory, visual and phonological processing. *Reading & Writing*, 17 (1–2), 153–85.

Kim, M. (1994) Referential management and activated memory in Korean discourse. *Interdisciplinary Journal for the Study of Discourse*, 14 (1), 5–21.

Kim, M. (1998) Theme and subject in Korean. In B. Caron (ed.), *Proceedings of the 16th International Congress of Linguistics* (Paper No. 340). Oxford: Pergamon.

Kim, M. (2002) Thematic management in Korean narrative (pp. 137–56). In M. Louwerse & W. van Peer (eds.), *Thematics: interdisciplinary studies*. Amsterdam, Netherlands: John Benjamins Publishing Company, 2002.

Kim, S. (1995) Types and sources of problems in L2 reading: a qualitative analysis of the recall protocols of Korean high school EFL students. *Foreign Language Annals*, 28(1), 49–70.

Koda, K. (1998) The role of phonemic awareness in L2 reading. *Second Language Research*, 14, 194–215.

Koda, K. (2000) Cross-linguistic variations in L2 morphological awareness. *Applied Psycholinguistics*, 21, 297–320.

Lee, C. & Chard, D. (2000) Lexical decision-making in Korean words: educational implications of learning to read words. *Psychologia: An International Journal of Psychology in the Orient*, 43, 165–175.

Lee, G. (2002) The role of Korean parents in the literacy development of their children. *International Journal of Early Childhood*, 34(1).

Lee, H. (1999) A discourse-pragmatic analysis of the committal -ci in Korean: a synthetic approach to the form-meaning relation. *Journal of Pragmatics: An Interdisciplinary Journal of Language Studies*, 31, 243–75.

Lee, I. & Ramsey, S. R. (2000) *The Korean language*. New York: State University of New York Press.

Lee, J., Park, E., & Kim, H. (2000) Literacy education in Korea. *Childhood Education*, 76, (6), 347–51.

Lee, N. P. & Lee, S. W. (1970) Construction of children's association frequency table. *Korean Journal of Psychology*, 1, 149–51.

McBride-Chang, C., Cho, J., Liu, H., Wagner, R. K., Shu, H., Zhou, A., Cheuk, C. S-M., & Muse A. (2005) Changing models across cultures: associations of phonological awareness and morphological structure awareness with vocabulary and word recognition in second graders from Beijing, Hong Kong, Korea, and the United States. *Journal of Experimental Child Psychology*, 92, 140–60.

Mori, Y. & Nagy, W. E. (1999) Integration of information from context and word elements in interpreting novel kanji compounds. *Reading Research Quarterly*, 34(1), 80–101.

Muljani, M., Koda, K., & Moates, D. (1998) Development of L2 word recognition: a connectionist approach. *Applied Psycholinguistics*, 19, 99–114.

Nagy, W. E. & Scott, J. A. (2000) Vocabulary processes. Handbook of reading research, Vol. III, pp. 269–84, Mahwah, NJ: Lawrence Erlbaum.

Nam, K., Seo, K., & Choi, K. (1997) The word length effect on Hangul word recognition. *Korean Journal of Experimental & Cognitive Psychology*, 9, 1–18.

Pak, M. K. (1997) A comparative analysis of middle-class Korean and middle-class White American children's story production and comprehension. Dissertation Abstracts International Section A: Humanities & Social Sciences.

Park, E. C. (2004) The relationship between morphological awareness and lexical inference skills for English language learning with Korean first-language background. Unpublished doctoral dissertation, Dissertation Abstracts International, 65 (05), 1761. (UMI No. 3131518)

Park, K. (1996) The role of phonology in Hangul word recognition. *Korean Journal of Experimental & Cognitive Psychology*, 8, 25–44.

Park, K. & Vaid, J. (1995) Lexical representation of script variation: evidence from Korean biscriptals (pp. 327–39). In I. Taylor, & D. R. Olson (eds.), *Scripts and literacy: reading and learning to read alphabets, syllabaries and characters*. Dordrecht: Kluwer Academic.

Park, T. (1997) Relation between implicit memory and lexical processing. *Korean Journal of Experimental & Cognitive Psychology*, 9, 95–118.

Perfetti, C. A. & Bell, L. (1991) Phonemic activation during the first 40 ms of word identification: evidence from backward masking and priming. *Journal of Memory and Language*, 30, 473–85.

Perfetti, C. A., Bell, L., & Delaney, S. (1988) Automatic (pre-lexical) phonetic activation in silent reading: evidence from backward masking. *Journal of Memory and Language*, 32, 57–68.

Simpson, G. & Kang, H. (1994) The flexible use of phonological information in word recognition in Korean. *Journal of Memory & Language*, 33, 319–31.

Simpson, G., & Kang, H. (2004) Syllable processing in alphabetic Korean. *Reading & Writing*, 17(1–2), 137–51.

Sohn, H. (1994) *Korean*. Cornwall: T. J. Press.

Sohn, H. (1999) *The Korean language*. Cambridge: Cambridge University Press.

Song, J. & Won, H. (1998) Working memory, short-term memory, word-reading speed, and syntactic knowledge of Korean children with reading-comprehension disability. *Korean Journal of Clinical Psychology*, 17, 105–21.

Taylor, I. & Olson, D. R. (1995) An introduction to reading the world's scripts (pp. 1–18). In I. Taylor & D. R. Olson (eds.), *Scripts and literacy: reading and learning to read alphabets, syllabaries and characters*. Dordrecht: Kluwer Academic.

Taylor, I. & Park, K. (1995) Differential processing of content words and function words: Chinese characters vs phonetic scripts (pp.185–98). In I. Taylor, & D. R. Olson (eds.), *Scripts and literacy: reading and learning to read alphabets, syllabaries and characters*. Dordrecht: Kluwer Academic.

Taylor, I. & Taylor, M. (1995) *Writing and literacy in Chinese, Korean, and Japanese*. Philadelphia: John Benjamins.

Yoon, H. K., Bolger, D. J., Kwon, O. S., & Perfetti, C. A. (2002) Subsyllabic units in reading: a difference between Korean and English. In L. Verhoeven, C. Elbro, & P. Reitsma (eds.), *Precursors of functional literacy*. Amsterdam/Philadelphia: John Benjamins Publishing Company.

10 Looking back and thinking forward

Keiko Koda

With rapidly growing numbers of language minority students in schools in the U.S. and other countries around the world, there is a critical need for ensuring that these students achieve high levels of literacy in their second languages. If, through research, we can clarify how second-language reading skills develop, then there can be significant steps towards more effective models of instruction and assessment. With this goal in mind, this volume has provided theoretical perspectives for conceptualizing and examining the impacts of prior literacy experience on second-language reading development.

The approach taken here began by establishing a theoretical foundation for identifying the learning-to-read requirements imposed by universal properties of reading, and then, illustrated how such requirements can be altered by the linguistic and orthographic properties of a particular language. These clarifications are vital in understanding what constitutes "prior literacy experience." Since literacy learning is a complex undertaking, without such clarifications, it is virtually impossible to isolate various elements of "previous literacy experience," and then determine on which elements to focus in subsequent investigations.

On the methodological front, the volume has provided detailed descriptions of the dominant linguistic and orthographic properties that are directly related to reading acquisition in five typologically diverse languages. These descriptions form the basis for systematic comparisons across the languages to identify cross-linguistic variations in the "literacy experience." Through a melding of two contrasting, yet complementary perspectives—i.e. reading universals and cross-linguistic variation—the volume presents procedures for identifying and describing the key competencies gained through prior literacy experience that are available to the learner when learning to read in a second language.

Theoretical underpinnings

Second-language reading is a complex, multi-dimensional pursuit, involving a variety of operations in two or more languages. Inevitably, its inherent complexities impose serious challenges both on theory construction and empirical validation of those theories. Thus, this volume represents an attempt to initiate systematic efforts in dissecting the interwoven factors affecting second-language reading development, by outlining a principled approach to conceptualizing, analyzing, and empirically testing the impacts of prior literacy experience on second-language learning to read.

As noted above, the current approach is grounded in the concept of reading universals. The notion of universality is critical because it specifies the requirements imposed on all learners in all languages, and in so doing, provides the common categories, shared across languages, for cataloguing learning-to-read experiences. As a case in point, the "Universal grammar of reading" (Perfetti, 2003; Perfetti & Liu, 2005; Perfetti & Dunlap, this volume) contends that in all languages, reading is embedded in a spoken language and its writing system, and as such, its acquisition universally requires all learners to make links between language elements and the graphic symbols representing them. The current approach, therefore, has concentrated on such linkage-building as the focal domain of "literacy experience."

Metalinguistic awareness is also central in the current approach, and serves as the focal construct in the analyses. The significance of this construct lies in its capacity for enabling learners to analyze and segment language forms. Through its analytic capacity, metalinguistic awareness guides learners in detecting regularities in input, and then identifying corresponding, co-occurring, elements in those regularities (Ku & Anderson, 2003; Kuo & Anderson, this volume; Nagy & Anderson, 1999). In addition, the construct provides major methodological advantages. Because of its reciprocal relationship with literacy—particularly, its reliance on print experience for "fine-tuning," the language-specific facets of metalinguistic awareness are seen as outcomes of literacy, closely attuned to the linguistic and orthographic properties of the language in which literacy is learned. The clear implication of such reciprocity is that the metalinguistic competencies directly involved in learning to read in a particular language can be identified through careful analysis of its linguistic and orthographic properties. Once identified, moreover, these competencies can be compared across languages, which, in turn, will illuminate the similarities and differences in literacy experience in diverse languages.

Learning to read in a second language presumably is also constrained by the universal properties of reading, and its requirements can be assumed to be the same as those in a first language. Metalinguistic competencies, developed through first-language literacy, should be readily available for use in learning to read in another language. However, linguistic and orthographic properties differ between the first and the second languages, and therefore, those differences should determine, in large part, the extent and manner in which the prior literacy experience contributes to the development of metalinguistic awareness and reading skills in the second language (Koda,

2005; Koda this volume). Systematic cross-linguistic comparisons of the relevant metalinguistic awareness thus can provide an empirical basis for conceptualizing: (a) which competencies are transfer-ready at a given point in time; (b) to what extent prior literacy experience facilitates second-language learning to read; and (c) how such facilitation varies among learners with diverse literacy experience in their first languages.

Metalinguistic awareness and reading development in diverse languages

The facilitative roles of metalinguistic awareness in early reading development among monolingual readers are widely recognized. Measuring this construct, however, is challenging, because it is multi-faceted, with each facet uniquely linked to a specific linguistic feature. Empirical examination of the construct, therefore, requires clarification of how its facets are defined, identified, and measured. The volume's five language chapters (Chapters 5–9) provide such clarification for each language analyzed by describing in detail the language elements graphically encoded in the writing system and the specific method of encoding them. Through the descriptions and analyses, these chapters offer a basis for comparing the critical metalinguistic facets involved in learning to read in these languages, and in so doing, collectively demonstrate possible cross-linguistic variations in the "literacy experience" in these languages. The sections that follow outline the key findings.

Phonological awareness

It is commonly assumed that the ability to segment spoken words into their phonological constituents plays a crucial role in learning to read English. The volume's language chapters generally suggest that their basic consensus can be extended to other languages, even non-alphabetic Chinese. Since the ability stems from children's understanding of the segmental nature of spoken words, it does not necessarily entail insight into the precise phonological unit (e.g. phoneme, syllable) represented in individual graphic symbols. Inasmuch as segmental understanding evolves from a similar developmental sequence, and also consistently relates to initial reading development across languages (Ziegler & Goswami, 2005), it is viewed as a by-product of oral language development and not specific to any particular language. As such, it is additionally presumed to be a precursor of literacy, serving as an enabler in learning basic mapping principles.

Studies of bilingual children consistently demonstrate high correlations between first- and second-language phonological awareness, as well as first-language phonological awareness and second-language word reading ability (e.g. Cisero & Royer, 1995; Durgunoglu *et al.*, 1993; Gholamain & Geva, 1999; Gottardo, 2002; Quiroga *et al.*, 2002; Wang *et al.*, 2005). These findings generally are interpreted as suggesting that once developed, phonological awareness transfers across languages, thereby creating facilitation, as a shared resource, in additional languages. However, whether such resource sharing constitutes "transfer" is open to question. Inasmuch as the studies on cross-language relationships in phonological awareness are almost all correlational, it is difficult to argue on the basis of the available data that the reported relationships are actually indicative of the hypothesized dependency of phonological awareness in the second language on that in the first. Although correlational analyses presume the variables to be correlated are independent of each other, the assumption has never been substantiated. Conceivably, therefore, the high correlations could simply imply that phonological awareness tasks in the two languages may have assessed the same underlying ability, or that phonological awareness in the two languages may be independent, but related indirectly, through third party factors. Since each interpretation yields different implications, it is essential that the research go well beyond correlations in clarifying the cross-linguistic relationship in phonological awareness.

Grapho-phonological awareness

Grapho-phonological awareness refers to insight into the way phonological information is graphically represented in the writing system. Accordingly, its acquisition requires substantial word reading and spelling experience. Writing systems vary both in the unit of phonological information represented in each graphic symbol and in the regularity of sound-symbol correspondences. Such variations are aptly demonstrated in the language chapters. For example, reflecting the dual-unit representation in the Hangul script (alphabetic-syllabary), Korean children are sensitized to both syllables and phonemes. In the consonantal Hebrew, however, children develop stronger sensitivity to consonants than vowels. In logographic Chinese, moreover, grapho-morphological awareness is a stronger predictor than grapho-phonological awareness of children's initial success in reading.

The language chapters also show systematic cross-linguistic variations in the extent to which phonological skills relate to decoding performance. As an illustration, reflecting varying regularity in grapheme-phoneme correspondences, word reading ability is differentially related to phonological skills in Hebrew and English. The relationship between the two has been found to be considerably stronger in phonologically less regular English than in highly regular Hebrew. Similarly, different phonological skills predict word reading ability in English and Korean. While phoneme and syllable manipulation skills are both strong predictors of word reading ability among Korean children, phonemic competence is more strongly associated with decoding performance than with syllable-based skills among English-speaking children.

Given these variations, it is reasonable to presume that grapho-phonological awareness shaped in one language is not instantly serviceable in another language. Assuming that first-language awareness is available to literate second-language learners, the core issue is how its impacts can be captured and studied. From the transfer point of view, grapho-phonological awareness and phonological awareness are critically different; while the former is language-specific, the latter may not be. It is essential, therefore, that the two be distinguished both conceptually and methodologically. While phonological awareness, presumably non-language-specific, is readily functional in any additional languages, grapho-phonological awareness could only provide limited support in learning to read in another language. Although systematic efforts have been initiated in describing grapho-phonological awareness among monolingual children (e.g. Li *et al.*, 2002), the two constructs are rarely differentiated in studies involving bilingual readers.

Incorporating grapho-phonological awareness in second-language literacy research is beneficial for several reasons. Inasmuch as it is attuned to the sound-symbol relationship in the second language, once acquired, it can significantly enhance efficiency in extracting phonological information from unfamiliar words and inferring the pronunciation of novel words. Moreover, since its acquisition necessitates substantial print experience, such dependency makes it possible to project the *initial* form of this awareness, which has been shaped through first-language literacy, as well as project its *subsequent* form, which will be acquired through second-language literacy. Thus, grapho-phonological awareness can serve as a window through which the coalescence of literacy experience in the two languages can be systematically explored.

Grapho-morphological awareness

Grapho-morphological awareness refers to the ability to identify, analyze, and manipulate morphological information in print. Since morphemes provide grammatical, syntactic, and semantic information, the value of this awareness lies in its capacity for assisting learners in identifying the grammatical category of words, inferring the meaning of unfamiliar words, and accessing stored lexical information (Carlisle, 2003; Koda, 2005; Ku & Anderson, 2003). Although a tacit grasp of the morphological structure stems from the use of spoken language, its explicit understanding develops mainly through encoding and decoding morphological information in print.

As evident throughout the volume, languages vary considerably in regard to the grammatical information to be signaled and the method of signaling. They also differ in the basic unit of word formation and the principles governing its processes. Variations occur in the way morphological information is encoded in the writing system. Further, there are more morphemes than phonemes in language, and grapheme-morpheme mappings are more varied than grapheme-phoneme mappings. The multitude of variations clearly suggests that grapho-morphological awareness is highly language-specific, and as such, requires substantial input—both oral and print—in accommodating the morphological and orthographic properties of the language to be learned.

On the assumptions that first-language grapho-morphological awareness is available to learners, and that it plays a role in second-language learning to read, it is further presumed that the transferred awareness undergoes extensive adjustments. Since such adjustments rely on input exposure and experience in the new language, second-language grapho-morphological awareness should offer an exceptional opportunity to dissect the impacts stemming from linguistic input and print experience in the two languages. Specifically, analysis of this construct should allow systematic explorations of three-way cross-linguistic interactions among the transferred first-language awareness, second-language proficiency, and evolving second-language awareness. Capitalizing on such an opportunity is a sensible tactic in clarifying the unique, cross-linguistic, nature of second-language reading. Furthermore, grapho-morphological awareness is directly associated with critical operations during comprehension, such as lexical inference, syntactic analysis, and lexical access. Systematic probing of this construct can promote much-needed research on comprehension sub-skills development.

Research gaps

The reviews of literacy studies in the languages described in this volume make it plain that considerable differences exist in both the research quantity and quality among these languages. There is considerably more information available in Chinese and Hebrew than in Arabic and Korean, and virtually no scientific research on literacy development in Khmer. The studies reviewed, moreover, vary widely in both their theoretical perspectives and methodological approaches, making it difficult to compare their findings. At present, the scant evidence on hand does not permit any generalizations regarding cross-linguistic learning-to-read variations. Without accurate descriptions of how reading skills develop in these and other languages, we cannot grapple with even the most fundamental issues of transfer—that is, what skills are transferred and how they alter reading development in a second language. In short, if we are to build a viable theory of transfer, we must establish a stronger research base which informs reading development in languages other than English.

Another arena of shortcomings is the general lack of guiding principles in research on reading skills transfer. In the absence of an explicit theory, transfer research, over the past thirty years, has been guided, in the main, by two theoretical formulations: the Contrastive Analysis (CA) hypothesis (Lado, 1957) and the developmental interdependence hypothesis (Cummins, 1979, 1991). Although both have been highly influential, neither has provided an adequate basis for theory construction. The CA hypothesis contends that learning difficulties arise from structural differences between the two languages involved. However, the differences in this formulation only concern the presence or absence of particular grammatical features—say, plurality marking—with no attention to how they marked. Therefore, it offers little to explain how particular information is extracted from either oral or print input. It is thus highly unlikely that such simplistic treatments can reveal either reading skills transfer or sources of learning/reading difficulty.

The developmental interdependence hypothesis, on the other hand, emphasizes academic language competence, including literacy, developed in a first language, as a major source of facilitation in developing corresponding competence in a second language. Its central contention is that the development of such competence in any language is supported by a set of non language-specific cognitive capacities, referred to as "common underlying proficiency." The development of second-language academic language competence is thus determined, to a major extent, by the degree to which the "common underlying proficiency" has developed in the primary language. Although the hypothesis has inspired a considerable amount of valuable research, it is problematic in that no clarification is offered as to what constitutes "common underlying proficiency." Lacking a clear definition of the central construct, subsequent studies examining the hypothesized interdependence vary considerably in virtually all aspects of the research design, including participants' characteristics (age, language background, ethnicity, academic status), cognitive/academic skills measured, and assessment tools used, disallowing systematic syntheses of research findings. Viewed together, the shortcomings of these formulations clearly suggest the strong need for a theory of transfer in initiating and promoting further empirical studies on cross-linguistic relationships in first- and second-language reading development.

Another conspicuous gap in second-language literacy research is the uneven attention to reading sub-skills. Under the componential approach, isolating and measuring reading sub-skills is becoming a common practice in contemporary studies involving bilingual readers. However, many of these studies have focused mainly on phonological awareness and decoding, and as a result, second-language reading development has been conceptualized primarily based on a highly restricted range of sub-skills. The limited scope is troublesome because decoding development can occur independently of other aspects of linguistic knowledge, such as grammar and vocabulary, particularly in phonologically shallow orthographies.

In fact, it is important in this regard to recognize that decoding competence alone does not guarantee comprehension success, among first- or second-language readers. Moreover, the acquisition of comprehension sub-skills requires distinct sets of linguistic knowledge and metalinguistic insight. More studies are needed to explore the functional relationships among metalinguistic awareness, linguistic knowledge, and comprehension sub-skills development, both within and across languages. Ultimately, comprehension ability is of greatest consequence in content learning. Extending the componential approach to explorations of comprehension sub-skills will likely yield useful information directly contributing to improved literacy instruction for language-minority students.

Finally, second-language studies generally provide limited information on the participants and the circumstances involved in their literacy learning. Since literacy does not occur in a vacuum, it is essential that the outcomes be interpreted by taking into account who the learners are and how their literacy is learned. Such information is particularly important in the study of second-language literacy because learners begin to acquire literacy in their second language at different ages, with a wide range in levels of literacy in their first language. Thus, for example, at the outset of instruction, learners are likely to have experienced different lengths of schooling in their first language, to have attained disparate levels of first-language proficiency, and to have available varying degrees of support for first-language literacy learning and/or maintenance. Given that these factors influence reading acquisition in significant ways, it is difficult to accurately gauge the impacts of prior literacy experience on second-language reading development without adequate information on how literacy was acquired in the first language. It is thus vital that a consensus be reached among researchers regarding what constitutes the minimally required information essential to understanding the circumstances of literacy learning among a particular group of second-language learners.

Future research directions

To reiterate, the primary goal of the volume is to explore a principled approach to examining the impacts of prior literacy experience on second-language reading development. The dual-lens perspective proposed here incorporates both reading universals and cross-linguistic variations. Through this perspective, "prior literacy experience" in a first language has been operationally defined as comprising metalinguistic and other literacy-related competencies that have been shaped through the universally required learning-to-read task—that is, the task of linking spoken language elements with units of graphic symbols. Although this approach represents a restriction in scope, in that it does not encompass the full range of experience associated with literacy learning, the restriction was necessary in order to disentangle the many complexities inherent in second-language reading. Now that a foundation has been established, the scope can be extended to additional related factors. Future research agendas can be built to purposefully expand the current scope of "prior literacy experience." Three areas seem particularly promising: (a) incorporating a wider range of literacy-related competencies; (b) examining the learner-external factors affecting "prior literacy experience;" and (c) tracking the long-term impacts of such experience.

Incorporating a wider range of literacy-related competencies

The recent research on reading transfer has begun to address one of the most fundamental questions—the question of which skills are transferred. Currently, the investigative goal is almost exclusively focused on cross-linguistic relationships in phonological awareness and decoding. Reading, however, goes well beyond decoding. In order to gain a more comprehensive understanding of the impacts deriving from prior literacy experience, it is critical to incorporate other sub-skills. Such sub-skills might include, for example, those required for extracting non-phonological (e.g. semantic and grammatical) information from print, as well as those needed for integrating the extracted information to construct meaning at the phrase, sentence, and discourse levels. Since each of these skills depends on specific facets of metalinguistic awareness and related linguistic knowledge, there should be exploration of their functional and developmental interconnections, both within and across languages. Such investigations should yield significant additional insights into how second-language reading skills evolve, beyond print information extraction, explaining the manner in which ongoing inter-actions between the transferred first-language competencies and the second-language print input contribute to the development of second-language literacy.

Examining learner-external factors affecting prior literacy experience

A number of learner-external factors are involved in literacy learning, which collectively shape the prior literacy experience among second-language learners. Three such factors—the onset of second-language literacy learning, home-school language discrepancy, and first-language literacy instruction—are particularly relevant to variations in prior literacy experience among second-language learners.

The onset of learning refers to the age at which second-language literacy learning commences, and is especially critical because one of the major conditions for transfer is the extent to which particular competencies have been established through prior literacy learning. Put simply, other things being equal, older learners are likely to possess more transfer-ready competencies, and as a result, their second-language literacy learning is likely to be more strongly affected by prior literacy experience than that among younger cohorts. Given that different competencies are available for transfer at different points in first-language literacy development, it is highly conceivable that learners at varying stages face fundamentally different challenges when learning to read in a second language. Documenting such differences, therefore, should further clarify the nature and magnitude of the impacts stemming from prior literacy experience.

Although age is a general indicator of literacy achievements in a first language, caution should be exercised in taking age at its face value. Obviously, not all students can achieve the expected competencies at the same rate. Therefore, we cannot simply assume that the same range of competencies is available for transfer among learners at the same age and/or grade level. Furthermore, not all students have had similar schooling in their primary language, as in the case of many Cambodian students recently immigrated in the US with minimum schooling in their home country. Without adequate formal literacy instruction, even upper-grade students are not likely to possess the expected, grade-equivalent, literacy skills in their first language.

Home-school language mismatch also affects literacy learning and its outcomes. While in monolingual contexts, it is commonly assumed that literacy builds on spoken language, such continuity cannot always be taken for granted in multilingual societies. As in the instances of Arabic and Chinese literacy, children learn to speak a local dialect at home and then learn the societal language (e.g. Mandarin and Modern Standard Arabic, respectively) for both oral and written communication at school. Their primary literacy thus occurs in their second language. Oral proficiency (particularly, vocabulary and grammatical knowledge) in the school language presumably varies among those children, and such variation in all likelihood affects their literacy development. Hence, more information is clearly needed regarding the extent and manner in which home-school language mismatch impinges on reading acquisition in the societal language.

Reading instruction is another factor influencing literacy experience. Literacy skills are taught differently from one culture to another, and even from one region to another within a single culture. Since these differences stem from predominant convictions as to how literacy is learned and how instruction can best promote its development, instructional approaches are also believed to play a major role in shaping the literacy experience. As a case in point, different levels of phonological awareness among children in Beijing and Hong Kong have been attributed to the distinct teaching methods in their schools—namely, the use of Pinyin, a phonemic coding system, in the PRC and the emphasis on rote memorization in Hong Kong (Huang & Hanley, 1994). Further explorations of instructional effects could shed substantial light on the relationship between literacy experience and learning outcomes.

Tracking long-term impacts

Reading comprises a number of sub-skills, which develop at different rates in accordance with their respective timetables. Many sub-skills, moreover, are developmentally interdependent in that their acquisition depends on the mastery of other sub-skills. These interconnections obviously make it difficult to uncover the true impacts of prior literacy experience if the sub-skills are only measured once, at a given point in time. To more fully appreciate what it means to have additional resources in learning to read in a second language, it would be important to pursue longitudinal comparisons of particular sub-skills among second-language learners with contrasting "prior literacy experience."

As an illustration, orthographic distance effects can be traced longitudinally by comparing decoding efficiency among second-language learners with contrasting (related vs. unrelated) first-language orthographic backgrounds. In such a study, it would be of considerable benefit to determine the extent to which developmental acceleration is associated with orthographic similarities between the two languages, and then explore how differential acceleration affects the subsequent comprehension skills development. To date, orthographic distance is known to be largely responsible for decoding efficiency among second-language readers. However, in the absence of longitudinal data, little information is available as to how the initial efficiency differences resolve over time. The differences may close over time, entailing no perceptible consequences for comprehension development. Conversely, however, it could have lasting impacts, inducing diverse procedures for print information extraction among second-language learners. Despite their direct bearing on interventions, these and other speculations have not been adequately addressed. Clearly, the long-term impacts of prior literacy experience should be systematically studied through longitudinal observations of multiple skills development.

Final remarks

By way of summary, this volume has suggested a principled approach in exploring the impacts of prior literacy experience on second-language reading development. Based on the assumptions that in all languages, reading builds on oral language competence, and that readers are universally required to make links between their spoken language and writing system, the current approach has focused on linkage building as the focal task of learning to read, and metalinguistic awareness as the dominant construct in the analysis because of its facilitative role in the linkage building. The volume's language chapters illustrate what is actually involved in the linking task in these languages through detailed descriptions of the major elements to be linked in each language and its respective writing system. In so doing, the chapters also demonstrate how the universally required linking task can be altered through those language-specific elements. In the current approach, such alterations are viewed as variations in "literacy experience" among individuals literate in these languages.

The development of second-language reading ability, presumably, is also subject to the universally required linking task. However, linkage building in the second language differs from that in the first because it involves two spoken languages and their writing systems, and thus requires multiple bridges for connecting language elements and graphic symbols both within and across languages. Obviously, dissecting the multitude of intra- and linterlingual linkages is an extremely challenging, but vitally needed, research endeavor if we are to gain a clearer understanding of second-language reading development.

References

Carlisle, J. F. (2003) Morphology matters in learning to read: a commentary. *Reading Psychology*, 24, 291–322.

Cisero, C. A. & Royer, James M. (1995) The development and cross-language transfer of phonological awareness. *Contemporary Educational Psychology*, 20, 3, 275–303.

Cummins, J. (1979) Linguistic interdependence and educational development of bilingual children. *Review of Educational Research*, 49, 222–51.

Cummins, J. (1991) Interdependence of first- and second-language proficiency in bilingual children. In E. Bialystok (ed.), *Language processing in bilingual children* (pp. 70–89). New York: Cambridge University Press.

Durgunoglu, A. Y., Nagy, W. E., & Hancin, B. J. (1993) Cross-language transfer of phonemic awareness. *Journal of Educational Psychology*, 85, 453–65.

Gholamain, M. & Geva, E. (1999) Orthographic and cognitive factors in the concurrent development of basic reading skills in English and Persian. *Language Learning*, 49, 183–217.

Gottardo, A. (2002) The relationship between language and reading skills in bilingual Spanish–English speakers. *Topics in Language Disorders*, 22(5), 46–70.

Huang, H. S. & Hanley, R. J. (1994) Phonological awareness and visual skills in learning to read Chinese and English. *Cognition*, 54, 73–98.

Koda, K. (2005) *Insights into second language reading*. New York: Cambridge University Press.

Koda, K. (this volume) Contributions of prior literacy experience in learning to read in a second language. In K. Koda & A. M. Zehler (eds.), *Learning to read across languages: cross-linguistic relationships in first and second-language literacy development*. New York: Routledge.

Ku, Y. & Anderson, R. C. (2003) Development of morphological awareness in Chinese and English. *Reading & Writing: An Interdisciplinary Journal*, 16, 399–422.

Kuo, L. & Anderson, R. C. (this volume) Conceptual and methodological issues in comparing metalinguistic awareness across languages. In K. Koda & A. M. Zehler (eds.), *Learning to read across languages: cross-linguistic relationships in first- and second-language literacy development*. New York: Routledge.

Lado, R. (1957) *Linguistics across cultures*. Ann Arbor: University of Michigan Press.

Li, W., Anderson, R. C., Nagy, W., & Zhang, H. (2002) Facets of metalinguistic awareness that contribute to Chinese literacy (pp. 87–106). In W. Li, J. S. Gaffney, & J. L. Packard (eds.), *Chinese children's reading acquisition: theoretical and pedagogical issues*. Boston: Kluwer Academic.

Nagy, W. E. & Anderson, R. C. (1999) Metalinguistic awareness and literacy acquisition in different languages (pp. 155–60). In D. Wagner, R. Venezky, & B. Street (eds.), *Literacy: an international handbook*. New York: Garland.

Perfetti, C. A. (2003) The universal grammar of reading. *Scientific Studies of Reading*, 7, 3–24.

Perfetti, C. A. & Liu, Y. (2005) Orthography to phonology and meaning: comparisons across and within writing systems. *Reading & Writing*, 18, 193–210.

Perfetti, C. A. & Dunlap, S. (this volume) Learning to read: general principles and writing system variations. In K. Koda & A. M. Zehler (eds.), *Learning to read across languages: cross-linguistic relationships in first- and second-language literacy development*. New York: Routledge.

Quiroga, T., Lemos-Britton, Z., Mostafapour, E., Abbott, R.D., & Berninger, V. W. (2002) Phonological awareness and beginning reading in Spanish-speaking ESL first graders: research into practice. *Journal of School Psychology*, 40, 85–111.

Wang, M., Perfetti, C.A., and Liu, Y. (2003) Alphabetic readers quickly acquire orthographic structure in learning to read Chinese. *Scientific Studies of Reading*, 7, 183–208.

Ziegler, J. C. & Goswami, U. (2005) Reading acquisition, developmental dyslexia, and skilled reading across languages: a psycholinguistic grain size theory. *Psychological Bulletin*, 131, 3–29.

Notes on contributors

Richard C. Anderson is Professor of Education and Psychology and Director of the Center for the Study of Reading at the University of Illinois. He also has appointments at Beijing Normal University and Hong Kong Polytechnic University. With co-authors, Anderson has published 200 books, book chapters, and journal articles. Recent publications appear in *Cognition and Instruction, Journal of the Learning Sciences, Elementary School Journal, Educational Psychologist*, and *Journal of Educational Psychology*.

Susan Dunlap is a doctoral candidate at the University of Pittsburgh. Her research interests include phonological awareness in reading acquisition, cross-linguistic differences in reading, and adult second language learning.

Michael Fender is an Assistant Professor of Linguistics at California State University, Long Beach. His research interests include first and second language reading development and psycholinguistics, and some of his research on the acquisition of ESL word and sentence level reading skills has appeared in *Language Learning* and *Applied Psycholinguistics*.

Esther Geva is Professor in the Department of Human Development and Applied Psychology at the Ontario Institute for Studies in Education of the University of Toronto. In recent years her research interests have focused primarily on theoretical and clinical aspects of language and literacy development in elementary-level English-language-learning children. She co-edited special issues of *Reading and Writing: An Interdisciplinary Journal* and *Journal of Scientific Studies of Reading*. Her work has appeared in journals such as *Annals of Dyslexia, Language Learning, Applied Psycholinguistics, Reading and Writing: An Interdisciplinary Journal*, and *Dyslexia*. Esther was one of the authors of the national literacy panel report.

Keiko Koda is Professor in the Department of Modern Languages at Carnegie Mellon University. Her research on second language reading and biliteracy development is published widely in journals, books and book chapters. She has edited and co-edited special issues of *Language Learning* and *Reading in a Foreign Language*. Her recent publications include *Insights into Second Language Reading* (Cambridge University Press, 2005) and *Reading and Language Learning* (Blackwell, 2007).

Li-jen Kuo is Assistant Professor of Educational Psychology at Northern Illinois University. She was a Spencer Fellow during the 2005–2006 academic year and a two-time Fellow at the Summer Institute of the Linguistic Society of America. Her research area focuses on the development of metalinguistic awareness in children with diverse language backgrounds. Her most recent publication is *Morphological Awareness and Learning to Read: A Cross-Language Perspective* in *Educational Psychologist*.

Eunyoung Christine Park is a Social Science Research Associate at Stanford University. Her research focuses on morphological awareness and literacy development in school-age English language learners. She has presented at Second Language Research Forum and American Association for Applied Linguistics conferences.

Charles Perfetti is University Professor of Psychology and Associate Director of the Learning Research and Development Center at the University of Pittsburgh. His research on reading and language is published widely in journals and in two books. He has also co-edited four books on literacy topics. He is the 2004 recipient of the Distinguished Scientific Contribution Award of the Society for the Scientific Study of Reading.

Saloni Sapru, independent consultant, has worked on a number of program evaluations and research studies on minorities, immigrants, and English language learners. Her research articles include Parenting and Adolescent Identity (*Journal of Adolescent Research*, 2006), Identity and Social Change (*Psychology and Developing Societies*, 1998), and with Nimmi Hutnik, The Salience of Ethnicity (*Journal of Social Psychology*, 1996).

Min Wang is Assistant Professor of Human Development at the University of Maryland, College Park, USA. She has published her work in various journals relating to language and literacy including *Cognition, Journal of Educational Psychology, Scientific Studies of Reading, Applied Psycholinguistics*, and *Language Learning*.

Chin-Lung Yang is an Assistant Research Professor of Linguistics at the University of Hong Kong, Hong Kong. His research interests include sentence processing, word-to-text information integration, neurocognitive indicators of reading abilities, and discourse comprehension. He has authored and co-authored 13 research articles in *Applied Cognition, Journal of Experimental Psychology*, and *Handbook of East Asian Psycholinguistics*.

Annette M. Zehler is a Senior Research Associate at the Center for Applied Linguistics, Washington, DC. Her work has focused on language and education, especially the education of English language learners. She has been project director and senior researcher on national studies of English learners, and has conducted research on the role of first language experience in second language acquisition.

Index